'It's a brave, well-written and often very funny story of a full and interesting life . . . Her stories of life in Australian theatre are as entertaining as those of her adventures with her lovers and husbands . . . She's risqué and witty and not afraid to make fun of herself.'

Gillian Lord, *Canberra Times*

'There's plenty of vicarious fun to be had reading about Jacki Weaver's rollercoaster life. There's always another drama, comedy or romance to keep the action coming—and that's just off stage darling . . . With her cheerful sexiness, Weaver comes across like a mini Mae West.'

Michelle Griffin, *Sydney Morning Herald*

'From the beginning Jacki's tone is conversational and intimate, and totally engaging. I was laughing by page two and crying by page 50 . . . while Jackie's style is often self-deprecating, she is refreshingly honest about her "dark side" . . . I loved this book—so easy to read, informative and accessible. It's well worth adding to your collection.'

Ruth Wykes, *Women out West*

Much love,
Jac
x

JACKI WEAVER

ALLEN&UNWIN

Allen & Unwin
Sydney, Melbourne, Auckland, London

83 Alexander Street
Crows Nest NSW 2065
Australia
Phone: (61 2) 8425 0100
Fax: (61 2) 9906 2218
Email: info@allenandunwin.com
Web: www.allenandunwin.com

Cataloguing-in-Publication details are available
from the National Library of Australia
www.trove.nla.gov.au

ISBN 978 1 74237 775 9

Set in Sabon by Midland Typesetters, Australia

Lyrics reproduced on pp. 260-1 from the musical
I'M GETTING MY ACT TOGETHER AND TAKING IT ON THE ROAD
By Gretchen Cryer and Nancy Ford Charles
Copyright © 1980 by Gretchen Cryer

FSC
Mixed Sources
Product group from well-managed
forests and other controlled sources
Cert no. SGS-COC-3047
www.fsc.org
© 1996 Forest Stewardship Council

The paper this book is printed on is certified by the © 1996 Forest Stewardship Council A.C. (FSC). SOS holds FSC chain of custody SGS-COC-3047. The FSC promotes environmentally responsible, socially beneficial and economically viable management of the world's forests.

Printed and bound in Australia by The SOS Print + Media Group.

10 9 8 7 6 5 4 3 2 1

Dedicated to the men I love, you know who you are

Contents

1. The Golden Girl from the West   1
2. Portrait of a Very Young Actress   30
3. Wouldn't It Be Nice   49
4. The Mancunian Lothario   71
5. The Smallest Fag Hag in Australia   90
6. Show Us Some Suburban Lust   111
7. Nothing's Impossible   126
8. Human Headline Rammed by Battlestar Galactica   143
9. Rollering Through the Good Times   166
10. Hurricane Hinch   185
11. Intimations of Mortality   205
12. Twilight of the Gods   230
13. Fear No More   245
14. And the Show, of Course, Goes On   259

Epilogue: Living National Trevor   262

Professional biography   274

Acknowledgments   280

chapter one

The Golden Girl
from the West

I WROTE A COLLECTION OF SHORT STORIES WHEN I WAS SIX
years old, but it wasn't until I was nine that I wrote my first
novel, filling a forty-page exercise book with an HB copperplate pencil in newly learned running writing. My novel was
about a little girl who runs away from home in Sydney,
becomes a stowaway on an ocean liner and wakes up in
Paris, where she eventually and incredibly finds her long-lost
real parents and discovers that her real name is Françoise not
Vicki. It took me a while to pull all the loose strands of the
plot together, but in the end it wasn't a bad read.

Sadly, *Françoise, Lost in France* wasn't snapped up by a
publisher but Miss Annie Jones, headmistress of Percival
Street Primary, accorded it an enthusiastic public reading
and ninety-nine per cent in the Year 3 half-yearly exams. My

piece of fiction had also made Miss Jones curious about my home life. She needn't have worried. I still think my father is the third most handsome and the best man I've ever hugged, and my mother the cleverest and most gracious of women. She could also be rather frightening, when she chose to be.

My mother Edith met my father Arthur in an English pub in Lichfield when she was still a teenager. He was a 21-year-old Australian, flying Lancasters for the RAAF over Europe. My daddy was also a war hero (isn't everyone's?). He was awarded a DFC but I didn't know about this myself until I was in my thirties. He was very modest about it.

Just now I rang my nephew Nick Weaver in Balmain for the exact wording of Dad's citation. It's in my brother's house (even though I thought it was going to be left to me!), framed on his wall along with all Dad's other medals. Here is what my nephew read out to me over the phone:

HONOURS AND AWARDS
DISTINGUISHED FLYING CROSS
Pilot Officer Arthur George Weaver 424247
Citation: Pilot Officer Weaver has completed numerous operations against the enemy in the course of which he has invariably displayed the utmost fortitude, courage and devotion to duty.

My mother came from the Lake District in Cumbria, joined the air force and became best friends with Belle, a gorgeous blonde from Durham. One night Ede and Belle were out on the town and hitched up with Art and his mate Charlie, possibly in a fish shop. And they all lived happily ever after. Belle is the only one of the quartet still with us, in Canberra to be exact, still an adorable goodtime girl. Her daughter Jude and I are great pals.

I have a love letter written in my father's distinctive copperplate hand to 'Edie my darling', dated 10 December 1944. I found it in my mother's bedside drawer just after she died in 1991, and my father said I could have it. It's very long but in part it says:

If I close my eyes I can imagine you right beside me, you seem very close tonight. Your laughter, your lovely smile, that joy of living that I love so well are all with me as I dream of you in the quietness about me here by the fire.

You know, I don't believe I started loving you when first I met you. It started long before then—a time when I never imagined there would be a person to fit that picture and yet deep in my heart I knew that somewhere I would find you—a gay, laughter loving, blue-eyed girl waiting to be loved and to love. I'm more than glad I've found that same girl just as I pictured her and that by a stroke of good fortune I did win her heart. One day that picture will be complete when you are mine forever. I don't think anything could change my love for you darling, for in my heart of hearts I know that you are my only true love, which could brave the changing future and unknown ways—for true heartfelt love is born in heaven and out of such divine guidance the future is known and the unknown ways are safe.

3

I'm wondering if this rambling of mine sounds readable for if not then I'll forgive you if you begin to think I'm a trifle unhinged by the solitude. It's strange the thoughts that hold sway when sitting by a warm fire on a cold winter's night. Can you imagine a different Christmas with no fires, no overcoats, without snow and in the middle of summer. Well my sweetheart that's something we will both have to get used to, but enough of that: homesickness! Sweetheart darling, you were born to be cherished and made happy. I do love you more than I could ever express with all my heart.

Artie

Artie was twenty-three at the time he wrote this letter and just eight weeks later he bombed Dresden. My mother remembered how he wept when he told her about the rumour that they were going to 'do Dresden'. And she told me that her own mother had often had to comfort him after he'd had terrible nightmares, when he used to sleep on their sofa before they were married—horrible dreams about death and mayhem and bombs dropping.

Perhaps it should be mentioned here that Art had left behind two fiancées, one in Australia and one in Canada where he did his air force training. Twenty years later the Australian jiltee was teaching me French at Hornsby Girls High School. She never gave me good marks.

After their wartime courtship Ede and Art were married on 28 April 1945, not long before the war ended. In the wedding photographs he looks dashing in his uniform and she looks beautiful in an ice-blue ensemble that shows off her long slender legs. Charlie was the handsome best man.

Eventually Art was sent back to Australia on a troopship with thousands of other young Australians who had fought in Europe. Some of them, like Art, had war brides, who followed them months later. These war bride ships always docked in Australia in a blaze of publicity and excitement, the sexual anticipation palpable. Ede and Art's reunion photo, taken at Circular Quay by a news photographer who plucked them randomly from the overexcited throng, made the front page of the Sydney *Daily Mirror*. After being forcibly separated for months by the War Office, the young couple look ecstatically in love.

As a child, I once heard my father being asked: 'How long was Ede in Australia before she became pregnant with Jacki?' And he replied: 'Twenty minutes.' But years later my father informed me that I was conceived at the Hydro Majestic Hotel in the Blue Mountains. I like both stories and can't choose between them, but there was no helicopter service running from Sydney to Medlow Bath in 1946 so I can't claim both.

Ede and Art were living in Sans Souci when I was born on 25 May 1947 in a Hurstville private hospital, in the foyer just inside the busy front door. My mother had had little warning of the impending birth, so when I emerged she was still wearing all her clothes. She never forgave me for the embarrassment.

My young parents were in for another shock, the day they brought me home from hospital, when they discovered that my toes were webbed. They still are. The old army song 'Be Kind to Your Web-Footed Friend' could've been written for me.

Soon after my birth Ruth Simpson, my grandmother in England, wrote to my mother Edith: 'Thanks for the photos of baby Jacqueline Ruth. You and Arthur are so good-looking it's surprising you have such a very plain-looking baby.' For years afterwards Daddy would remark wistfully, 'It's a shame your granny didn't live long enough to see that you didn't turn out to be so very plain after all.'

My mother took me to visit my grandmother Ruth in England just before Ruth died of cancer aged forty-eight. I was two years old and the trip took us six weeks by ship. Every morning a group of stewards, probably Friends of Dorothy, would spirit me away and take care of me. Throughout the day my mother would catch brief glimpses of me being dressed up, being taught ridiculously camp songs and generally cosseted, culminating in a first prize at the ship's talent quest, dancing topless in a hula skirt and singing 'Buttons and Bows'. A dear gay friend still refers to me as 'The Smallest Fag Hag in Australia'. Back then, aged two, it would seem I was 'The Smallest Fag Hag in the *World*'. And the youngest.

After Ruth's death, her husband Jackson Simpson (my grandfather) and her ten-year-old daughter Georgina (my aunt) both came back with us to settle in Australia, travelling on the same ship with my mother and me. There was a severe postwar housing shortage in Sydney and at first my grandfather had to live in various lodgings and Aunt Georgina was sent to boarding school, Roseville Ladies College, but only for a few months until we found somewhere with enough room for all of us. Long-term rental accommodation was so scarce that we seemed to be forever on the move and we lived in several places in my early years—Bondi, Dover Heights, Manly, Chatswood, Lane Cove and, of course, Sans Souci.

I'm fond of boasting that I've lived in twenty-nine suburbs in Sydney throughout my life, except for twelve years in Marvellous Melbourne (four suburbs) in the eighties and nineties. Puzzlingly, people often mistake me for a Melbourne native. Cheryl Barassi refused to believe my denial saying: 'Come off it, Jac. You're a Sunshine Girl if ever I saw one!' I was highly flattered, thinking she meant I have a sunny disposition, not realising that Sunshine is a suburb of Melbourne. When a doubting Pom once scoffed at me, 'Oh tosh! Sydney doesn't *have* twenty-nine suburbs!' I checked the Gregory's and there are at least five hundred.

My grandfather was a true gentleman of solid working class stock—he'd been a miner in England, courteous and impeccably groomed, and with a North Country accent so thick that I had to translate everything he said to my friends into Australian so they could understand him. He lived with my mother and father from 1950 until he died in 1980. Jackson (obviously I was named after him and Ruth) was always buying me books, an average of one a week. I think he had an almost mystical belief in the power of reading and loved my tendency to bookwormery. He bought me everything from Enid Blyton to Emily Brontë. He bought me my first Patrick White (*Tree of Man*), my first Christina Stead and my first Zola, and when I enjoyed something he would comb the bookshops for everything else by the same author, like a man on a mission.

Gone with the Wind probably wasn't suitable reading for an eight-year-old, however. And all that reading meant that I knew about SEX earlier than most of the other kids, which probably accounts for a great deal of what happened afterwards. I told one of the boys over the road where babies come from when we were seven. He told his mother; she told mine and I was thoroughly scolded.

Apart from filling my room with books, my grandfather filled the house with a constant supply of chocolates, probably a reaction to all that wartime rationing. Cartons of Polly Waffles, Kit Kats and Violet Crumble Bars from Parry's milk bar in Kogarah (see Clive James' *Unreliable Memoirs*) crammed the kitchen shelves. Visiting playmates found them irresistible but I soon tired of them and to this day I'm not fond of chocolate, for which I feel very grateful to my grandfather. Otherwise I could be the size of a garage, or a medium-sized tool shed.

My mother gave me a box of pennies when I was four. An hour later she found me sitting on the front fence giving them away to passing children on their way home from school. A socialist? *Moi?*

My parents were keen subscribers to the Sydney Symphony Orchestra all their lives. Not surprising then that Dad took me to my first symphony concert when I was two years old and apparently I danced in the aisle of the Sydney Town Hall to Schwanda the Bagpiper. Obnoxious? *Moi?*

When I was three my grandfather took me to see the pantomime *Aladdin* at the Tivoli Theatre. It starred the fabulous Jenny Howard as the Principal Boy with her hands on her hips in the customary garb of tights, jerkin and high-heeled boots ready to take on all villains. It was that magical experience that made me determined, aged only three, to be up there on the stage one day, telling stories just like Jenny Howard. Indeed, my friend Noeline Brown says I still have Principal Boy legs: sturdy with trim ankles. When she played Aladdin Jenny Howard wore beautiful green satin boots, which Maggie Blinco found twenty-five years later at an auction of old theatre costumes and generously presented to me. They still hang on my bedroom door by their green laces, a little worse for wear since the dog chewed them. Jenny Howard would boast on TV chat shows well into her eighties that she had inspired both Nancye Hayes and me to follow a life upon the wicked stage.

My mother, always hoping to improve my looks, had me on diets from an early age, packing me a lunch of Vegemite on VitaWeet diet biscuits and, for play lunch, an apple. At the age of six I was kissing Graham Morris behind the wash shed in exchange for his Peak Freens custard creams, exacer-bating my chubbiness while honing my love-making skills as a possible vocation.

My first kiss was at North Bondi kindergarten with another three-year-old, called Charles. I felt sorry for him because he was nearly always crying, except when I kissed him and he smiled. This was an early insight into how to treat the male of the species that has served me well (the insight, not the species, though I'm not complaining). From then on I always loved boys, sometimes even wanting to *be* one. The day I started school at Carlton Central in Percival Street near Bexley, none of the five-year-old girls were crying but all of the five-year-old boys were sobbing as if their heart would break. I longed to kiss every single one of them (and probably did, eventually).

A comely six-year-old chap called Cliffy lived in Warialda Street and we used to play Superman and Lois Lane in his backyard. One day he said he loved me and that he'd do anything to make me love him in return. I promised I'd love him if he could fly. So he adjusted his cape, jumped off the roof and broke both his arms. I then told him that I didn't love him because he couldn't fly after all. Callous? *Moi?*

Twenty-five years later I told that story to a disbelieving audience on the Mike Walsh *Midday Show* and a chef from the New South Wales South Coast called the station to confirm it. It was Cliffy.

My brother Rod was born when I was five. My mother's pregnancy was a difficult one. She was anaemic and spent her last two months prior to giving birth in St George Hospital. Children were not allowed into maternity hospitals in those days, so I didn't see her for eight weeks. I was sent to live with my father's former foster mother, Connie, in Cabramatta and I cried for my mother every night.

My dad, who was working for the Postmaster-General and studying law full-time at Sydney University, would make the long trek by train out to St Johns Road, Cabramatta, to see me a couple of times a week. He brought me a box of paints and a painting book but, when he was told I was painting my face with them, on his next visit he brought me a cigar-box of proper stage greasepaint (a 5, a 9, a Carmine and a Lake, a black eyeliner pencil) and some cold cream.

Connie, or 'Auntie Connie' as we called her, was a widow and she lived in a Housing Commission fibro cottage with her daughter Clarice, her son-in-law Albert and her son Leonard. Another daughter, Mavis, lived with her husband and children nearby. There were apricot-coloured satin festoon curtains hanging across the glass front door, which I thought rather glamorous. I would spend hours amusing myself performing on their front porch, which I felt was rather like a stage—singing, dancing, making up stories and being lots of different people. They had no dress-up box but Leonard kindly lent me his old windcheater and work shorts and Albert let me use his umbrella as a walking stick.

One day I was sitting on the front step taking a breather (it must have been interval) when I overheard Auntie Connie and her daughters Clarice and Mavis talking about me. One of them said: 'Do you think she's *all there*?' Another said, 'Yes she's *all there*—she's just *unusual*.' Next time my dad came to visit me, I asked him what the word 'unusual' meant, and remember being relieved when he told me, 'It means *special*.' I suppose it's not surprising that I may have given the impression of being a little odd at that time. And let's not forget I was barely five years old—I actually turned five while I was living in Cabramatta. Jovial Uncle Albert—a dear man who, what's more, was a fireman—once remarked to my dad, 'She's a real character, isn't she!' and I clearly remember thinking, no, no, I'm *lots* of characters.

One Sunday they took me all the way out to St George Hospital and, because I wasn't allowed in, Dad put me on his shoulders and stood in the garden so I could wave at Mum, who was barely visible leaning out of a second-floor window. She told me years later that she wept at the pathetic sight of me in the distance looking like Little Orphan Annie because Auntie Connie had let down the hem of my best dress 'for the sake of Modesty'. Whoever Modesty was.

When I was twenty-two and expecting a child without being married to the father, Dad finally told me about his own background. He was born out of wedlock in 1921 to a teacher called Grace Weaver, in Goulburn, New South Wales. He never really knew who his father was but suspected it might have been a William Onions, a local rogue who had something to do with the Goulburn Cinema. Maybe he was the owner. Or the projectionist . . . or the cleaner . . . Whatever.

Grace kept Arthur until he was seven. But then hard times hit rural Australia and he was diagnosed with malnutrition, taken from Grace and made a ward of the state. He never saw his mother again though he once ran away to find her but was caught before he made it to Goulburn. Connie and her husband, with three children of their own, fostered Arthur, though he always refused to be adopted by them, hoping to return to his mother one day.

In 1932 my dad rode his bicycle across the Harbour Bridge the day it opened. He was already a pupil at Fort Street Boys High School. Connie's family lived in Marion Street, Leichhardt (this was before they moved to Cabramatta in the early 1950s), and with them he attended the Salvation Army citadel. Dad learnt to play several brass instruments proficiently and was a member of a number of different bands all his life. Brass bands now make me weep for my dad. I can't listen to them.

Connie's entire family often reminded Art that he was 'a child of sin', which probably accounts for his anxiety about my own son's wellbeing. My mother said that when Art confessed that he was a bastard, just before they were married, he was expecting her to break off their engagement. Instead she laughed at his concern. A typically commonsense, practical and irreverent response from Ede, God bless her.

I heard a different story about my grandmother Grace from someone who'd lived in Goulburn: that when Grace was fifteen she was working as a maid on a property in the area and that the owner, her boss, a man in his fifties, was my dad's sire. Which would have made her only fifty-six when I began working in television and appearing in the newspapers. Did she ever wonder if we were related, and how did she feel about it? Grace was small and fair-haired, like me; added to that, I resemble my father, so it would have been easy for her to make the connection. Who knows?

Finally I left Cabramatta and Auntie Connie when Ede brought my baby brother home from hospital. After my two months' separation from Mummy, an eternity in the life of a five-year-old, I felt very shy when I first arrived in Kogarah, home at last. The blinds were down and a navy blue pram stood in the middle of the room with a mosquito net over it. 'Look what I've got,' she whispered to me, carefully lifting a tightly wrapped bundle of tiny infant from the depths of the pram. For me it was adoration at first sight. 'What's his name?' I asked. 'Rodney,' she said. I was totally enchanted with him. The perfection of him, his lips, his eyelashes, his stillness. When the local GP circumcised him on the green laminex and chrome kitchen table, I was sent to play in the lounge room. His screams of pain and distress were ear-piercing and I can still hear them now. Crying with rage myself, I swore then that if I ever had a little boy of my own, *nobody* would be allowed to do anything so barbaric to him.

At six weeks my brother contracted whooping cough and almost died. No one in the house slept much during this crisis. My grandfather would snatch my baby brother by the ankles and turn him upside down when he started to choke.

My dad graduated in law from Sydney University when I was about six and he was also admitted to the Bar. I remember being told he was now a barrister and being shown his Bachelor of Law degree. Somehow I got the words confused and solemnly announced at Sunday School that my daddy was a bachelor, which was a cause for considerable mirth amongst the young teachers in St James' Parish Hall that particular Sunday.

Mine was a fairly run-of-the-mill 1950s Sydney childhood, for me a flashing kaleidoscope of impressions: blistering heat--

waves without the relief of airconditioners (*airconditioning—what's that?*), the ear-splitting din of a million cicadas, billy-carts with ballbearing wheels and rope steering reins careering down Union Street. Bare feet stained black from running on hot bitumen, squeals of pleasure playing under the garden hose on the front lawn, grubby faces sticky from eating huge crescents of watermelon.

Paddle Pops had only recently been invented and not everyone could afford them, so the people in the corner shop on Percival Street sold homemade ice blocks straight from their fridge. Outside that very corner shop is where I got drenched one afternoon during a thunderstorm, dancing in the gutter, trying to be Gene Kelly singing in the rain for the amusement of the other kids waiting under the leaky awning for their mothers to come and collect them with their rain-coats. I was in the full flight of performance when a hand suddenly appeared from nowhere and grabbed me by the scruff of the neck. It was my furious mother, totally un-expected, who then dragged me home in the teeming rain. An ignominious finale for the would-be Gene Kelly. How was I to know she'd come to collect me? She'd never done it before.

Television didn't arrive until I was nine and my parents resisted buying one until I was twelve so the wireless was our major source of entertainment. Much of the 1950s was spent listening avidly to the radio serials like 'Tarzan', 'Search for the Golden Boomerang' and 'Superman' (but not 'When A Girl Marries', which my father banned; how ironic when this girl marries often), the Sunday night plays and 'The

Argonauts'—I was Ancona 15, and Phideas twice gave my paintings a good critique and a blue certificate, Phideas being the pseudonym of the great Australian painter Jeffrey Smart.

Memories of being nurtured by a teacher I adored called Miss Bliss, hot fresh bread delivered by the baker on a horse and cart, exchanging the old wooden ice chest for a Crossley Shelvador Refrigerator, watching fascinated as my arm slowly went through the wringer of the Wilkins Servis washing machine up to my elbow before Mum rushed into the laundry to extract it (an experience many of my generation seem to have had), helping Dad wash the 1938 yellow Dodge and later the blue FJ Holden, a midget fox terrier called Twink and a blue budgie called Nicky Popov.

I spent months lying awake at night, frightened about the Kingsgrove Slasher, a serial prowler who broke into women's bedrooms and slashed them with a razor blade while they were sleeping. There was an annual pilgrimage out to the Royal Easter Show at Moore Park, always damp and muddy, where Dad insisted we tramp doggedly through endless horse and cow stalls to 'feel the country', he said. Every year at the Police Exhibition in the Hordern Pavilion I would stand transfixed before the grisly, lurid photos of the famous Pyjama Girl murder victim's charred body, thus ensuring I had nightmares for weeks to come.

One day in the school holidays I sat fascinated on an upturned crate for hours watching a sign-writer paint a twenty-foot high Kinkara Tea lady ringing her bell on the wall of Rothman's grocer shop. We kept in touch with world events by watching flickering black-and-white newsreels at the State theatrette in Market Street. I liked helping Mum fill hampers of food—tinned peaches, dried apricots and sultanas—in David Jones' Food Hall to send back to ration-stricken England, food hampers paid for by my grandfather, who was now working as a fitter and turner in a factory at Rhodes, near Ryde, and whose work clobber always had a strange chemical aroma. I remember morning teas at Repin's where my mother always had cinnamon toast, and lunches at Cahill's in Castlereagh Street where my brother once tipped an entire lime spider drink into her best pig-skin handbag. Holidays in Ulladulla, Coolangatta, Adelaide, Griffith, Dolls Point, Summer Hill and, of course, in Canberra staying with Belle and Charlie. The kids over the road used to go to a place oddly called Sussex Singlet. Or so I thought. I was quite surprised when I finally realised they were referring to Sussex *Inlet*, and that it hadn't been named after some strange British undergarment.

My mother used to wear a beautifully tailored, figure-hugging black overcoat with fox-fur cuffs. Whenever she held my hand, my cheek would fit neatly against her wrist, so I must have been about three or four. How vividly I can conjure up the sensation of the soft fur against my face and the feeling of safety and comfort I derived from it.

Ede was a strict disciplinarian and a frequent smacker. She was a charming and civilised woman but she was also given to volatile and fearsome bouts of temper. Much of my childhood was spent striving to stay in her good books—no easy task. She was a stickler for good manners, especially at the dinner table and in cafés. I carried a longstanding resentment of her strict rule that the bottom of the milkshake —the frothy residue, arguably the best part of the experience— must be left in the bottom of the metal container because to suck it up through the straw made a rude noise. I vowed then that, in the distant future, any child of mine would not only be allowed, but encouraged, to finish the milkshake to the last drop regardless of the cacophony of noisy bubbles that might accompany it. I shall be just as permissive with my grandchildren, if I'm fortunate enough to be blessed with them.

Bea Miles, the legendary Sydney eccentric who was immortalised by Kate Grenville in her novel *Lilian's Story*, arrived in our street one morning having refused to vacate Mr McCormack's taxi. The notorious Bea Miles sat under the house with us kids and gave us sweets. She was enormous, with a booming voice, but not a bit frightening. By play-lunch time, the police came and took her away and they sent us to school.

On a shopping trip into the city, Mummy and I saw the famous and mysterious *Eternity* man, later revealed as Arthur Stace and celebrated in fireworks on the Sydney Harbour Bridge on New Year's Eve 2000. He was already a legend in the 1950s and we actually witnessed him in the act of writing '*Eternity*' in chalk on the footpath outside Bebarfalds department store, opposite the Sydney Town Hall. We often saw the writing, but the writer himself was always elusive, except for that one magical glimpse when Mum said, 'Look, Jac, it's the Eternity Man,' as he chalked the final flourish and disappeared in a moment.

Even though a horrible boy vomited on my best kilt when I was waiting in the queue outside the Carlton Odeon, I used to love going to the pictures every Saturday. In fact I was drummed out of the Brownies for wagging three Saturdays in a row to catch the Esther Williams Festival at the Kogarah Victory: great classics like *Dangerous When Wet*, *Million Dollar Mermaid*, *Neptune's Daughter* etc. I would skulk off with my shilling for Brownies and hand it over to MGM. When I was found out, the Brown Owl, Mrs Prebble, said there was no place for a deceitful Brownie in the Bexley chapter and I was stripped of my epaulettes.

My mother had an English accent but it wasn't broadly North Country like my grandfather's because in the 1930s, when she was at grammar school, there was a policy to discourage regional accents, if not to stamp them out altogether. It wasn't until the 1950s that such accents became fashionable again, along with gritty kitchen-sink dramas.

I was about nine when Ede decided I needed elocution lessons, to spruce up my increasingly Ocker vowel sounds, even though I was desperate to tap-dance instead. She took me to Joy Mead in Allawah, who had me recite for her and then sent me from the room before informing my mother: 'That child was *born to act*!' To which Ede replied: '*Oh my god, no!*' She was to utter exactly the same words thirteen years later when told I was pregnant.

My mother was as unlike a stage mother as it was possible to be. Although my parents were quietly supportive, and I guess they felt my future as an actor was inevitable, at no time was I ever pushed into performing or ever made to feel

I was responsible for vicariously fulfilling some frustrated ambitions of their own, as is often the case with stage mothers—and stage fathers, for that matter. But from then on I was allowed to attend classes at St George Children's Theatre in Kingsgrove, and I had a terrific time there acting in plays, taking classes in voice, movement and improvisation, doing re-enactments of Scott of the Antarctic (I was usually Amundsen, though I secretly longed to be Oates, because Oates sacrificed his life for his friends with the line 'I'm just going outside, I may be some time', then disappeared out the tent flap into a raging blizzard never to be seen again) and the dramatic abduction we'd all seen on the newsreel in the Petrov Affair (I was always Mrs Petrov).

I'd already had some stage experience before an audience. Keith Smith, the radio star, came talent-scouting to our school to choose children to be on his very popular national show called 'The Pied Piper' and I was recommended to him by my teacher. After auditioning me Keith Smith then nabbed me to do several episodes. It was supposed to be ad-lib and spontaneous but he did run us through the questions beforehand and, if the cute riposte didn't quite measure up, he'd be rather stern and say: 'That's a boring answer! Think of something better than that.'

The program was done live on-stage in front of an audience of four hundred in 2GB's Macquarie Auditorium in Phillip Street. The best part was being allowed to stay around afterwards to watch the recording of the 'Macquarie Hour', a different play each week with the cream of Australia's actors reading from scripts into microphones. Glamorous stars like Margo Lee, Ray Barrett, Neva Carr Glynn, Leonard Teale, Nigel Lovell, John Ewart, and John Meillon, all wearing tuxedos and evening gowns. Quite an education for a seven-year-old. I resolved then and there that I wanted to do exactly that when I grew up.

I was also the Quiz Kids' spelling champion for a couple of weeks, but I stopped bragging about that after I heard a professor say that good spellers are usually fascists. Or punctual train drivers.

The house we then lived in at Union Street, West Kogarah, was a little crowded, though I never noticed at the time. My aunt Georgina and I shared one bedroom, my parents and my baby brother the other, and my grandfather slept on the open verandah, which was chilly in winter. It was an ugly semi-detached, black brick cottage built in the 1930s and owned by Uncle Arch, who lived next door with his girl-friend Auntie Em (in those days it was thought polite for children to address their elders as Auntie and Uncle even if they were not related). Uncle Arch had made a packet buying up lots of property in Sydney's beach suburbs—Rose Bay, Bondi, Coogee—during the war after the Japanese torpedoed a ship in the harbour, killing eighteen sailors, and shelled surrounding areas, thus causing people to take fright and sell their real estate for a song.

Our house always smelled of Pine-o-Cleen, 4711 cologne and stale cigarette smoke which hung around every room like a pall. Both my parents and my grandfather were heavy smokers. My mother lit a cigarette first thing each morning, and even smoked in the bath. The three children who lived in that house—my aunt Georgina, my brother Rod and I—grew up to be confirmed non-smokers. How I loathed that putrid stench from the thick clouds of continual Craven A's. How sullen I became when told to fetch an ashtray even though I was constantly chastised for being melodramatic when I couldn't hide my revulsion for the filthy stink of the butts. 'Don't just do as you are told, Jacqueline, do it with *good grace*,' they admonished me.

Aunt Georgina was a strikingly pretty teenager, besotted with James Dean and Richard Burton. She was also ineffably sad, probably because her mother had died when my aunt was only ten. I used to spend a lot of time trying to imagine what that must have been like.

Georgina and I used to play a game in bed where I had to scratch messages on her back with my finger for her to decipher. It's a good game that I still enjoy, though not with Georgina, who now lives in Queensland with her husband Uncle Harry; they have five grown-up daughters. Harry Lozan, blond, good-looking and a tennis coach, was a champion tennis player who had competed against the likes of Lew Hoad and Ken Rosewall. He was so good he'd even beaten them occasionally. Harry and Georgina's wedding reception was at Sydney's Metropole Hotel, where Chifley Square now stands. That wedding reception is also where I tasted my first oyster, at that moment ensuring that oysters became one of my rare enduring passions.

Recently, on one of those tell-all surprise TV shows—Channel 9's *This Is Your Life*, to be precise—my aunt

Georgina revealed that at the age of seven I used to sit in front of the mirror and practise weeping, a memory that totally eludes me, though I don't doubt Georgina's story. On the same TV program another relative told a tale about me that I know to be demonstrably false. Time and retelling had made it authentic for the narrator so I didn't refute it, in case denying it might be construed as lack of grace under pressure.

Similarly, one of my ex-husbands often regales me with accounts of entire vivid conversations we've had, and I don't recall a single scrap. 'Memory, dear Cecily, is the diary we all carry about with us,' said Oscar Wilde. Pity that it's full of fibs, half-fibs and stuff that's disappeared into the ether.

The family legend goes that my father taught me to read when I was a toddler and at age four I would recite passages from Swift. My mother, ever the sceptic, was scornful. Her contention was that I'd memorised entire chapters and was merely repeating them, not reading them. She may have been right. All I remember is that I loved *Gulliver's Travels*. I identified with the Lilliputians. (For those who don't know, I'm impossibly small.)

Another family story is that at age four I was reading that awful Sydney rag, the *Sunday Truth*, one morning after Sunday School and Daddy said: 'May I have the paper, Jacki?' and I replied: 'Please just wait until I've finished reading Dramas of the Criminal Courts.' Precocious? *Moi?*

My dad also used to read me stories from Shakespeare by Charles and Mary Lamb. Lambs' *Tales From Shakespeare* was the first pun I knew and understood:

Q: What's for dinner?

A: Lambs' tails from Shakespeare. (Shakespeare was the butcher in Bexley.)

My favourite Lambs' tale was *Twelfth Night*. Though aged only four, I could identify with Viola's predicament and share the dangerous thrill of pretending to be someone else, especially a boy. And I would weep with sympathy at Malvolio's humiliation. I also loved *A Midsummer Night's Dream*, delighting in the fact that Bottom was a Weaver, just like me.

By the time I'd started school, Dad was reading me Shakespeare's plays from the huge leatherbound volume I still keep on my bookshelf alongside Dad's *Complete Works of George Bernard Shaw*, which he would also read to me. *Arms and the Man* was the first one. My mother scoffed: 'She can't possibly understand Shaw at her age!' She was probably right but I do remember enjoying it, hanging on his every word and never being bored. I still find Shaw a bit of a puzzle sometimes, more than fifty years later.

I do remember reading the lesson in church when I was only six or seven and needing a milk crate to stand on to see the Bible. Not long ago outside Wynyard Station a sweet woman grabbed my arm and said, 'You won't remember me—I was your Sunday School teacher in Bexley when you were three years old. At the Christmas concert we had you picked to play the Christmas tree fairy but you were insistent that you wanted to be a black child instead. So we had to tie all your white curls into a black bathing cap and colour your face with burnt cork and you sang "Lulla Lulla Bye Bye".

Only three, mind you! And you were adamant! It wouldn't be allowed now!'

So there I was, a character actress at three. I remember my father carrying me home that night after a triumphant performance in St James's Parish Hall; I remember crying with overexcitement and Daddy saying, 'You have stripes on your face where the tears have streamed.' From then on, making my face black with burnt cork and a bit of my mother's cold cream became a favourite pastime. She was surprisingly patient about this odd habit.

I'd never met a black child, or a black adult for that matter. After all, it was Sydney in the fifties. However, I can still see in my mind the poster of Jesus on the Sunday School wall with several children of every possible race and hue surrounding him and sitting on his lap. The black child was the closest to him. I became very attached to that picture and studied it for hours—well, years in fact.

My fascination with what made other people tick, wanting to get inside their skins, becoming someone else for a time, was deeply ingrained in me almost from infancy. I would wander up to the Kogarah Station ramp, visit the Italian greengrocer and his wife, and pretend that I was Italian too. I would tell them about my imaginary family in great detail, in an Italian accent of course. The Italian mama would always hug me and give me a banana or an apple.

Or I'd drop in on the cobbler on the other side of the road and pretend I was French, with a completely different set of family circumstances and a Parisian accent, or the closest I could imagine at the ages of five, six and seven. I still love the smell of shoe repair shops.

In the newsagency where I was sent to collect the papers, I would use my grandfather's broad North Country accent and sadly tell them about the harsh postwar rationing in England that I'd recently left behind me to come to sunny Australia. This usually got me a free packet of Lifesavers and once even a box of caramel sweets called Columbines. Not that I masqueraded as other people for reward. The joy and danger of the make-believe were enough and the perks were just an added treat. It seems hard to believe now that I got away with it but, looking back, I can only assume all those retail folk believed me or were terrific actors themselves.

Although no longer regular churchgoers my parents were still confirmed Christians, my mother Church of England and my father a young veteran of many years in the Salvation Army. Dad knew his Bible inside-out and back-to-front (what an odd expression; taken literally it means from Revelations to Genesis). At the age of eight weeks, I had had a proper church christening wearing the Simpson family ancestral christening gown, with two officially designated godmothers, Peggy Griffiths and Flo Drury. Peggy, who'd befriended my mother on the sea trip out from England, was a tiny livewire so accustomed to wearing very high heels that on the rare occasions when she removed her shoes she would still walk about on tiptoes. I would grab these moments of opportunity to practise teetering about in her stilettos like a tiny stilt walker, which has stood me in good stead for more than fifty years. Even now I still wear five-inch heels on an almost daily basis. But at times it's been a strain on my back and feet, and five-inch heels still only elevate me to shorter than average.

However, the best part about Auntie Peggy, apart from wearing her high-heels, was her broad Scottish accent, which I loved. I would spend hours listening to her, watching her mouth, fascinated by her every phrase and cadence; then I would try to reproduce the same sounds, much to her delight.

My other godmother, Auntie Flo Drury, had been a friend of my dad's since they were in amateur theatre groups as teenagers. Flo is Australian but with Irish parents—Mr and Mrs McIllhagger, who used to live next door to her in Kingsgrove. I loved crawling under the loose paling in the back fence, going through Mr Mac's vege garden—spinach, rhubarb, *real* tomatoes—for visits to Auntie Flo's mum, who would pound the piano in the front parlour and insist I sing along to her accompaniment as she talked nonstop in her beautiful Belfast brogue. As soon as I got home from these visits my mother could hardly wait to hear me recount everything Mrs Mac had said, in an Irish accent, of course.

Auntie Flo, or Flossie as her family calls her, is now eighty-four, still a well-groomed vivacious redhead with stunning legs. She recently came to one of my performances and backstage afterwards told me: 'You're a good-looking woman, Jac, but never the beauty your mother was.'

As children we had a lot more freedom to wander about the neighbourhood during the 1950s. From the age of six I was allowed to catch the trolley bus to Dolls Point for a day at the beach with Sandra Telford, who was the same age. Not advisable these days.

Our customary pit stop for pale-green lime milkshakes was at Parry's milk bar on the other side of Kogarah Station. However, much as I wanted to, there was no way I could set about masquerading as a Greek in Parry's milk bar. The Parrys were Greek friends of my grandfather's and would have dobbed me in straightaway the next time he was in the shop, which was every afternoon on his way home from work.

The travelling player Thea Rowe used to visit our school a couple of times a year to perform in the big kindergarten room. It cost sixpence and was money well spent. She must have been middle-aged; my dad said he remembered her coming to his primary school in Leichhardt. She carried a big basket of costumes and told stories, becoming each character with a simple change of garment. I enjoyed her immensely. The Rayner sisters were another acting treat who'd entertain small children on the school circuit. I adored their visits.

My aunt Georgina loved to dress me up and paint my face (I loved it too; I still love it) and for a fancy dress competition at my school she spent a lot of time transforming me into a miniature Nell Gwyn, Charles II's mistress, complete with long tight frock, huge picture hat, rouged cheeks and a beauty spot, ie a fake mole drawn with eyebrow pencil.

Uncle Arch and Auntie Em next door said I looked more like Mae West. My aunt was scornful: 'But she's carrying a basket of oranges to sell at Covent Garden—she *must* be Nell Gwyn!' Whether Nell Gwyn or Mae West, I was already masquerading as a sex symbol at the tender age of seven.

Union Street, West Kogarah, was full of Irish Catholic kids, except for me, my baby brother and the Jewish grocer's daughters, Lena and Louise Rothman. So for a time I thought that being Protestant and being Jewish were much the same, in that the Catholic kids disapproved of us. Though I did wonder, when I overheard the girls' grandmother refer to me as a gentile, if she meant I was some kind of lizard.

I vividly remember attending a screening of the Charlton Heston version of *The Ten Commandments* with the Rothmans' parents, Phil and Miriam, and a large group of their friends and family. When the Angel of Death passes over the Jewish homes and Moses says, 'This event will be celebrated for thousands of years,' many of the grown-ups began to weep, including some of the men. I realised I was witnessing something very significant, without fully understanding it. It wasn't until my teens, when I read Leon Uris' *Exodus*, that I wanted to be Jewish.

The Catholic kids in Union Street numbered more than twenty. They would often remind us solemnly, 'The Pope says you'll burn in hell.' For a time I would fervently pray every night that I'd wake up next morning and be a Catholic—a magical nocturnal transformation. But it never happened.

When the nuns awarded my rabbit David first prize at the St Patrick's Pet Show, my grandfather remarked that they were probably just trying to convert me. To this day I prefer to believe that David was the best rabbit there.

chapter two

Portrait of a Very Young Actress

LIKE HUNDREDS OF OTHER LITTLE GIRLS, I WAS SEXUALLY molested. I was seven years old and he was a man in his forties married to a friend of my mother, with three daughters of his own slightly younger than I was. It was horrible, very painful and I was terrified of him. He threatened me into secrecy by saying that, if I told my parents, he would deny it and say he had caught me touching myself.

For four years I had frightening nightmares about him and lived in dread of the next time he'd be babysitting when my parents and his wife went out together. I hated the sound of the front door closing when they left the house and I would lie there in the dark very afraid, pretending to be asleep.

He would wait until his own children were asleep and then carry me into his lounge room, where he would do what he liked to me. And he hurt me. I would always cry and plead with him to stop, but that only seemed to make him more determined. His tongue smelled of tobacco and beer.

When my parents and his wife arrived home he'd be holding me on his lap reading me a story and say, 'As usual, I couldn't get her to go to sleep.' One day, when I was eleven, I told him he must not come near me anymore or I would tell. He was nasty and sneered at me, but he must have believed me because he never did it again.

That is all I intend to say on the subject now and forever. Perhaps this is partly because of my strong reluctance to be unwillingly cast in the role of a victim or as some kind of spokesperson. Maybe it's also due to a feeling that denial and forgetting have proved to be my best ways of coping with a trauma that I believe I've successfully put behind me. Apart from confiding in a few close friends, I've kept it secret for more than fifty years, even from my parents, my brother and my son. I hope I don't regret having revealed it now. The sort of cruelty I endured is still sadly prevalent—selfish adults without conscience preying on prepubescent children. There was a time in my twenties when I was so consumed with hatred for my tormentor that I fantasised about doing him bodily harm. He's dead now. I'm over it, almost forgetting, though not quite forgiving. The subject is closed and shall remain within the pages of this book. To delve any further would only cause further pain, not just to me but to other people as well.

When I was ten, we moved to West Pymble, to a War Service home that was 'architect-designed' by Peter Swan. Lots of glass, cork floors, a flat roof and a Mondrian-inspired design in primary colours—red, blue and yellow—painted by my father on the wall of the carport.

West Pymble was mostly bushland then. Ryde Road was a two-lane road, not the six-lane arterial it is now, and De Burghs Bridge was a rickety, narrow little crossing slung low over the Lane Cove River. The houses were set so far back from the road that it was impossible to see them, so there were markers on the gum trees to help you work out where your driveway was. My father found thirty-two funnel-webs in the backyard in a single afternoon when he was clearing weeds to plant vegetables. I once trod on a brown snake on the way to school and one day a blue-tongue lizard terrorised my mother at the kitchen door. Flocks of lorikeets and kookaburras would descend onto the Hills hoist every afternoon and the occasional wallaby would wander in and sniff the azaleas.

Ryde Road, where we lived, was part of a new housing estate built with War Service loans for returned servicemen, a couple of miles from the real Pymble on the other side of the North Shore railway line. The wrong side of the tracks, literally, according to Auntie Beryl, a childhood friend of Dad's who lived with Uncle Frank, a Changi veteran, in a cul-de-sac off Livingstone Avenue, a more desirable part of Pymble but still the unfortunate side of the railway line. We didn't even have sewerage for the first year and the night soil carter would visit twice a week to pick up and deliver the pans. (I have no idea why it was called *night* soil when most folk shit in the *morning*.) One night he tripped and dropped his full load on Mrs Winkle's patio.

I still went to Sunday School, now at St John's Anglican Church at Gordon, where my teacher was Mr Waters. I was confirmed there and I even taught Sunday School briefly. I loved the rector, Roy Wotton—indeed, I still love him. He's more than ninety years old now and sometimes comes to see me in shows. His daughter Judy remains a good friend.

Around the time that we first moved to West Pymble my father went to Canberra to work for the Crown Solicitor. When I became unwell, the doctor's diagnosis was that I was fretting for him, so at weekends I was flown to Canberra to see him by TAA, unaccompanied. Glamorous air hostesses with platinum-blonde French rolls and legs like Grace Kelly would hold my hand and once, after I'd been sick, a dashing pilot cradled me down the stairs of the DC3 straight into the waiting arms of my father. It turned out they'd been in the air force together.

In retrospect I think my malaise of spirit could also have been related to a sadist of a teacher at Gordon West Public School, who regularly humiliated and chastised me in front of the class in a misguided attempt to bring me down a peg or two. Maybe she was right; maybe I deserved it. But it's true I used to wake up in tears on Tuesdays, Wednesdays and Thursdays, when she taught us, and be perfectly happy on Mondays and Fridays, when the headmaster taught us. Anyway I got my own back. I was dux of the school in sixth grade, out of one hundred and twenty sixth-graders.

Then came Hornsby Girls High School. When I began First Year (Year 7) there I couldn't reach the tuckshop counter. I was twelve and a half years old and four feet seven (139 centimetres). Then I shot up four and a half inches (about 11 centimetres) in the next year. And never grew another skerrick. Ever.

One of my best friends at school was Jenny Hoffmann, who is a stunning six-foot redhead. We used to go to drama school together, to the Rathbone Academy, where I went after I moved to the North Shore and left the St George Children's Theatre. We must have made an odd couple. When she was seventeen she fell in love with a novelist who was described by Mrs Hoffmann with a certain amount of alarm as 'a writer of erotic stories', much to my mother's amusement. His name was Frank Moorhouse.

When my father saw Jenny and me in our graduation play he said, 'You were very good, darling, but Jenny was brilliant and will be a star.' And he was right. Jen reinvented herself as Roxy Beaujolais, ran Ronnie Scott's jazz club in London for twenty years and now runs the best pubs in the West End.

Another of my school friends was Susan Kessler, who became a great singer to much acclaim on the international circuit. Loved all over the world for her beautiful classical voice, she died while only in her forties. Sue and I sat together in choir practice every morning for five years singing soprano. It was Sue who decided my stage name should be Jacki without an *e*—she wrote it on my spectacles case and that's how it's been ever since. I wish I'd left it as

Jacqueline. Much better. Jacqueline is a beautiful traditional French name with connotations of mystery, glamour and romance. Jacky is a sweaty, sleeveless flannelette shirt worn by shearers. (Not that I have anything against shearers. Those *arms*!)

The West Pymble to Gordon Station bus was a hotbed of adolescent intrigue. Young hearts and straw boaters were broken in the back seat of the bus on a daily basis, only to be mended and rebroken on the train to Hornsby. And the gossip raged like a bushfire. A piece of graffiti on the back window of the bus declared 'Jacki Weaver is the Sex Symbol of West Pymble'. Which some bright spark altered to read: 'Jacki Weaver is the Sex *Thimble* of West Pymble'. As I don't have a lisp, it must have been a reference to my size. I was thirteen years old at this time.

On Friday nights in the Loftberg Hall the YWCA held dances which became a teenage hormone fest that neither the organisers nor the unsuspecting parents could possibly have imagined. The stroll home via Loftberg Oval included kissing. 'Darcy' was my first love.

Some psychologists might say that being sexually molested from the age of seven led directly to my being sexually active by the time I was twelve and a half but, after many years of pondering this, I don't believe the two matters are related. For a start I adored 'Darcy', who was only thirteen and little more than a child himself. Everything that happened between us was willing and consensual, with no question of coercion. Nearly every day after school Darcy and I would make love in his mother's bed; but by the time she arrived home from work, we'd be diligently doing our homework. Soon after that, Darcy and I would ride our bicycles home to my house before it got dark. In summer we would sometimes detour through the bush and make love again beside the creek.

My mother was very fond of Darcy and approved of our friendship and the way he looked after me and helped me with my homework; he was very scholarly and a year ahead of me at school. In her eyes we were innocent children. And we *were* children. Children indulging in very adult recreation. And avoiding unwanted pregnancy more by luck than good management. I was infatuated with Darcy for a long time. I also loved 'Angus' who was Darcy's friend at school. We formed an odd trio and spent a lot of time together. Angus the romantic film buff imagined we were a reflection of the story of Jules and Jim, the Truffaut classic about two men in love with the same woman. I don't know what's happened to Darcy but I still love Angus more than forty years later. I also love Angus' wife and his two children, and see them all regularly.

In 1960, I arrived home one night from a YWCA dance wearing lipstick for the first time, in a shade called Rock 'n' Rose. My mother scolded me for wearing lipstick. She'd have been appalled if she'd known what else I was up to. I was the naughtiest girl in high school. That's what many people said anyway, especially the tuckshop mothers. I'm not sure if I really *was* the naughtiest girl in the school, but I was certainly a major contender.

By 'naughty' I don't mean drugs and shoplifting, or even smoking, but there is documented evidence that I was heavily involved, from an early age, in rock'n'roll and regular detentions. I was given so many detentions a plaque should have been erected in the detention room in my memory. Detentions for misdemeanours as various as wagging sport, reading novels during algebra, giggling in French, giggling in Latin, giggling in assembly, letting the dog eat my homework, and the most serious offence of all: talking to boys on the train while not wearing my gloves. The sight of a schoolgirl's bare hands could send any mild-mannered Knox, Barker or Normanhurst boy into a marauding frenzy.

I don't think I was a wicked girl, even though some people told me I was. I think I was just high-spirited and adventurous and an undeniable source of anxiety for many of my teachers at Hornsby Girls High School. Because my marks were usually good, my rebellious and defiant behaviour seemed to be of even greater concern to everyone.

I avoided sport at school like the plague. No ball skills. With girls anyway. I used to spend the whole sports period sitting in the lavatory reading novels or lying in the sick bay pretending to suffer from period pain. Miss Saddington once said to me: 'Weaver, you're the only female I know who menstruates fifty-two weeks of the year.'

Once, for no apparent reason, a trumpet-playing bully bashed me on the shins with her hockey stick during a stupid hockey match. Forty years later she had the temerity to come backstage uninvited and say, 'You look really ugly on-stage.' Some people never learn to be kind.

I was often sent in disgrace to the headmistress, Miss Cahill. Miss Cahill was a wise and wonderful woman, who would sit me down in her office and for ten minutes discuss whatever I was currently reading—usually one of the Russian or French masters, not ever Mills & Boon—and then send me, chastened, back to class until I transgressed again a few days later. So when, about a decade ago, I received a message to call the current headmistress at Hornsby High, Mrs Johnston, I will admit to a frisson of trepidation—just like the old days of being summoned to the principal's office. I wondered if it would be the same office, with the same carpet to be carpeted on by stern authority. As it happened, Mrs Johnston simply wanted me to address her girls at a speech day at Sydney Town Hall.

I agreed to do this, but at the same time I couldn't help remembering our speech days in the 1960s—all of us dressed in pristine white, all of us wilting from excruciating boredom in Sydney Town Hall (which was not airconditioned at that time), all of us wondering of the guest speaker: Where did she get that horrid outfit? How old is she? What's her *real* hair colour? Does she have children? Etc, etc.

In the 1960s Hornsby Girls High was a first-rate school, just as it is now. It was one of the few selective high schools in Sydney, meaning a certain standard of excellence was required for enrolment. I've always joked that there must have been lapses in the criteria if I got in, but in my first year at high school I did come fifth in the year overall out of about two hundred. So academically I started off okay, but I just went steadily downhill from there. We had the best choir in the state, under the baton of Miss Cunningham, and a lively debating club, both of which I must admit I loved. I realise now that I loathed school mainly because all I really cared about with unequivocal passion was acting, which I was then learning outside school hours. I couldn't wait to flee the shackles of school and get on with it. Acting, that is.

My aunt Georgina had taken me to see the film of Olivier's *Richard III* when I was only seven and I'd loved it, but I had nightmares about it for weeks afterwards. I can also recall my dad talking wistfully about the John Alden Shakespeare Company when I was quite young and lamenting its demise. But the Young Elizabethan Players used to visit us at Hornsby Girls High, where the sight of a young man in tights was enough to provoke a sort of genteel low-key hysteria.

Later, my final year English class went to see *Hamlet* at the Old Tote. I was so captivated that my dad took me to see it a second time. I went alone to see it again. And again, and again, and again. Six times altogether. John Bell was Hamlet. In his book *The Time of My Life*, John is very dismissive of that Hamlet but, believe me, he was brilliant. My mother remarked dryly: 'All the other seventeen-year-olds are in love with the Beatles. Jacki's in love with Hamlet.'

As a youngster I must have performed Juliet's balcony speech for at least a dozen auditions. I got a lot of work out of it, but I never got to play Juliet. Which always saddened me as I think I might have made a wise and earnest little Juliet, given the chance. Meanwhile, at our school drama studies consisted of one play a year—the annual school play, which took six months of arduous rehearsal and was more like a military exercise than a creative experience. It was directed by a terrifying woman called Miss Rosalie Collins, who would only ever cast me as a child because I always looked young for my age. That was very frustrating; indeed, it was a frustration that was to haunt me for years to come because I was still playing children when I was into my thirties, when I was aching to play a woman my own age. At last that no longer matters.

Compare then with now, if you will. Today dramatic art has become so valued and respected that it's an important part of the school curriculum, rather than being looked on as a frivolous hobby as it was in my day. Young people interested in theatre and film now, even if their eventual career is destined to be elsewhere, are fantastically lucky to have such opportunities.

Late in 1962, the year in which I turned fifteen, there was an article in the *Daily Mirror* about a search being conducted by Sydney's Phillip Theatre for a Cinderella to play opposite the Prince, to be played by Bryan Davies, an eighteen-year-old singing heart-throb who already had his own eponymous TV series. I was a little scornful of his wholesome image but my mother persuaded me to audition just for the experience, not really thinking I'd get the role. My father's secretary Mary coached me in the song 'I Feel Pretty' from *West Side Story*; I took a rare day off school, wore a lacy 'Sissy' blouse, tight tweed skirt and black stilettos, and caught the train to Museum Station.

By then the Phillip Theatre had moved to Elizabeth Street, opposite Sydney's most exclusive department store, Mark Foys (now the Downing Centre Law Courts). The Phillip Theatre had originally been located in Phillip Street of course, and had been the very successful home of satirical revues and contemporary plays starring a cavalcade of luminaries including Ruth Cracknell, Barry Humphries, Gordon Chater, Reg Livermore, Gloria Dawn, Maggie Dence, Noeline Brown, Barry Creyton, Wendy Blacklock etc. The list is endless. Many long and illustrious careers had begun at Phillip Street. My parents loved going to their shows. I was still too young to go but Dad would perform some of their sketches for me when they got home, and I would reproduce them for uncomprehending friends later. How I must have bored some of my tiny colleagues. At age seven I knew every word of the record album 'Noël Coward in Las Vegas'.

But back to my audition at the Phillip Theatre. I sang and read for the writer and director Bill Orr and for composer and musical director Dot Mendoza (who later became my singing and music teacher) and they were very sweet to me. The next day, when I arrived home from school late—another detention for some misdemeanour—my mother was excited and impatient: 'The Phillip Theatre called and want to see you again tomorrow at 3.30. But you can't take another day off school—you'll have to go in your school uniform.' My first callback!

So I duly turned up the next day, expecting to have to audition again. But instead I was offered Cinderella. By far the biggest surprise was the huge reaction of the producers,

Eric Duckworth and Bill Orr, to my school uniform. For some reason they weren't expecting a school uniform and found it charming and adorable. So of course the publicity in the tabloid papers made much of my being a schoolgirl and I even had to pose for photos wearing the wretched uniform, which I found irksome in the extreme.

The following week, at my first wardrobe call, I met my leading man and Prince Charming, Bryan Davies, and I didn't hide the fact that wholesome boys with their own TV shows didn't impress me. Probably as a direct result of my indifference (let's not forget he had thousands of adoring fans), he was immediately smitten. But, to be fair, I was equally smitten with him within a few weeks and remained so for three years. There was a lot of publicity about our romance. He would pick me up from school in his red Jaguar, until the headmistress banned him because hysterical girls once mobbed the car. So after that he had to collect me from Gordon Station.

The actress Deborah Kennedy, who followed a few years after me at Hornsby High, says that at her time there was a regulation known as 'the Jacki Weaver Rule', which proclaimed that boys were not only forbidden within the school gates but they weren't even allowed on the nature strip around the school fence.

Because I was underage, my father had to sign the contract with the Phillip Theatre. I had to provide twelve performances a week (two shows daily for six days) for 30 pounds a week, a small fortune at a time when my pocket money was one pound a week. I joined Actors Equity at this time, in 1963, so I have spent more than forty years pretending to be other people and getting paid for it. And much longer doing it for free. Playing Cinderella with that cast of fine seasoned professionals was quite possibly the best debut imaginable for a fifteen-year-old tyro like me. I learned a great deal in those three weeks of rehearsals and six weeks of performing in twelve shows a week from people like Neva Carr Glynn and Dolore Whiteman (the Wicked Sisters), Janet Brown, Robina Beard and Earle Cross, who all looked after me and taught me so much about discipline, routine, stagecraft and responsibility. Plus the added fun of dressing up in gorgeous costumes, wearing make-up, telling a good story, singing with a band, pretending to be a sad angel who turns into a princess, and being adored both on-stage and off-stage by a handsome young TV star. I also learned to love audiences. Still do.

At this time the newest and best agency was Gloria Payten's International Casting Service (ICS). She already had Ruth Cracknell and Reg Livermore, and everyone said she was the one to be with. I arrived at the 4th floor, 147A King Street, Sydney, for my appointment with her one afternoon after school (again in that wretched school uniform) and she signed me up, and I'm still there to this day. Strikingly beautiful, exotic, Greek, Gloria was brought up in Germany. One night when she was a teenager she was forced to flee the bombs being dropped by my father, as well as by hundreds of other Allied airmen, during the infamous raid on Dresden—so my father nearly killed my agent. If it hadn't been for Gloria I'd never have bought my first house in

Paddington, and then my apartment in Darling Point that she found for me in the same block that she lived in. She was like a mother to me and I was shattered when she died in 1989. 'You were Gloria's baby, Jacki,' her sister Irene cried the day she died.

Gloria had started ICS in 1961 and over the years she employed a small coterie of staff to help her look after the large stable of actors she eventually came to represent. Many of these staff moved on to become successful agents in their own right, including June Cann, Hilary Linstead and Anne Churchill-Brown of Shanahan's. ICS is now run by Philomena Moore and Pauline Lee, close friends of Gloria, and they've been there for thirty-five and twenty-five years respectively.

In 1962 I still had another two years of school left but Gloria had me working every school holidays, playing everything from Gretel in ABC-TV's production of the opera *Hansel and Gretel* by Humperdink to Jill in *Mother Goose and the Three Stooges*, starring Pee Wee Wilson and the Delltones. When I was Gretel (playing a nine-year-old, though aged fifteen) the technical producer Jim Lyons brought his enchanting six-year-old daughter Susan in to watch us filming. We were immediate pals. She is now of course the actress Susan Lyons, former head of Actors Equity and a very dear friend to this day.

I was also Gadget in *Once Upon a Surfie*. This was amongst the dubious panto offerings in 1963 at the Palace Theatre in Pitt Street, where the Hilton Hotel is now. I was earning ninety pounds a week! Admittedly for eighteen shows a week, which nearly killed me, but the Palace boards were lovely boards to tread. The dressing rooms there could be a little uncomfortable, however. They were underground, built over the Tank Stream, and whenever it rained the stream rose and the dressing rooms were six inches under water. We had to apply our stage make-up while standing on Shelley's Lemonade crates. A young singer making her stage debut in that show was Little Pattie, who had a current big hit with 'He's My Blonde Headed Stompie Wompie Real Gone Surfer Boy'. Being two years older and one inch taller, I taught her everything I knew about eyeliner and mascara.

Of course, now she's Patricia Amphlett OAM, highly respected union official with MEAA (the Media Entertainment and Arts Alliance). Other cast members included pop stars like Lucky Starr, Dig Richards, Rob EG and my boyfriend Bryan Davies, as well as a few showgirls from Chequers nightclub wearing fur bikinis. Indeed. It wasn't Ibsen. I was actually too shy to wear a bikini on-stage and opted for a one-piece bathing suit with a little skirt.

In the September holidays of 1963 I played the child of a broken marriage in an ABC-TV drama directed by Ken Hannam of *Sunday Too Far Away* fame. My parents were glamorous Diana Davidson and gorgeous Leonard Teale, who'd been my childhood radio serial idol. I couldn't believe that Superman, faster than a speeding bullet, more powerful than a locomotive, was playing my father! I was thrilled. Just as thrilled as I would have been if it had been Ray Barrett. On the wireless, he was Tarzan, King of the Apes. The scripts were American, I imagine, but the productions and the actors were all Australian, including Tarzan and Superman.

By this time I was attending classes at Dame Doris Fitton's Independent Theatre in North Sydney, where one of my favourite teachers was Doreen Warburton, who'd worked with the great Joan Littlewood in London before migrating to Australia. Doreen opened my eyes and ears to text and gave me insights that nobody else had up until then. She gave me the keys to the secrets about becoming someone else.

And it was in 1963 that I was sitting at my desk pretending to do calculus homework when Mrs Cunningham called over our West Pymble back fence: 'President Kennedy's been shot!'

That year I was still involved with Bryan Davies, who wisely but feverishly waited until I was sixteen before knowing me carnally. The day of my sixteenth birthday was the first time I ever saw Mighty Melbourne. Bryan took me to Melbourne on a TAA Fokker Friendship for a surprise birthday lunch at the newly opened and rather glamorous Southern Cross Hotel. And then home to Sydney in the afternoon. It was to be another three years before I set foot in Melbourne again, but I was already besotted with that beautiful city.

The following year Bryan Davies was offered a management and recording contract with Norrie Paramour, who was Cliff Richard's manager. He didn't want to go to London, but it was a terrific offer that his mother wouldn't let him refuse and, besides, she was determined to wrest him away from my evil clutches. So Bryan made a tearful departure for England, where he spent several sad months, made a couple of good records and wrote to me every day. I still have the letters.

This was also the year the Beatles came to Australia. I watched them on TV arriving in Adelaide one freezing dark morning as I was putting on my school uniform in front of the radiator. When Paul's umbrella blew inside out I was doing up my suspender with my black stockings—it was before we had regulation school pantihose.

When they came to Sydney, Angus took me to see them at the Stadium because Bryan was in England. A girl we knew was the envy of all because she had a romance with John Lennon. Around that time, another famous pop group came to Australia and I had a brief but torrid liaison with the lead singer, which Bryan didn't know about so I'll have to tell him tomorrow before he reads about it here.

Not to mention the handsome Scott from Kensington, who distracted me from the straight and narrow after Bryan's aunt introduced us: 'He's just lost his mother, Jacki, so be kind to him.' So I was kind to him. Very kind.

I did the Leaving Certificate (the equivalent of today's HSC) at the end of 1964. This was when New South Wales still only had five years of secondary school. In early 1965, my friends Barb and Tracy enrolled in pharmacy at Sydney University and I landed a regular role playing a thirteen-year-old adventuress in a seven-part ABC-TV mini-series directed by Ken Hannam called *Wandjina*, to be shot on film (unusual in those days) on location in the outback. One of the stars was a terrific actor that I had a crush on and I followed him around like a wistful puppy. He was always charming to me, but one afternoon in the bunkhouse he finally said: 'You're too young for me darlin'. Come back to see me when you're

47

older.' Alas it never happened. His name was Mark McManus and he went on to star as Taggart in the hit TV series. And alas, he died too young.

The focus puller on that shoot was a teenager called John Seale, now one of the top cinematographers and directors in Hollywood. *Wandjina* rated well on British TV and I received fan mail from a lot of young English schoolboys, who of course didn't realise that I was now eighteen years old.

By the end of my teens I'd had thirteen years of regular tuition from many different drama teachers. I still feel a bit stumped for an answer when asked why I didn't go to NIDA, but actually many of the teachers at NIDA had already been teaching me for years elsewhere, both off-stage and on-stage: people like Keith Bain, Alan Edwards, Robin Lovejoy, Doreen Warburton and Alexander Hay.

chapter three

Wouldn't It Be Nice

In 1965 Linda Lee Records, a subsidiary of Festival Records, signed me up to a recording contract after a much-publicised 'Australia-wide search' for male and female talent. They also signed up Billy Thorpe and the Aztecs, who then had a huge hit with 'Poison Ivy', selling many thousands of copies.

I did an old Etta James song called 'Something's Got a Hold on Me', with Buddy Holly's 'Raining in My Heart' on the flip side. It sold 159 copies. However, it led to numerous singing gigs on TV's *Bandstand* and the *Johnny O'Keefe Show* and numerous TV variety shows with Barry Crocker, Don Lane and Jimmy Hannan. I enjoyed that work, but really only cared about acting.

I did a couple of days' shooting on the movie *They're a Weird Mob* with the great British director Michael Powell (*The Red Shoes* and that scary movie about the photography murders, *Peeping Tom*, now a cult classic). If you blinked during *Weird Mob* you'd miss me—indeed, one of the scenes hit the cutting room floor—but Michael Powell sent me a letter (now framed) saying:

Thank you for playing those two parts. I hope you are convinced you are no longer a child actress. I am quite sure anyway that you are headed for great things.

Yours sincerely,
Michael Powell

A few months later I screen-tested for Michael Powell for the part of the young girl in *Age of Consent*. Even though I was the right age, he said I looked a bit too young. Nevertheless, it still came down to a choice between me and Helen Mirren—and it's no disgrace to have lost out to Helen Mirren.

I skitingly showed off that letter from Michael Powell to my good friend Ken Hannam, who'd directed me in *Wandjina*. He penned me this teasing note to keep my feet on the ground:

Darlingest Jack,

Just to say thanks for all your hard work in our recent concert.

I think I've overtold you how talented, charming and worldly you are—anyway I feel sure that Michael Powell will have remembered anything I've forgotten.

I hope now you realise that you are STILL a child STAR!

Lots of luck in '66,
Ken

Ken Hannam died in early 2005.

In 1965 I passed the notoriously difficult ABC Radio Drama Audition after three attempts, which was a little discouraging until I heard that the mighty Peter Finch had failed five times before he got in, as was the case with many of our radio luminaries.

Soon I began to work in radio drama and children's programming. This led to a foothold in the commercial voice-over area, where I did a lot of character and children's voices. I was the voice of Snap, Crackle and Pop for a year, and was a sultana for Sultana Bran. However, I was sacked (the only time I've ever been sacked) from a gig for Heinz 57 Variety, where I was cast as an asparagus, because I couldn't stop laughing. The producer told my agent that my behaviour was the most unprofessional he'd ever experienced (he should have got out more). I was deeply ashamed but, in fairness, it was a classic case of miscasting to make me an asparagus. A squash, maybe; but an asparagus? Never. I tried to get them on unfair dismissal but didn't have a leg to stand on.

An advertiser once paid me $1000 just to laugh for two minutes for a voice-over because he'd heard me laugh on a talk show and liked the sound of it, which was great. I also did a TV commercial for the Nabisco breakfast food Rice Krinkles, and had my face on the packet, looking like a complete idiot. Good money, though. However, many of the advertising people and their clients were terrible tossers who didn't have a clue. Once one of them actually asked me if I could 'get more *feeling*' out of the word 'soap'!

There was a stint in a satirical revue at Kings Cross's Copenhagen restaurant, which was located opposite the Chevron Hotel in Macleay Street, near the old Sheraton where the Beatles stayed when they were in Sydney. Norman Kessell's review of my efforts in the Sydney *Sun* was head-lined: 'Jacki scores in new field'. This gave me my first taste of playing several different characters in the one show, which I love doing to this day.

Then came *Be Our Guest*, an ABC-TV series set in a motel where the regulars interviewed, danced and sang with 'guests' in the motel. It was a shocker—a sort of sitcom/inter-view/variety/mishmash/'seemed like a good idea at the time' show. I was a regular with Lorraine Bayly, Sean Scully, Jack Allen and Gordon Glenwright, and it aired four nights a week at 6.30 pm. It was quite a workload so there were four different directors. One of them was David Price.

Boyishly handsome, David was born in Cheyne Walk, Chelsea, London. He was the only child of a beautiful woman, Ray, a painter, and Eric Theodore Wren Price, so named because Eric's father, David's grandfather, had been a close friend of the notorious 'Red Ted' Theodore (former Premier of Queensland, Federal Treasurer in Jim Scullin's Labor Government and business partner of Kerry Packer's grandfather). He had also been a friend of the equally notorious John Wren (about whom my future friend, Frank Hardy, wrote his bestseller *Power Without Glory*).

David had grown up in Melbourne in privileged circumstances, but he was sent to board at Scotch College when he was five. *Five years old!* I still can't get over that. I loved both his parents very much (I've always been lucky with in-laws), but I do not understand sending a child to boarding school at any age, never mind *five*.

David's career had begun promisingly at ATV in London, after a stint studying drama at the University of California. He was a talented ice-skater and represented Australia at the 1960 Squaw Valley Winter Olympics, in doubles figure skating. He raced sports cars, had competed at Brands Hatch in a Lotus, and was a keen surfer.

The first day we met, he invited me to go out with him. I asked him his age and, because I was only a teenager, he apologetically replied: 'Twenty-seven. Is that too old?'

I laughed. One thing I could never be accused of is being ageist. I accepted but I had to open a fete at my old primary school at Gordon West, so he drove me there in his silver Alpha (I sound obsessed with cars—I'm not) and then he took me to dinner.

Seven weeks later, to the day, we were married. Crazy, huh? Yes, he asked me to marry him on our first date, and the sex was so good I said yes. (I believe in sex on a first date, otherwise how do you know if a second date is worth the effort?)

My parents were horrified. I only saw my mother weep on two occassions in my life, and that was one of them. As I was still a teenager, my father could have refused to sign the consent form but, being a lawyer himself, he realised that a magistrate could overturn it in a few minutes. Instead Dad took a pragmatic approach. He suggested we just live together—quite a radical and progressive notion in the mid sixties. But both David and I wanted to marry. I've always been a believer in marriage, believe it or not. Apart from the firm and holy commitment, I need formality, ritual and ceremony.

And so the arrangements for the marriage were made. My mother took me to a kindly doctor in East Gordon, who prescribed sedatives for her and oral contraceptives for me (quite new in those days). He also gave me a gentle little talk about 'marital relations' and said that in happy marriages the wife will always 'submit' to her husband's physical demands, even when she may not be 'in the mood'. I wanted to laugh but managed to refrain. He told my mother that I only looked about fourteen, and seemed to exude avuncular concern for me.

One of the big songs around at the time was the Beach Boys' 'Wouldn't It Be Nice', which summed up our feelings, along with 'God Only Knows'. The ABC's publicity department (often referred to as the Secret Service) was cock-a-hoop. Here was an opportunity for some great press coverage handed to them on a platter. Both the Sydney *Sun* and the

Daily Mirror had page-two photos of David and me with big smiles. The headlines shouted: 'TV Star to Wed!' (alas, my hair needed a wash) and 'Australia's Most Promising Young Variety Actress [whatever that is] to Wed Her Producer'. Blah, blah, blah. *People* magazine had a four-page photo spread of me, which they trumpeted as: 'No Honeymoon for Cinderella!' while *Pix* ran with four pages of 'My Break with Jacki: Bryan Davies Tells'. The exposure was big.

During that seven weeks of preparation the *Australian Women's Weekly* featured my picture on their front cover sitting in a tree in Clifton Gardens wearing a white trouser suit and a mauve hat, a story based on an interview I'd done with them weeks before. There was a fashion spread of me inside wearing four different outfits and an article by Kerry Yates (later Skye Yates) with a quote from me proclaiming: 'I love hats! One of my favourites my boyfriend calls: "Jacki's Going to Town Hat when Bryan's not going".'

Mildly droll. But on another page, in the TV section, was a piece by Nan Musgrove containing the news of my whirlwind engagement and upcoming wedding to David. 'Love At First Sight!' gushed the headline. The *Sydney Morning Herald* pointed out the gaffe and scoffed at the lack of communication between the *Weekly*'s departments. The editor of the *Weekly* was not amused and Kerry Yates phoned to reprimand me. I was slightly embarrassed, but events had moved so quickly that this discrepancy was unavoidable. I didn't think to question Kerry Yates about the fact that all the clothes I'd worn in the photo shoot were from a shop managed by her mother. Conflict of interest wasn't much of an issue in those days and, anyway, the *Weekly* was held in much the same esteem as the Bible. The *Women's Weekly* didn't touch me for some time after that, and who can blame them? They've been very good to me in recent years, however, saving my bacon to an extent that they probably don't even realise when they actually paid me generously for an interview that I was very reluctant to do.

My mother was never happy that I married David Price, partly because I broke Bryan Davies' heart, a fact Bryan never fails to remind me of whenever I see him every few years— most recently last week, nearly forty years later. He should be grateful (and he is) that it enabled him to marry the beautiful Tracy Bailey, my school friend and a much better wife than I would have been. They live in Lindfield, are still happily together with two great children. Beautiful kids in fact.

My co-actor in *Be Our Guest*, Sean Scully, was David's best man and my schoolmate, Barbara Hay, was my brides-maid in a pale rose-pink silk mini-dress and matching coat. I wore a white silk crepe mini-dress (ie above the knee) and matching coat with a collar of the finest ostrich feathers and a stupid pillbox hat that I regret to this day. (It was Tracy's fault—she told me that brides look awful with their hair down, so I had to put it up.)

We kept the guest list small, but there was still a big crowd outside the Wayside Chapel. The wonderful Reverend Ted Noffs officiated and the reception was at the very swish Caprice restaurant in Rose Bay.

There was no time for a honeymoon as we had to be back in front of, and behind, the cameras on Monday. So the wedding night was spent in our rented flat at Queenscliff Road, Queenscliff, no doubt listening to the Beach Boys and 'Good Vibrations'. The next day, Sunday, a large photo of David and me dominated the front page of the Sydney *Sun-Herald* with the headline 'Hiccup at the Altar'. Apparently I had hiccups during the ceremony. 'Mini-skirt Wedding!' announced the *Telegraph*. 'Actress Weds in Mini-Dress!' said *TV Week*. Such attention to hem length when it was in fact of quite discreet proportions with just a smidgin of patella on view.

A few weeks later a woman claiming to be a nurse at Royal North Shore rang my mother to say that David and I had been seriously injured in a car smash. And might die. She and my father frantically made their way to the hospital only to find we weren't there, so they assumed they'd gone to the wrong hospital and spent a terrible day trying to find us. Meanwhile David and I, oblivious, were at the cinema. If mobile phones had been invented back then, they would have saved a lot of anguish. We never found out who the hoaxer was.

Over the years I've had my share of stalkers and cranks from time to time, most of whom eventually fade away as mysteriously as they surface. Some write pages and pages of illegible scrawl, often badly spelt, occasionally perfectly spelt, sometimes threatening, spiteful and distressing. Others are harmless but unsettling, like the man who used to send me beautifully executed but frankly obscene sketches he'd done of me.

Then there are the benign and genuine fans who remain loyal for decades and come to every show, often more than once. Dear souls like Rex the Dandy, George the Knitter, the chap who sent me a live lobster on a silver platter delivered to the theatre by a young waiter wearing a tuxedo, the young student who declared himself so besotted that he sent me a tape of himself singing Sondheim's beautiful 'I'm Going Out of My Mind'. Not forgetting eleven-year-old 'Mitzi' whose mother sent me a note in 1980 saying that Mitzi had become obsessive to the point that not only were the walls of Mitzi's room covered with my photos, but she would only answer to my name; even her teachers at school were forced to call her Jacki if they wanted a response from her. Her mother asked if I would meet her after the matinee that week. We met and stayed friends—Mitzi still comes to all my shows, and twenty-five years later she's a lawyer.

In 1965–66 I had more work offers than I could possibly accept. I was too lucky probably. For a while there, everything just seemed to fall into my lap. I went to Melbourne to be murdered in my first episode of *Homicide* for Crawfords. I think, all up, I was done in about nine times in *Homicide*. As well as having some very narrow escapes.

The Old Tote engaged me in three classics in quick succession—Pinero's *The Schoolmistress*, Molière's *Imaginary Invalid* and *You Never Can Tell* by George Bernard Shaw Esq. The Old Tote Theatre was a forerunner to the Sydney Theatre Company and produced some terrific stuff at the atmospheric 'tin shed' theatre in the grounds of the University of New South Wales in Kensington and later across the road in Anzac Parade at the Parade Theatre, which eventually became part of NIDA.

In my teens I had seen many Old Tote plays with my parents, who were subscribers; these included a memorable *Who's Afraid of Virginia Woolf?* with the wonderful Jacqueline Kott (later Mrs Gordon Samuels, wife of one of the most popular Supreme Court judges and then Governor of New South Wales) and the redoubtable veteran, Alexander Hay, as George. As well as seeing John Bell's marvellous *Hamlet*, I saw some great plays by Joe Orton, John Osborne, Brecht and Shaw, among others, and a controversial impressive first effort by a very young Alex Buzo called *Norm and Ahmed*. I was a very fortunate teenager.

Anyhow Alex Hay himself directed *The Schoolmistress*, my first play at the Old Tote, and I was Dinah, a sixteen-year-old schoolgirl who is secretly married. The schoolmistress was played by Clarissa Kaye, who'd been a contortionist in the circus before Hayes Gordon discovered her and made her a star at the Ensemble Theatre. Clarissa's warm-up before every performance consisted of twisting her body into the most alarming shapes in the Tote's tiny dressing room. She refused to allow Deirdre Rubenstein (now one of the best actors of our generation), who played the maid, to address her by her first name even though the rest of us did, because Deirdre was still a NIDA student and it was 'against regulations', which was quite cow-ish of Clarissa, I thought, especially as Deirdre was so sweet and respectful and it made her a little tearful.

When actor Helen Morse married Sandy Harbutt there was a photo of them in the newspaper with Helen dressed in a fetching white pantsuit, rather daring at the time. We young actors were all admiring the photo in the dressing room and saying how much we liked the fact that Helen had worn trousers to her wedding but Clarissa was very disapproving of Helen's outfit. 'That's the kind of behaviour that gives the acting profession a bad name,' she told us firmly. Though Helen Morse is blessed with a gentle sense of good-humoured mischief, she's also an unassumingly dignified person so it's impossible to imagine Helen could give anything or anyone 'a bad name'. Clarissa Kaye later married actor James Mason after they met during the filming of *Age of Consent*, directed by Michael Powell. I don't know what Clarissa wore at her wedding but let's hope it wasn't a trouser suit. Mustn't let disrespect rain down on the profession.

In those days they couldn't afford understudies (most productions can't afford them these days either) so NIDA students understudied all the roles as part of their training. Kate Fitzpatrick understudied me in *The Schoolmistress* in her last year at NIDA and copied me assiduously, down to the last detail. She even went cross-eyed at certain points, not realising that for me it was not a choice.

At this time I was playing Peter Pan during the daytime at the Independent. Also in the cast, playing Wendy's brother John, who becomes one of the Lost Boys, was twelve-year-old John McCallum, now the *Australian*'s principal Sydney theatre critic and lecturer in theatre, film and dance at the University of New South Wales. David Goddard was a gorgeous Captain Hook and Bill Shanahan, the late great much-mourned theatre agent and founder of Shanahan's, was Smee the boatswain. I loved being Peter Pan. The only disadvantage was that my chest had to be tightly bound in elastic bandages to flatten it entirely. Okay, it was 32DD, or 10DD in current sizes. All the little Lost Boys seemed fascinated by the process.

Critic Norman Kessell lamented 'Jacki Weaver's Peter Pan is earth-bound in more ways than one' because he didn't approve of my suntanned bare legs, instead of the green tights Peter Pans traditionally wore. But his words were almost prescient because at one performance the flying apparatus malfunctioned and I fell with a thud onto the stage, bottom first. Bruised and embarrassed, I managed an ad-lib—'Fairy dust isn't foolproof'—to a round of applause from the anxious mothers in the audience.

Robin Lovejoy directed Molière's *Imaginary Invalid* at the Tote with Ron Haddrick as Argan, the invalid. Others in the cast included Helen Morse, Kirrily Nolan, and Jennifer Hagen, all of whom were recent NIDA graduates. In that respect, I was the odd one out. There was a big magazine spread of us girls with the headline: 'Is This the Prettiest Quartette Ever to Grace the Sydney Stage?' The production got rave reviews, especially Kirrily as Toinette, Jennifer as Beline and Ron in the lead. Three of the critics described me as having 'exquisite timing'.

Jim Sharman was the director of Shaw's *You Never Can Tell*. I loved working with him and the rest of the cast, especially Ross Thompson, who was incredibly beautiful and mischievous. We were the twins. I did very well out of that show, with the critics and the public alike. Rex Cramphorn wrote in the *Bulletin*: 'Join the queue to fall in love with Jacki Weaver.'

Pity I wasn't doing so well in my two-year-old marriage. David Price and I were now living at Palm Beach—Ocean Road, right opposite the sea. I was working at the Old Tote in Kensington six nights a week, and a few days a week as well, on radio serials, voice-overs etc. So some days I'd commute to the city and back twice in a day—quite a bit of driving, Palm Beach being about 50 kilometres from the eastern suburbs, I would estimate.

David was working at the ABC at Gore Hill, but most nights he'd be coaching ice-skaters or training himself at the ice rink in Strathfield. With his unruly hair, good looks, great body and fine technique he looked like a Nureyev on blades. He was gorgeous. I used to love watching him skate. He bought me an expensive pair of skates and some groovy skating gear, but I was hopeless. For me skating was very difficult and often painful. Especially when you hit the deck and make contact with the icy slush.

David would also disappear for days at a time with his surfboard and some mates, including an amiable chap called Flick the Fireman, and they would drive miles and miles up and down the coast looking for the perfect wave. I didn't love watching David ride his surfboard. I particularly resented sitting on the cold sand at Bell's Beach, Victoria, freezing and wind-bitten, clutching a blanket around me, gazing out at the pounding grey surf for hours while my wet-suited husband sought the perfect damned wave.

It wasn't a conventional marriage. We used to take illegal amphetamines, which weren't considered as harmful then as we now know them to be. David knew a tame chemist in

Narrabeen and another in Collaroy, who'd supply us with methedrine, sometimes benzedrine and dexedrine. I loved speed. If it were legal and safe for my heart, I'd still take it; but it's not, so I don't. But I have always loved going at a thousand miles an hour.

I also loved driving at a hundred miles an hour down the Wakehurst Parkway, usually coming home to Palm Beach from the theatre after work late at night. One night some hoons spotted me on the Spit Bridge and then followed me all the way home to Palm Beach. I managed to elude them for a time and get to our place, where I locked myself in. Then they arrived, circling the house and yelling out, until they finally gave up and left long after midnight. It was quite nerve-racking.

There were no neighbours around—it was winter, so all the holiday homes were deserted. And on top of that, my husband wasn't there. He'd gone on another surfing safari in the red Lotus Elan (I repeat, I am *not* obsessed with cars) on the spur of the moment. In those days, before mobile phones, it was different from now and there was minimal contact between us while he was away. David still hadn't returned the following night and my parents, concerned for my safety, drove to Palm Beach and took me back to West Pymble to my old bed.

When David came back to Palm Beach the next evening with a bottle of French champagne under his arm, he found a note saying that I was staying with my parents for a while. Dejected, he drank all the champagne and ate three bowls of cornflakes.

He went straight off on another surfing trip to Melbourne for a couple of weeks, or maybe it was a skating competition, and when he returned I was firmly ensconced at my parents' home, in the middle of a very sedate twenty-first birthday party they'd organised for me, mostly with their friends and neighbours. Tired and emotional, David turned up unexpectedly and had to be mollified by my dad and my brother outside. I think the words 'Give me back my wife!' may have been uttered.

Later that night he tried to climb in through my bedroom window. When I protested, fearing my parents' disapproval, David expostulated: 'But we are *married*, for God's sake!' I must admit he had a point.

A détente of sorts was reached. David agreed to leave his beloved beach and move closer to the city, to Hardie Street, Neutral Bay, in fact. He wanted me to concentrate on television and was working on a few ideas to develop for me. I was enamoured of the theatre, but he was much less so and he especially resented the time it consumed. He was particularly unhappy when I accepted a gig at the 1968 Adelaide Festival in Eleanor Whitcomb's *The Runaway Steamboat*, playing a twelve-year-old urchin who disguises herself as a boy. Out came the old elastic bandages again, to bind up my recalcitrant chest.

Back in Sydney, a favourite cool hot-spot for after-show suppers where you could get an illegal drink in a coffee cup until dawn was Vadim's in Challis Avenue, Potts Point. It was a haunt for actors, writers and assorted ne'er-do-wells. And the occasional do-very-wells, like Barry Humphries. He had been an idol of mine since the first time I saw him at the Theatre Royal, when I was fifteen. Edna Everage was still a Mrs in those days, not a Dame, and Sandy Stone was endearing as ever. So imagine my delight when Barry said to me one night at Vadim's, after he'd seen me in *You Never Can Tell*, the Shaw play: 'You have great comic talent.'

An endorsement from the Almighty Humphries! I was thrilled. When I breathlessly reported this compliment to my husband, he was singularly unimpressed: 'He only said that because he fancies you,' he said. I was totally deflated and, stupidly, accepted his judgement.

I related this story years later, when Barry Humphries and I were appearing on Michael Parkinson's chat show. Barry paused for a second and graciously admitted, 'Yes, I *was* trying to get into your pants, but I *also* think you have a great comic talent.'

A couple of months ago I remarked in passing to my friend Andrew Ross, who is Barry's pianist, that I felt a tinge of curiosity that I never took Barry up on the flirtation. Next day Andrew called and inquired: 'Barry wants to know if it's too late.'

My husband David's put-down was matched only by one from my own dear mother, who said to me after the opening night of the Shaw play, 'I must admit you were very funny tonight and you looked *beautiful* on-stage.' This was a compliment she'd never paid me before and I was gobsmacked: 'Thank you, Mummy.' At which point she added: 'You've got the sort of looks that look better from a distance.'

Even my sixteen-year-old brother felt moved to defend me: 'So have you, Mum. About twelve miles distance.'

In fairness to my parents, they probably felt it was their duty to keep my feet on the ground so I wouldn't get too conceited, but sometimes over the years their efforts did bewilder me. Like the time when I was six and won the physical culture prize and asked my father, whose good opinion was the only one I cared about, if he'd clapped when my name was called out. 'Yes. But I clapped harder for the girl who came second,' he said firmly.

I clearly recall my heart-stopping disappointment. Years later he explained that he just didn't want me to get too big for my boots. A very Australian ambition to have for one's offspring, especially in the 1950s. Well, it didn't work—I *am* too big for my boots. But at least they're very small boots.

Moving to Neutral Bay only helped my marriage to David temporarily. I'd begun to be beset by the bouts of in-effable sadness that would dog me for the rest of my life. One afternoon I sat on the window ledge of our eighth-floor apartment for thirty minutes, contemplating my bare feet swinging against the red brick wall, thinking how easy it would be, and what a relief, to just fly out into thin air.

Reality hit when a woman in the street below began to gesticulate wildly at me. The thought of my mother's devast-ation was the main motivation that forced me to go back inside and pull down the window. And lock it.

Everyone deals with melancholy in their own way. I have never considered my particular form of despondency to be unusual, assuming, perhaps mistakenly, that everyone goes through bouts of sadness to varying degrees. While not scorning those who seek professional help, I have never felt moved to seek counselling myself, preferring to deal with my sadness privately. Perhaps an inherited British 'stiff upper lip' from my mother? Or maybe a reaction to 'It is our duty to be cheerful' from my dad? Two of my close girlfriends from school are now respected consulting clinical psychologists, and a casual natter over a sociable lunch with one of them seems to be enough to keep me serene for a few months. I have other friends whose reliance on counselling and/or medication has literally saved their lives, and yet others who have found no relief anywhere for their internal anguish. We are all so different and so complex, no solution is universal.

Slowly and inevitably David and I were drifting further and further apart in diametrically opposed directions. One day two American boys came to the door wearing suits and selling Bibles. I was craving company but I also felt sorry for them and invited them in for a cup of tea. Two hours later they were still there when David came home from work. He quickly got rid of them. 'They could have been murderers!' he scolded me. They were only Mormons. And I was lonely. With the black dog of despair snuffling at my heels. But I resisted conversion to the Latter-Day Saints.

My slough of despond was exacerbated by the fact that I was in a bit of a hiatus workwise. I was employed for a few days in 1968 filming an episode of the TV series *Animal Doctor*, shot in the sleepy Hawkesbury River hamlet of Brooklyn near Gosford, halfway between Sydney and

Newcastle. The storyline was about a Bengal tiger with toothache because of his penchant for sweets, and I was the ice-cream girl at the window of a Mr Whippy mobile ice-cream van. I was pretending to feed him a choc-top ice-cream, but it was actually a piece of rump steak in a cone.

He was an enormous, fiercely handsome beast, moon-lighting from his real job in the circus, and his great gulps of the fake ice-cream came closer and closer to taking off my tiny hand with each take we filmed. My sense of security was further undermined by the fact that, in the interests of safety, the entire film crew, including the director, were filming from inside a mobile cage on wheels and I was on my own out there, exposed and unprotected from this huge man-eating tiger. Oh yes, except for a puny seventeen-year-old boy with a rusty rifle who couldn't disguise his nervousness. He was the Third Assistant Big Cat Trainer but was there on his own because the Head Trainer was running late—by several hours.

The gun-toting boy warned me that, unlike lions, whose whims are easy to foresee, tigers are terrifyingly unpredict-able. But he reassured me that, once the Head Trainer arrived, there'd be nothing to fear. Finally a car pulled up.

'It's the Head Trainer,' announced the callow chap to everyone's relief. Which quickly evaporated when the Head Trainer stepped out of the car and we all saw he had only one arm.

I missed out on three roles I really wanted after being one of the last two actors left in the running for the job, which was a blow after things had been going so well for me in terms of work. One of these was the lead in *The Fantasticks*; it was between me and another girl but, after countless auditions, they chose her. I was very disappointed. This show became the longest-running musical on Broadway, only closing in 2002 after about forty years (many say it stopped because its signature song—'Try to remember, the kind of September'— was too painful for audiences there after 9/11).

One night in 1968 I was watching the TV news coverage of Robert Kennedy's assassination when David arrived home with the news that he'd been sacked by the ABC for providing information about inefficient work practices to Hal Lashwood at Actors Equity. The ABC's General Manager, Talbot Duckmanton, sacked David personally—'with regret, due to disloyalty'—which he was able to do because David was a contracted employee and not permanent. I believe David's motives were noble. At that time the ABC was top-heavy and bureaucrats outnumbered creatives by ten to one. A woman in finance had once had the gall to retort: 'We're not just here to make programs, you know!' Duh?

David went on to have a brilliant career in commercial TV. He was the Price part of Hayden Price associates, Mike Walsh's company, which produced the Nine Network's *Midday Show* for about a decade. David also went on to marry MJ, and they have a son. One of the big thrills for me at my surprise *This Is Your Life* party in 2002 was to see David and his wife. I hadn't seen them for years and they'd driven hundreds of kilometres just to be there on the night.

But, back to 1968. Having by now slumped into a mire of discontent, through no fault of David's, I finally told David that, with my friend Rona Coleman, I was moving into a flat in Randwick owned by Bryan Davies' father, Dr Norman, and his wife Margot. Norm and Margot were going to spend a year's sabbatical at Cambridge University and needed someone to stay in their home. David tried to dissuade me, but my mind was made up.

And by now I'd met John Walters.

chapter four

The Mancunian Lothario

EVERYONE WARNED ME AGAINST JOHN WALTERS.

A genuinely witty, intelligent, smooth-talking autodidact, he was a fifty-ish (though he claimed to be forty-ish), hard-drinking, chain-smoking newcomer from the UK. He had dark, slick hair and a thick moustache that gave him the air of a Victorian music hall villain. Photos of him in his youth bear a passing resemblance to Laurence Olivier—the same craggy Celtic brooding brow and deep-set eyes. Indeed, when John Walters worked at London's National Theatre during Olivier's tenure, Olivier himself jokingly referred to John on several occasions as 'my illegitimate son'.

Channel 7 brought John Walters out from England to produce and direct a new groundbreaking drama by Jon Cleary called *You Can't See Round Corners*. John auditioned an inexperienced young beauty from Brisbane, gave her the lead role, put her on the front pages and made a star of her overnight. Her name was Rowena Wallace.

The show was a huge ratings success for the channel and John Walters very quickly acquired a certain guru-like status in the industry. Meanwhile he was cutting a swathe through the actresses of Sydney like some kind of Mancunian Lothario. (I doubt he would like that description. His accent was pure London—well, Central School of Speech and Drama London anyway—but his origins were definitely in Manchester.) Women seemed to fall at his feet by the bedful. His conquests were many and varied, from naïve maidens to mature married women in every age group. And not all actresses either. There were musicians, writers and a couple of casting directors thrown in for good measure.

I screen-tested for John out at Channel 7 in Epping for a role in *The Battlers*, but lost out to Janice Dinnen, who'd played Ophelia to John Bell's Old Tote Hamlet and later, tragically, was killed in a London bus accident. After the screen test John told me he liked my work and invited me for a drink. 'I'm married,' I told him huffily and stalked off.

He then came to see *You Never Can Tell*, the Shaw play I was in at the Old Tote Theatre, mentioned in the previous chapter. He saw me rush out of the stage door after the show and trip over headlong into the shrubbery; he remembered being surprised at the vividness of my curses. (One of my flaws has always been my extravagant swearing which, most of the time, I now manage to curb by dint of huge attempts at self-control.)

Not long afterwards I chanced to see John Walters at Vadim's with a group of others late one night after work. Of course he turned on the charm; he was interesting and amusing, and I was fascinated by him.

'Not rushing home to your husband tonight?' he teased me, referring to the last time he'd seen me at the theatre.

'Actually, I'm living apart from my husband for a while,' I confided to this attractive paternal figure. WRONG! (But I was only twenty-one, remember.)

'I thought you seemed a little sad,' he murmured sympathetically. 'Let me treat you to dinner at the Jade Terrace next week to cheer you up.'

One of my girlfriends, who'd been amongst his myriad conquests, cautioned me that he was a callous bounder and a cad. She begged me not to succumb to him. I was scornful, assuring her that I would enjoy a pleasant evening of dinner and conversation with him and that would be that. No middle-aged Casanova was going to bewitch *this* highly sophisticated woman of the world, thank you very much! For goodness sake, I was now old enough to *vote*! John Walters was *not* going to be able seduce *me*! Thus determinedly armed, I went to dinner with him.

The meal, the wine, the conversation were splendid. So was the man. Then came the crunch, when he asked me back to his apartment for a coffee.

'I'm *not* going to go to bed with you,' said I, firm and resolute.

Coldly, he informed me that not only did he have no *desire* to go to bed with me, but that he would definitely *not* be going to bed with me. Deflated and disarmed, not to mention a little surprised, I meekly accompanied him home for coffee.

Reader, he had *lied* to me. He didn't even *have* any coffee.

It would be remiss of me to neglect to mention that the experience was nothing short of spectacular, in spite of the lack of coffee. Within a few months an affair had burgeoned. A full-blown love affair. What does Stanley say to Stella about 'seeing coloured lights' in Tennessee Williams' *A Streetcar Named Desire*?

John Walters lived in a flat in Upper Pitt Street, Kirribilli, with a harbour view. Some nights, when the air was still, you could hear the lions roaring across the water from Taronga Park. Within days John had begun to shed all his doxies.

One of his girlfriends heard that we'd been seen together and demanded furiously: '*Are you fucking that midget?!*' Many of his other women were similarly unimpressed, particularly one of Australia's leading casting directors, who has never given me a job in forty-one years.

It's true John Walters and I made an unlikely couple. Wherever we went, I was invariably mistaken for his daughter. Indeed, he was older than both my mother and father, who were at first, naturally, alarmed. But they were quickly won over by John's charm and great sense of humour. Also, it was probably quite obvious to them that John Walters loved me and wanted to take care of me.

He courted me diligently. Candlelit dinners at two of Sydney's plushest restaurants—Prunier's and Primo's—and romantic lunches in the garden of the exquisite Belvedere Hotel, which was eventually demolished to make way for the Kings Cross tunnel (the same fate which befell the Jade Terrace, where we had our first date). He could be irascible and volatile and difficult, but then I could be a handful myself. No bigger than a handful, though.

In 1969 he bought a brand-new flat in Avenue Road, Mosman, which Janet Hawley, in an article about me in the *Australian*, referred to scornfully as '*Pseudo* Spanish'. Duh, Janet. The only way it *couldn't* have been pseudo Spanish is if it had been in *Spain*, right?

I moved out of the flat I was sharing with Rona Coleman in Randwick and set up house with John Walters in Mosman. I learnt to make crème brûlée, osso bucco, bouilla-baisse and the best and crunchiest roast potatoes in the universe; and to grind his coffee beans by hand each morning before doing his kippers just the way he insisted.

I lay on the sand at Balmoral Beach in my pink string micro-bikini while he sat beside me doing the *Times* cryptic crossword. I washed and ironed his clothes and cleaned the house. I was Mrs Brady without the six kids. And I wanted a baby.

In 1969 I did two good plays with John Derum for the Q Lunchtime Theatre at Circular Quay—*The Applicant* by Harold Pinter, and *See the Pretty Lights* by Alan Plater. The Q Theatre, brainchild of the marvellous Doreen Warburton, was a very successful venture located in the original AMP building opposite Circular Quay; they served sandwiches, soup and coffee and provided forty-five minutes of live theatre every lunchtime to office workers in the Sydney CBD. We were almost always packed out.

I played Nancy in *The Knack* by Ann Jellico in a terrific production for the Theatre Royal in Hobart directed by Anne Harvey. In England *The Knack* launched the acting career of Rita Tushingham, who also appeared in the film. It's a gem of a role—hyperactive, complex, poignant and funny. I loved it.

I've performed in about eighty different theatres in Australia and Hobart's Theatre Royal remains my favourite. It's also our oldest theatre, though the Theatre Royal Ballarat would dispute that on a technicality, and Ballarat may well have a point. Whichever is the older, they are both beautiful examples of first-rate Victorian architecture—great venues to play in, with perfect acoustics. Why can't they build them like that today, the old codgers want to know.

The producer of *The Knack* was a Hobart visionary who's now a psychiatrist. This was Rod Morice, whose six-year-old daughter Tara used to spend a lot of time in my dressing room. She was very bright, very sweet and wanted to be an actress. And now, of course, she is one of our best. Rod's ex-wife, Jan Morice, is still a dear friend. Jan's also a fine marriage celebrant. She married my father to my stepmother, then my stepbrother Nigel to his wife Kylie, and then Sean Taylor to me (but that won't be revealed until Chapter 14). Jan also officiated at my son Dylan's marriage to Makiko Matsumoto. Thus Jan Morice is our officially designated family celebrant.

But back to Hobart, 1969. One of my publicity calls was

an interview with Hobart's ABC-TV nightly presenter. Her name was Robyn Nevin. One of her questions to me was: 'What is your greatest ambition?' To which I replied: 'To give birth to a child.' Her disdain was palpable.

As it happened, Robyn Nevin, unbeknownst to me, had just given birth to a child. A few nights later, at a dinner party at the Morices', I spent most of the evening cuddling the newly minted Emily Crook, who arrived swaddled in her bassinet with her father Barry and mother Robyn Nevin, who didn't smile once all night. We had an excellent pumpkin soup served in tiny pumpkin shells.

Apart from receiving glowing reviews for *The Knack* in Tasmania, I also received glowing love letters from John Walters, who was back in Sydney. I still have those letters.

The well-known English actor Alfred Marks came to Australia to star as a brigadier general in Peter Ustinov's *Halfway Up the Tree* at Sydney's Theatre Royal. Veteran British director Colin Gordon cast me as Alfred Marks' daughter—a spoilt, upper-middle-class teenager who is pregnant, unmarried and displays her rebelliousness by smoking cigars on-stage. Obnoxious. I'm a fan of Ustinov, but his play was not great and the critics and the punters didn't like it either.

At the same time I screen-tested for the late great director Tony Richardson, father of Vanessa Redgrave's daughters Joely and Natasha, and he cast me in his version of *Ned Kelly*, starring Mick Jagger. I was going to be one of the Kelly sisters but Mick had a minor shooting accident, hurt his hand and filming was rescheduled. I had to drop out because

I was already halfway through filming something for Crawfords (probably my seventh murder victim, I don't recall exactly) and I couldn't be released. Big disappointment.

ABC-TV engaged me for a Sunday night panel game show called *Would You Believe?*, which became so popular it ran for five years and I was with the show all that time. Two opposing teams told tall stories concerning Australiana and the other team had to guess which was the factual one, rather like the BBC's *My Word*.

Adman Peter Lazar was our compere. The novelist Frank Hardy, wine man Len Evans and actress Noeline Brown sat opposite historian Cyril Pearl, stockbroker Michael Baume and me, and I became mates with everyone, especially Frank and Noeline. In those five years Michael Baume transformed himself from a Labor Party member to a Liberal MP, and years later he became Consul General in New York.

All the stories I told on the program were written for me by my good friend John O'Grady, son of the author of *They're a Weird Mob*. John O'Grady junior wrote and produced *Would You Believe?* and was a stalwart of ABC-TV's comedy and light entertainment departments for decades. It's a measure of his skill as a writer that every word he wrote for me was exactly how I spoke, down to the last comma, and I never had to paraphrase his scripts. So if you think I sounded like a dill on *Would You Believe?*, blame O'Grady not me.

Then came *The Bandwagon*. It was 1970. The Phillip Theatre decided to bring out the redoubtable Peggy Mount to repeat her role in this play, which had just had a successful run on the West End in London. Peggy Mount was well-known for her stage and film roles, particularly *Sailor Beware*. She also starred in the TV series *George and the Dragon* with Sid James. She wasn't George. She had a huge Cockney voice, a formidable stage presence and great comic timing. The playwright, Terence Frisby, had already enjoyed international success with *There's a Girl in My Soup*, which was later a film starring Goldie Hawn and Peter Sellers.

The Bandwagon was another light comedy, a sort of working class sitcom with a good heart and a bit of a message. There was also a terrific role in it: Peggy Mount's daughter Aurora, a very plain, rather confused sixteen-year-old who is unmarried, pregnant and not entirely sure how it happened. When it's discovered that she's expecting quintuplets, Aurora becomes an unwilling celebrity overnight.

As soon as I read the script, I longed to be Aurora. My agent Gloria Payten sent me to audition for Eric Duckworth and William Orr, who'd cast me as Cinderella in my first professional role seven years earlier. The director was Robert Chetwyn, who'd also been imported from England. I did a good audition. Robert Chetwyn told me that he loved my reading but that I was *too pretty* for the part. *Too pretty!?* I was furious.

I managed to curb my anger and quell my tears of disappointment. By the time I got home, Gloria had already set up another audition with them for the following day. 'Make yourself as ugly as possible,' she ordered. I did another good reading, but by now they were thinking of someone else for the part.

The following day they called me back for a third reading and this time I was desperate. I rubbed oil in my hair, manu-factured dark circles under my eyes and psyched myself into a state of homely dejection.

On my fourth callback they said the magic words: 'You've got the part.' I was ecstatic.

Weeks later in rehearsal the director was chatting to the cast and said that he'd almost rejected me for being too pretty. 'What rubbish!' retorted Peggy Mount imperiously, as though she were the Queen in *Alice in Wonderland*. 'She's not too pretty at all!' I was never sure if this was a compli-ment or a put-down. I think it may have been a put-down.

As usual, John Walters was a great help to me right through rehearsals. He taught me a lot about timing; about staying focused, keeping calm and good-humoured. He taught me that having a sense of humour is largely to do with maintaining a sense of proportion regarding life in general. He kept my feet on the ground.

John's attitude to actors was deceptively simple and was the same as that of Nick Enright, who once told me that actors should be punctual, cheerful, serious and good. Occa-sionally it niggles when the bad-tempered, uncommitted actors who are always late still manage to prosper. Even if they're good.

The opening night of *The Bandwagon*, 6 March 1970, went well. John came backstage straight after the curtain call and was the most proud of me he'd ever been. I was sitting in the dressing room I shared with the beautiful flame-haired Bettina Welch. I was feeling stunned, exhausted and a little dazed. I knew I'd done a good job, but nothing could have prepared me for the praise that followed.

HG Kippax wrote in the *Sydney Morning Herald*: 'Miss Weaver, unrecognisable as the glum, dim-witted, touching little bundle of submerged humanity, Aurora, gives the performance of her career. She is brilliant.'

Katharine Brisbane echoed him in the *Australian*:

The Bandwagon is chiefly notable for one dizzy starring role—but not the one played by Peggy Mount. It is the teenager Aurora, played with a wonderfully funny and touching character by Jacki Weaver. This, above all the things she has done, is the part Miss Weaver has been waiting for, a part which makes use of her little girl look and her cracked baby voice without trapping it to them. She responds with a depth which from now on will enable her to put away childish things.

Yeah sure, if only! I was to continue playing children's roles for years, in fact.

Frank Harris in the *Daily Mirror* claimed that 'Jacki stole the show' and Robin Ingram in the Sydney *Sun* could only agree. Rex Cramphorn in the *Bulletin* chimed in with: 'The real centre of *The Bandwagon* is not Miss Mount's character but, rather, the daughter Aurora . . . [Jacki Weaver] resists every temptation to play the obvious comedy of situation and dialogue and achieves a surprisingly moving characterisation that is a credit to her and to her director.' And so the critics went on—these are just a few examples, but that's the gist. There were far more press reviews of the theatre back then than now, it seems, and all of them were good for me.

If I became a little too pleased with myself it didn't last long because, when we toured the play to Melbourne, the critics shat on me from a great height. It was to be several years before I received press plaudits in Melbourne equal to those I customarily got in Sydney; I still sometimes felt like some unwanted Sydney blow-in, even after I'd made Melbourne my home base for twelve years.

But back to Sydney and the Phillip Theatre in April 1970. I was working too hard to get conceited, and anyway I was too preoccupied. I had found out that I was pregnant. John Walters and I had discussed having children, so he knew how keen I was to be a mother. He encouraged me to stop taking the pill and within a microsecond, it seems, I became pregnant.

As soon as I suspected, I visited a Macquarie Street obstetrician for tests and returned a few days later for the result. In those days it couldn't be detected straightaway—tests had to be done with rabbits or something. When the pregnancy was confirmed, I was so excited that I rushed down to the foyer of the building, accosted a complete stranger by the public phone and said, 'Please give me ten cents. I'm pregnant!'

I phoned John at work to break the news and he was delighted. At that time he was working with John Laws out at Channel 7, but they were due to have lunch that day in the city. I met them at the Tai Ping restaurant in Haymarket. I think the astrologer Karen Moregold may have been there. I remember being very distracted.

I was very anxious about telling my parents. John assured me that he would handle it. He invited them over to Mosman the following Sunday. They arrived cheerful and happy to see us. When they settled down with their drinks, John dropped the bombshell: 'Jacki's pregnant.'

My mother was devastated. 'Oh my God, no,' she cried. I began to sob quietly. My father, grim-faced and businesslike, began talking about divorce. I was, after all, still married to David Price.

The next hurdle was informing my employers, the Phillip Theatre. Producer Eric Duckworth was also devastated, until I reminded him that I was a healthy 22-year-old and there was no reason why I couldn't continue playing a pregnant sixteen-year-old right up until the birth if necessary, provided my false pregnancy was reduced as my real pregnancy advanced.

However, it wasn't a good pregnancy; I hated being pregnant. I was ill every day for nine months—nauseous, aching, frequent cramps. The only good thing about it was that I talked to my baby constantly while he was in utero. Told him all sorts of things. I was thrilled to be having a baby, but miserable with the way I felt physically. And totally exhausted, though, admittedly, some of that could have been due to performing eight shows a week.

My pregnancy diet was impeccable. No alcohol at all. Loads of fresh fruit and vegetables and good healthy food, and exercise and a swim at Balmoral every day. But still I felt unwell—maybe some people are just not cut out to be breeders.

Then we went on strike. Young actors today are usually amazed when I inform them that, until 1970, we were not paid rehearsal money. This meant that producers could make you work a forty-hour week, for four to six weeks until the show opened, for NO MONEY. Then if the show ran for, say, only two weeks, you'd have worked six or eight weeks for only two weeks' money. That's just the way it was. So we, via our union (Actors Equity), decided to ask all the theatre producers to start paying us rehearsal money. I think the refusal was unanimous. We were told rehearsal money would 'destroy the industry'.

Our Equity meeting in the Phillip Theatre green room was tense. Peggy Mount was very vocal in her opposition to striking, saying that Actors Equity in England had done more harm than good. Her understudy, Maggie Kirkpatrick (yes, the Freak in *Prisoner*) was equally forceful in support. Most of the other members of the cast of ten agreed with Maggie. She was, after all, a good socialist, having trained at the New Theatre. As for me, I've always been a staunch unionist. So we decided to strike.

It was a very gentle strike. We simply held the curtain for half an hour for three nights only, but the effect of that thirty-minute delay in starting the show was amazing—audiences were very angry about it. So much so that, after only three nights, most producers all over town capitulated and we got our rehearsal pay.

A few actors were too fearful to join the strike, notably

at the Olde Music Hall at Neutral Bay, where proprietor George Miller (not to be confused with the two film directors of the same name, Dr George Miller of *Lorenzo's Oil*, and *The Witches of Eastwick* or the other George Miller, who directed *The Man From Snowy River*) threatened instant dismissal if they did. My parents used to enjoy the occasional meal and melodrama at the Music Hall but, after they heard about that, they never went there again.

After the Sydney run, *The Bandwagon* opened in Melbourne at the Athenaeum Theatre to lukewarm reviews. My tummy was growing rapidly but I was denying all the rumours. Most people didn't know I actually was pregnant. A friend of mine who was a cameraman at Channel 0 (before it became Channel 10) overheard a woman in the canteen talking about *The Bandwagon*: 'That little Jacki Weaver is quite good, but someone should show her how a pregnant woman really walks.'

I took a small flat in East Melbourne on the floor below Peggy Mount. But she ignored me most of the time, which made me bewildered and sad. I contracted a severe bout of bronchitis. Bettina Welch, Michael Laurence and Bernadette Hughson, who were in the show, were very kind to me.

John drove down from Sydney in the Valiant twice to see me. My parents came to stay for a few days and even my grandfather Jackson flew down to visit. By now my mother was knitting tiny garments.

By the time the show closed at the Athenaeum, my fake tummy had been altered three times and would actually move with the movements of the real baby. Finally it was a huge relief to get out of Melbourne. By now I was seven months pregnant.

My divorce a month later in the Sydney Divorce Court had an element of farce about it. I stood in the dock hugely pregnant in a white lace dress dubiously testifying that David Price had deserted me, while my mum waited in the court holding a bag of bananas, bananas being my particular pregnancy craving. (Potassium deficiency? I ended up with a baby who wouldn't touch bananas for years—obviously had had more than enough bananas in the womb, thanks.) These were the bad old days when one of the partners was forced to take the blame for a marriage breaking down, part of the uncivilised system that was in operation before the great jurist Lionel Murphy's reforms came into being, recognising that nothing is cut and dried, that blame is pointless and that sometimes partnerships just irretrievably break down and should be allowed to dissolve as painlessly as possible.

John Walters wasn't having a good time at Channel 7 in Sydney. One of the shows he was producing was *Beauty and the Beast* with John Laws. He employed me to edit and compile the letters for each one-hour program, five days a week for two months, for a modest remuneration. Nepotism, sure, but hey, I gave good correspondence. Most of the letters were total inventions, straight out of the dark recesses of my imagination.

Neither the 'Beauties' nor John Laws knew that only about 5 per cent of the letters were genuine and even then heavily edited by me. I couldn't help feeling gleeful whenever one of my fake letters led to heated debate from the panel.

And I laughed when Pat Firman once exclaimed: 'This is the most idiotic piece of mail we've ever received! Most of the people who write to us are so intelligent!'

I was looking forward to giving birth—to the organic experience of pushing out my baby, drug free, and to witnessing every detail of the event. I was well informed and primed up; I had regularly attended childbirth education classes, trained in the Lamaze method, practised all the breathing etc etc (one of the teachers was Wendy McCarthy, who later became Deputy Chair of the ABC). Thus on the great day it was a major disappointment to be told at 11.15 pm, after nine hours of labour, that my baby was in distress, couldn't move and that an emergency caesarean under a general anaesthetic was unavoidable.

Dylan was born at the Wahroonga Sanitarium (now Sydney Adventist Hospital) at 11.25 pm on Friday, 4 December 1970, nine months after *The Bandwagon* had opened (on Friday 6 March). He weighed nine pounds (4.08 kilograms) and I'd gained 50 pounds (23 kilos), but I was very happy. I spent a week in hospital.

I wanted him to be called Benjamin but John demurred, saying Benjamin was 'too Jewish'. John wanted to call him Brendan but I objected, saying I didn't want him named after an Irish drunk (playwright Brendan Behan). So we compromised and named him after a Welsh drunk and a Jewish folk-singer.

The press leapt onto our good fortune like lard-seeking seagulls. One of the glossy mags ran a story with a huge banner headline: 'Jacki's Love Baby: Scoop Picture', which we proudly hung over Dylan's cot. My mother wisely remarked: 'If only *all* babies were love babies.' I was quite ready to wed John Walters but he was always unflinchingly opposed to the idea, a position from which he never wavered, saying he didn't believe in marriage. Sometimes I wondered idly if perhaps he had a secret wife hidden away in the UK and that was his reason, but there was never any evidence to back up this fantasy of mine. And anyway, I never doubted he adored me and so I was content to go along with his immovable stance against legalising our union.

Ann Churchill-Brown had just taken over from Hilary Linstead (when Hilary left to start M&L Casting with Liz Mullinar), helping Gloria Payten to look after the female actors at Gloria's agency, International Casting Service. Gloria usually employed at least six other people, but she always ran the place overall. Ann phoned me to say that film director Tim Burstall had offered me the lead in his movie *Stork* by a new Australian writer called David Williamson, but that they'd need to start shooting in March.

Tim sent me David Williamson's screenplay when I was still in hospital after having Dylan. Next day Tim rang me to ask what I thought of the script. I said I loved it, except for the smoked-oyster-up-the-nostril routine. Tim roared with laughter and shouted: 'Honey, the audiences are going to love the smoked-oyster-up-the-nostril routine!' And he was right. After we made it, I toured the country promoting that movie. I must have seen it twenty-five times. Wherever we went, the oyster gag never failed to provoke enormous hilarity, just as Tim predicted. Except in me. But I had a great time doing *Stork*. Bruce Spence was a darling, as were Tim and Betty Burstall and all the crew. They even engaged a nanny for Dylan.

When Dylan was only six weeks old I took him to Melbourne for a week as I was playing a twelve-year-old schoolgirl in an episode of *Matlock Police* for Crawfords. So much for 'putting away childish things'. Out came the old elastic bandages again, but this time there was breast milk involved.

Another of my frustrations with myself as a parent was that I only managed to breastfeed for three months, while my own mother had breastfed me for two years. Not a good breeder *and* with inferior feeding apparatus. But I adored my baby and I carted him everywhere with me.

John was an adoring and excellent father, especially as he'd never expected to become one. However, his career at Channel 7 had stalled; he was miserable and frustrated and quarrelling with me. I was very tired all the time.

Then I had a call to go to an interview with John Bell and a then unknown Richard Wherrett at the recently opened Nimrod Theatre in Kings Cross.

chapter five

The Smallest Fag Hag
in Australia

I MET RICHARD WHERRETT AT A BALMAIN CHRISTMAS PARTY IN 1970. He was the handsomest man I'd ever seen. Not that handsomeness has ever been a priority for me. Men I've fancied have ranged in looks from gorgeous to gorblimey. Beauty's fine, but not obligatory.

Richard had recently returned to Sydney to work at the Old Tote Theatre after several years in the UK, where he'd taught at East 15 Drama School in London and undertaken various directing gigs. He was a Sydney boy, originally from West Ryde; a Trinity Grammar schoolboy who later became a Trinity teacher after graduating from Sydney University, where his contemporaries were John Bell, Bruce Beresford, John Gaden, Ron Blair, Ken Horler, Leo Schofield etc. His extraordinary life, along with that of his brother Peter, is documented in their dual autobiography, *Desirelines*, and further in his beautiful follow-up memoir about his brilliant career, *The Floor of Heaven*.

Having been out of the Sydney loop for several years, he needed to reacquaint himself with the available thespian talent pool. So, since his arrival, he'd been interviewing local actors, but my agent Hilary Linstead had postponed my interview because of my pregnancy.

I took my three-week-old baby son Dylan in a basket to that Christmas party. After that Richard and I saw each other at different social gatherings and I was always taken by his seeming inscrutability and aloofness which, without warning, could burst into hilarity. He had a wicked sense of the ridiculous and the unusual ability to laugh until he cried—he would actually shed tears of mirth.

I was also struck by that devastatingly beautiful face and bearing. I wanted him to like me; I wanted to make him laugh; I wanted to make him laugh until he cried. And in that I succeeded, often without even trying, right up until the week he died.

In 1971 my agent Ann Churchill-Brown sent me to see Richard, John Bell and Ken Horler at the newly opened Nimrod Theatre (which of course was then located in Nimrod Street, Kings Cross, where The Stables now is; it had in fact opened during the week that Dylan was born). Richard was about to start directing for Nimrod, as well as for the Old Tote, and teaching at NIDA, and they were casting a quartet of plays.

Years later I read Richard's notes from that interview. He said 'Jacki Weaver: Good acting, good-looking, charming and more intelligent than she lets on.' Rather than being flattered, I was disappointed that I must have given the impression of being a bit of a dickhead. As a result of that interview, though, John Bell cast me in the first Sydney production of Williamson's *The Removalists*, Ken Horler put me into Jack Hibberd's *Customs and Excise*, Larry Eastwood directed me in Tom Stoppard's *After Magritte* and Richard gave me Alex Buzo's *The Roy Murphy Show*, alongside John Wood.

I clearly remember gazing at Richard during rehearsals in that steamy little space in Nimrod Street and being riveted by him. And also feeling a little insecure about his much more free and open style of direction compared with the mainly authoritarian directors I'd been used to up until then.

A few months later we were rehearsing Bob Ellis' and Michael Boddy's *The Legend of King O'Malley* for the Old Tote Company in a production that would go to the South Pacific Arts Festival in Fiji and then tour New Zealand. John Bell had directed the highly successful debut production less than two years earlier. The touring party comprised a stellar cast, including Reg Livermore, Chris Haywood, Bob Hornery, Terence Clarke, Edwin Hodgeman and musician Bill Qua. We were having a pun craze so when Bill lost his luggage we called him Poor Qua, amid much hilarity. Chris Haywood lost his temper in a cafe and declared: 'I hate puns! They're pointless! You might as well say: "Please pour me a chimney of wine!"' He was even crosser when we couldn't stop laughing.

During those rehearsals in Sydney, Bob Ellis did an unforgivable thing. Using his privilege as a playwright he came to watch a rough run-through of the play and then had the gall to review it (I think in *Nation Review*—some publishers have no scruples!) and utterly slammed us. The effect on company morale was devastating. Privacy in rehearsal is sacrosanct and Ellis had violated it. I still find it harder to rehearse if anyone unconnected to the production is present. The rehearsal period should involve taking risks and being allowed to fail. Outsiders can't always be trusted, and so they inhibit the process.

When we arrived to perform at the Arts Festival in Suva we found it impossible to sleep in our billeted accommodation because of the mosquitoes and the Tongan contingent having noisy coitus behind the partitions separating our bunks. There was also the issue of the turds floating in the shower stalls (cold water only). Richard and I opted for the luxury of the Sheraton, even though it cost more than we were earning, and we decided to share, on a platonic basis of course, a four-bed suite with Jane Harders and Sandra McGregor. By the time we reached Auckland, however, after that platonic week together in Suva, I was irrevocably and unequivocally in love with him. And he with me. I still have his love letters.

After the first night we spent alone together I crept back along the draughty creaking Auckland hotel corridor at 4 am to the room I shared with Jane. I was wearing nothing but a moth-eaten coat. Shivering, I slipped it off and slid naked under the sheets. From the other bed Jane opened one eye, cocked an eyebrow and inquired dryly, 'What've *you* been doing?'

'Just talking,' I said.

I returned to my baby and his father in Sydney after being away for three weeks. My guilt was immeasurable, but so was my love for Richard. I was obsessed.

I began working on Robin Lovejoy's Old Tote production of Peter Nichols' *Forget-Me-Not-Lane* with a big cast including Ruth Cracknell and Drew Forsythe. I was Ursula, ageing from thirteen to twenty during the course of the play. A picture of me as the thirteen-year-old in school uniform was on the front page of the *Telegraph*. I was actually twenty-four.

After a season at the Parade Theatre in Kensington we went on a country tour, including Wagga Wagga and Albury-Wodonga. Richie turned up by light plane in Wagga, much to everyone's surprise. Except for Ruth Cracknell, who was on to us from the start. Richie's lame excuse for being there was that he had relatives in Cootamundra. *Cootamundra!* Quite a distance from Wagga.

Another surprise was the writer Bob Ellis turning up in Albury to see me. I certainly wasn't expecting him. I think I was rinsing out a bucket of dirty nappies at some dingy motel when Ellis arrived unannounced. I had my baby Dylan on tour with me, which was hard work, even though he was the sweetest and most placid of infants. He was teething at the time and would often sleep in a skip full of costumes in the dressing rooms.

Bob Ellis was very peeved that I had to spend the only afternoon he had in Albury doing a publicity photo opportunity at the local dog food factory and he later sent me a classically Ellis vicious letter of bitter reproach. I was a little frightened of him for some time afterwards. All's fine now though. I like Bob very much—his cleverness, his often odd take on many of the ways of the world. His wife Anne Brooksbank is extraordinary, and a terrific writer.

I was just one of Bob's dozens of crushes back in the early seventies. I went out with him once only, to an afternoon screening of *The Last Picture Show*. However, I never even held his hand, never mind kissed him. Or anything else, for that matter. Yet to this day Bob Ellis is still telling people we had an affair. Only last week, in fact, he told my friend Manuela that he had 'had a fling' with me. 'Fling' means *sex*, Bob. And *sex* means *genital contact*. (Of *any* kind, Bill Clinton.) In ya dreams, Bob, you big fibber!

This is a pattern that has been repeated often in my life— strange men falsely claiming to have been my intimates. A curious thing. One night at ten thirty I was reading in bed when my old school friend 'Clare' phoned. She was in the middle of giving a posh dinner party in Mosman for her husband's advertising colleagues when my name came up in conversation: one of the chaps claimed to have had an affair with me and even went into detail, not realising that his hostess and I were close friends. That was when Clare slipped away from the table to phone me.

'Did you sleep with "Hieronymus Bosch"?' (not his real name) she demanded to know. I, ever honest, replied in the negative. My loyal friend, thus assured, returned to her dinner table to announce triumphantly: 'I just spoke to Jac and she says not only did she never fuck you, but she wouldn't touch you with a barge pole!'

I've lost count of the number of similar falsehoods I've heard about myself. That's why I never believe rumours about anyone, especially the famous. Some people invent stories about other people and that's a fact. Go figure.

Anyway—getting back to Bob Ellis, Wodonga and the dog food factory—I was by now so desperately in love with Richard Wherrett, so blinded by love, that I could barely see any other man never mind feel attracted to them. Within weeks of our return, Richard had smuggled me and Dylan out of John Walters' Mosman flat and moved us into Ann Churchill-Brown's flat in Edgecliff. I still feel great remorse for the grief I caused John by taking his baby son away. When he found out about Richard, he rang my parents in the middle of the night and shouted: 'She's deserting me for *a homosexual*!'

When my dear friend, actor Garry Scale, affectionately refers to me as 'the smallest fag hag in Australia', it's a tag I wear with pride. For some people, 'fag hag' is an unattractive and pejorative term, but I like it and take it as a compliment. When I compered the Gay and Lesbian Mardi Gras Night of Stars Concert at the State Theatre in 1996, *Sydney Morning Herald* reviewer James Waites referred to me and others like me as 'gay-friendly straights', which, let's face it, is just a polite way of saying 'fag hag'.

That's not to say I like all gay men—not at all. But the fact is that the majority of my close friends happen to be men of the *queer* persuasion. This is indeed the case with many women who work in the arts. In such a career the chances are you'll meet a greater proportion of gay men. It's simple statistics.

Left: My first birthday, 25 May 1948. 'Such a plain baby,' said Grandma.

Below: Ede and Art as they appeared on the front page of the *Sydney Daily Mirror,* August 1946, so much in love.

Left: Georgina and I playing with dolls in Sans Souci, aged 11 and 3.

Below: Aged two, farewelling Daddy Artie aboard the ship *Orion,* bound for England with Mum to see her dying mother.

Left: Martin Place, Sydney, wearing my Sunday best pink frock from Mark Foys.

Right: With my aunt Georgina at Bexley Physical Culture concert, impersonating Native Americans.

Left: In the backyard at West Kogarah. I'm on my tricycle with Rod in the background alighting from his dinky.

Below: With Rod and Dad at Brighton-le-Sands.

Above: At West Pymble. I'm 14. Rod, aged 9, had just finished three months in hospital after Dad ran him over with the car. *(Author's private collection)*

FROM SCHOOLGIRL TO CINDERELLA

SHE DARED TO BECOME A STAR

The main role in a Christmas pantomime this year will be played by a real Cinderella.

For a month, the magic wand of the theatre will transform Jackie Weaver, a 15-year-old schoolgirl of Hornsby, into a pantomime star.

Each night, in the glow of the footlights, Jackie, who is blonde and only five feet tall, will sing and dance the role of the fairytale character, her leading man a teenage TV star.

At the end of the month she will go back to Hornsby High School to settle down to a further two years' study.

Saved the day

Jackie, who has just finished her Intermediate — "I hope I've passed" — has had her eyes on a stage career since she was eight.

She auditioned for the part of Cinderella in the Phillip Theatre pantomime, A Wish Is a Dream, on a dare.

"My mother told me if I wanted to become an actress I had better start getting some experience at auditions and dared me to have a go for the role of Cinderella," Jackie said.

Jackie's last minute appearance at the audition saved the day for the pantomime.

Her two leading men, Bryan Davies and Terry Mitchell are only 18 and 17. Neither of them is tall.

"We had auditioned about 20 girls when Jackie turned up in her school uniform," said Mr. Bill Orr, the producer.

"But they were all very tall and older than their leading men. Jackie was just right."

How does Jackie feel about playing opposite Bryan Davies, the TV star?

"Well," she said, "I wasn't a fan of his until I met him. Now, I think he is wonderful."

DAILY MIRROR, THURSDAY, DECEMBER 6, 1962

Above: Aged 15. My first press interview in the *Sydney Daily Mirror*, the first of thousands of interviews. *(Author's private collection)*

Left: The cover of *Teenager's Weekly*, a magazine inside the *Australian Women's Weekly*, as Cinderella with two Prince Charmings, Bryan Davies and Terry Mitchell. *(Author's private collection)*

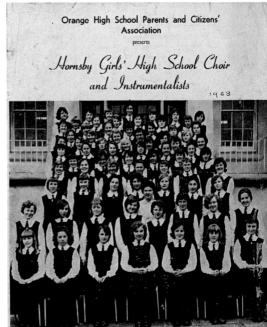

Right: Hornsby Girls' High School choir. I'm in the front row, left-hand end. Brillliant singer Susan Kessler is back row, left-hand end. *(Author's private collection)*

Left: Aged 16, in 1963, another publicity shot at Bondi Beach with lovely Bryan Davies, the Prince who turned into a Paramour (as opposed to a frog). *(Author's private collection)*

Below: ABC-TV opera of Humperdinck's *Hansel and Gretel* with Brian Gilbert (now a Harley Street, London, specialist) as Hansel. *(Author's private collection)*

Left: With Mum and Dad in Bankstown, where Dad had his legal practice. *(Author's private collection)*

Right: On stage at the Palace Theatre, Sydney (on the present site of the Hilton Hotel) with Rob E.G. (for example?) in *Mother Goose and the Three Stooges* by Ibsen (only jokin'!). Am holding a banana, obviously an important plot point which now escapes me. *(Author's private collection)*

Left: On the front cover of the *Australian Women's Weekly,* precariously seated in a tree at Clifton Gardens. There were two separate stories inside this issue contradicting each other about my love life. *AWW* editor not amused. *(Author's private collection)*

Below: Wedding to David Price at the Wayside Chapel, Kings Cross, with Reverend Ted Noffs. *(Author's private collection)*

Left: 1967, aged 20 at Tamarama Beach in a pink crochet bikini. This photo was published on page three of *News of the World* in the UK. I don't know who gave it to them but I certainly didn't.
(Author's private collection)

Right: Aged 21, in a sailor dress.
(Author's private collection)

Above: Aged 22, this (semi-nude) photo of me was always hanging on Richard Wherrett's bedroom wall, right up until the day he died. To see it there often took people by suprise. *(Author's private collection)*

Right: Excited expectant father John Walters listening closely to the Fruit of my Ute (i.e. Dylan). *(Author's private collection)*

Above: 1971, in Mosman. Dylan telling his dad a joke. (Me in the middle). *(Author's private collection)*

Right: Richard Wherrett aged 30, around the time I met him. *(Author's private collection)*

Above: Snapped by Robert Alexander at Whale Beach. Richard and Dylan playing 'This Little Piggy Went to Market'. I'm still wearing that frayed old crochet bikini. *(Author's private collection)*

Right: Rich and I at Barbara and Richard Butler's wedding at Coogee, where Rich was Best Man in his green velvet suit. *(Author's private collection)*

Above: At Bondi Pavilion, Dylan laughing at me, which he's been doing all his life. *(Author's private collection)*

Below: Wedding to Max Hensser at Sue and Bruce Moir's house in Greenwich, Bruce with his hand on my shoulder, Max on my right. *(Author's private collection)*

Above: Interviewing two brilliant legends, Garry McDonald and Gloria Dawn, for the Willesee program. *(Author's private collection)*

Below: My hair dyed black, as Masha in Chekov's *The Seagull,* Nimrod Theatre, Surry Hills, which became the Belvoir Street Theatre. *(Author's private collection)*

Above: With Phil Davis in Paris at the Moulin Rouge nightclub. *(Author's private collection)*

Below: Brother Rod with me in Newtown. Always good friends and close confidantes. *(Author's private collection)*

Another sad fact for me is that I've never been let down by my gay male friends in the way that I've so often been betrayed by girlfriends. Some gay men don't fancy women at all whereas other gays find sex with a woman an appealing idea. The label *bi*sexual has always been a vexing one for me, the *bi* bit of it seeming to imply an equal preference for both sexes whereas, from what I've observed, the so-called bisexual man is basically a gay man who also likes women to a degree. Cunt-struck queers, to be blunt. And that's emphatically not a criticism, but merely an observation.

I knew Richard was gay from the moment I met him but, by the time we fell in love, his homosexuality simply wasn't an issue between us. Our physical attraction was strong, mutual and fulfilling; our emotional connection was total. We were in love, and that was that.

Some of our friends and relatives were not so blithe about our union. My mother said: 'I'm very fond of Richard, darling, and I can understand why you love him. But he's simply not your *type*.' Which was the closest she could bring herself to saying the word *homosexual*. She also said that, yes, Richard was good-looking but his brother Peter was much better looking than Richard. I remember trying to explain to my concerned aunt, Georgina, exactly what homosexuality was but that Richard and I were committed to each other completely and faithfully. Some of Richard's friends were very disapproving, even openly hostile, fearing it would end in tears. We remained steadfastly in love.

One night at a party in Paddington, Richard was holding two-year-old Dylan on his hip when a drunk lurched up and sneered, 'Who do you think you're fooling, you faggot? Using that kid as a prop, you poser!' Richard ignored him, but then the man deliberately and pointedly ashed his cigarette on Dylan's head. In a split second Richard had hit the man with his free hand and knocked him sprawling across the floor. Dylan meanwhile simply gazed at this fracas wide-eyed, unconcerned and unscathed. We left the party soon afterwards.

A couple of my women friends who were among the most supportive had themselves experienced failed relationships with gay men, from which a couple of children each had been produced. And yet they encouraged and cheered me on. Fag hag solidarity, perhaps? Indeed there are dozens of such families out there, especially in Sydney circles.

In an effort to understand everything I could on the subject I began to read people like Denis Altman, who certainly helped enlighten me about gay politics. Twenty-five years later, Richard went on record in an interview as saying that his ideal lover would be a man from the waist up and a woman from the waist down, which makes me smile now, particularly considering the never-insubstantial size of my breasts (even when I was twenty-seven years old and weighed 41 kilos, which could explain why I became such an expert at bust minimisation). Richie put it more subtly in *Desire-lines*, the 1997 book he co-wrote with his brother Peter, in which he explored his reasons for feeling attracted to both sexes. It's in the chapter 'The Politics of Experience', where he also quotes his favourite dictum from EM Forster: 'Only connect the prose and the passion and both will be exalted and human love will be seen at its highest.'

Richard and I now knew we wanted to be together always. Around the middle of 1972 he left Sydney to take up a term teaching at East 15 Acting School in London and I was to follow when I'd saved up the fare. I did a Benson & Hedges cigarette commercial for TV, which proves how desperate I was because I've always been fairly militantly anti-smoking. Always thought smoking was disgusting, filthy and stupid. But it paid the fare to London.

My mother was very angry with me. The only people who saw us off at the airport were Bryan and Tracy Davies, because they felt sorry for us. But at least my mother was kind enough to lend me her good woollen overcoat for the London winter, even though it was about four sizes too big for me.

The Qantas flight was packed. Dylan, aged nearly two, sat on my lap for twenty-five hours, except for the forty minutes between Rome and London when he finally fell asleep and, exhausted, I limped up to the back of the jumbo to stretch my legs. Within seconds a steward sidled up to me and invited me to join the Mile High Club. I gave him the shortest shrift I've ever given anyone.

Richie used to say that, when he picked up Dylan and me from Heathrow Airport, he watched us coming through the arrivals gate looking like two pathetic orphans and he knew then that he would love us forever.

London was a great adventure. I was happier than I'd ever been. For a while we stayed with friends in a tiny Dickensian terrace in Shelton Street, WC2, near Covent Garden. Peter Cook and Dudley Moore were playing in

Behind the Fridge—their successful follow-up to *Beyond the Fringe*—in a theatre nearby.

London was putting on a glorious autumn and I was keeping house and playing Happy Families with my dear little boy and the man I adored. Each day Richie would catch the train to Loughton, Essex, to work while Dylan and I would shop, cook, clean and play. And religiously watch *Monty Python* on TV.

One day we had lunch with director Jim Sharman, who was having huge successes with Harry M Miller's productions of *Hair* and *Jesus Christ Superstar* both in Australia and the West End, where they were currently playing long runs. Soon he'd direct the first of many productions of *The Rocky Horror Show*. After lunch Jim and I looked around a sex shop in the West End, because I'd never been in one. Dylan in his pusher seemed unimpressed. No purchases were made.

Dylan gave me such pleasure. A happy, gentle two-year-old, always laughing, with white blond curls, crooked eyes and a ready smile for the camera. On weekends the three of us would have picnics at the zoo or Hyde Park. We were very contented.

By now we were living in a lovely flat in South Kensington. Even though our finances were very limited, Richard would still manage to take me out somewhere different every night while Byron, a six-foot four-inch (193 centimetres) acting student from a farm in Dayton, Ohio would babysit Dylan in return for all the food he could eat, which was usually the entire contents of the fridge. He was a preacher's son and was great with kids because he had five younger brothers and sisters back home in Ohio.

Many of Richie's female students had huge crushes on him, which was understandable and I didn't mind. Except for one really pushy number, who got right up my nose, not to mention in my ear—Ruby Wax. She was simply too keen on Richard for comfort. My comfort, anyway. Ruby Wax became a TV star and producer and often works with Dawn French and *Absolutely Fabulous*'s Jennifer Saunders.

We saw Olivier in *Long Day's Journey into Night*, a huge thrill; we saw Anthony Hopkins and Diana Rigg in *Macbeth*; we heard the LSO playing Mahler, and Janet Baker singing Schubert and *Tosca* at Covent Garden, where I wore the long lilac silk dress Richie had chosen for me at Biba. In Piccadilly he bought me a tiny pair of antique amethyst earrings, which I'm wearing as I write this. He nearly blew all our money— $800—on a wonderful hand-painted silk sunshine-yellow Zandra Rhodes dress that he thought would look good on me, before I stopped him in the nick of time.

I get irritated by self-appointed fashion fascists who declare seventies fashions were ugly. Some of the clothes were very beautiful. Richie had a bottle-green velvet suit that always looked fabulous. And I had some stunning clothes from Jenny Kee and Linda Jackson, from a Melbourne designer named Norma Tullo, and from the House of Merivale in Sydney.

We also went to rock concerts: Led Zeppelin, Slade and David Bowie as Ziggy Stardust at the Finsbury Park Rainbow Room. Plus a gala performance of *Tommy* with Peter Sellers,

Tina Turner and Roger Daltrey. Not to mention a bunch of weird Andy Warhol movies and Mick Jagger in *Performance*. And one night a glamorous late supper at the Café Royale and the first of many proposals of marriage from Richard.

Richie was earning 40 pounds a week, which was worth about $80, believe it or not; in 1972 the exchange rate was very different from nowadays. Our budget was tight because we were saving to go to New York. We had a terrific windfall one day when I received a cheque from Australia for $500 from the AFI Awards people for Best Actress for the film *Stork*. It was a huge help to us—thank you, Hoyts! The AFI gives only trophies now, when for many actors a cash prize would be hugely welcome. In some cases, essential.

I could have lived in London forever but Richie was itching to get home, especially after a letter arrived from John Bell saying there'd been dancing in the streets when Gough Whitlam had recently been elected.

On our way home we stayed in New York for a fortnight, firstly at the Algonquin Hotel in West 44th Street, in homage to Dorothy Parker and all the writers at the *New Yorker* magazine. Then we stayed with Richard and Barbara Butler in their apartment in the East 70s. Richie had been friends with Richard Butler and his brother Peter Butler at Sydney University and now Richard had a diplomatic post at the UN. When Richard and Barbara were married at Waverley in Sydney, Richie was the best man (in the green velvet suit). Richard Butler became Prime Minister Whitlam's Private Secretary, later a UN weapons inspector and then, controversially, Governor of Tasmania.

And so we returned home. I used to wonder whether, if we'd remained in England, we would have stayed together. Maybe.

We rented a tiny sandstone cottage in Adolphus Street, Balmain. We were very poor. Carillo Gantner and Nancy Black lived nearby and gave us saucepans and kitchenware. So too did Richard's mother Lyle and his auntie Sadie, both of whom I adored. Lyle once said to me: 'I know, whatever happens, you'll love Rich always.' And she was right. I did.

Richie was working again at Nimrod in Kings Cross. He and John Bell co-directed a terrific *Hamlet* starring John, with Anna Volska as Ophelia and Max Cullen as the gravedigger, with Larry Eastwood's ingenious mirrored set.

During production week I arrived home one evening from delivering Dylan to his father John for an overnight visit to find a note from Richie urging me: 'Please come to the theatre, I need your chirpy sustenance.' I loved that note. I raced to the theatre to hold his hand.

The following day my doctor told me I was pregnant. I'd seen him the week before because I'd been unwell, but this was the last thing I expected. There'd been no real symptoms and yet he said I was at least eight weeks pregnant, possibly more. I felt stupid for not realising and I was in turmoil. We had no money. Richie was less perturbed than I—we can get married, he said. I didn't want anyone to know and for a week I didn't sleep and couldn't think of anything else. I was very frightened, of what I'm not sure.

I began to prowl around Wynyard Station, like a stalker, spying on Richie's father Eric, who worked in the pharmacy there. I was probably trying to find a family connection with the baby growing inside me. It was bizarre behaviour, but I did it five afternoons in a row. Richard had been estranged from his father for many years and so I'd never had an opportunity to meet him. And here I was spying on him, a tall, balding man with a sad face.

And then one night in the bathroom in Balmain I lost the baby. So much blood. Richie took me to Crown Street Women's Hospital where my gynaecologist was the lovely Derek Llewellyn-Jones. They gave me a blood transfusion and kept me there for three days.

We didn't tell anyone what had happened. I think some people suspected I'd had an abortion, but I didn't even consider that option. Not with Richard's baby.

Richard picked me up from the hospital one night after his rehearsal, with Dylan sitting in the back seat, both of them pleased to be taking me home. I was very tired and very sad.

'I'll make you an omelette for dinner and put you straight to bed,' said Richard.

'I have a craving for some red meat,' I said.

As we had nothing in the fridge and the butcher was shut, Rich decided to call in on Ken and Lilian Horler in Suffolk Street, Paddington, to see if they could help us out. Dylan and I waited outside in the car while Richie went inside.

Generously, as usual, Lily gave us a fillet of beef she'd bought for a dinner party the following night. Richie put the meat in my lap and began driving. By the time we arrived home I'd eaten the whole thing, raw, with my fingers, like some ravenous carnivore. Obviously my body was demanding iron, and demanding it immediately.

The Horlers had a dear little girl about Dylan's age called Sacha, whom we'd sometimes babysit (yes, *the* Sacha Horler). We'd put them in the cot together and Sacha would jump around chattering endlessly while Dylan just sat and watched her, smiling like some two-year-old Buddha.

Years later, when they were ten and at Glenmore Road Primary School together, Dylan told me that Sacha had informed him that his dad, Richard, was homosexual. 'What did you say?' I asked. 'I said that I wasn't sure about that, but I thought he was just very gentle.'

Richard was a perfect nurse and carer after the miscarriage, but nothing was ever the same between us. We moved to Terry Clarke's house in Newman Street, Newtown, and we still loved each other, but a fresh tension had developed, as though the relationship had taken on a different dynamic. I was fragile emotionally and physically and probably suffering from post-miscarriage hormonal upheaval.

I was also working very hard. I was in three movies in a row—David Williamson's *Petersen*, directed by Tim Burstall; Margaret Fink's production of Williamson's *The Removalists*; and then Peter Weir's *Picnic at Hanging Rock*. I also did two plays for Nimrod and one for the Old Tote, all of them directed by Richard: Alex Buzo's *Tom*, Chekov's *The Seagull* and Tennessee Williams' *A Streetcar Named Desire*.

Over the entire thirty years Richie and I knew each other, we worked together in only about eight productions. Out of his total of one hundred and twenty-seven, this was surprisingly few, given that we were generally perceived to be joined at the hip. Most notably in *Born Yesterday*, *The Real Thing*, *The Seagull*, *A Streetcar Named Desire* and *The Girl From Moonooloo*, a musical movie written for ABC-TV by David Mitchell.

One of my best experiences as an actor was playing Stella in Richie's production of *A Streetcar Named Desire*. Robyn Nevin's Blanche was incandescent, probably the best work I've ever shared a stage with. She was truly magnificent. Everyone worked well in that production. The gentle giant Hugh Keays-Byrne, who'd come to Australia with the Royal Shakespeare Company in Peter Brook's famous *A Midsummer Night's Dream* and then stayed forever, was a powerful Stanley.

I almost didn't get the role because at first Richard didn't even think I was suitable for Stella, and wouldn't even audition me. So much for the casting couch. I was sleeping with him every night, and he wouldn't cast me! As well as pleading with him to audition me, I wrote him a three-page essay on Stella's character, as I saw it, in the context of the play, and why I thought I was exactly right to play her. Eventually he relented, I did a couple of good auditions for him and I got the part. But it was the essay that clinched it. Richie was always receptive to actors writing to him. He admired actors with the initiative to go after the work, instead of just waiting for it to come to them. And I didn't let Richie down. I did a reasonable job of it. It was sheer joy to be in that beautiful, wonderful play.

Rehearsals for *Streetcar* were fraught, though. Robyn was ill and needed time off work and I remember feeling very sorry for her. Dylan was four years old and we couldn't afford childcare, so he had to come to rehearsals each day, where he sat quietly on Richard's lap absorbing Tennessee Williams. He knew every word of Blanche and Stella's lines of dialogue, and quite a few of Stanley Kowalski's lines as well.

Robyn Nevin was newly married to the playwright Jim McNeill, who'd spent most of his life in jail. He'd had his plays discovered by Katharine Brisbane and produced by Ken Horler at the Nimrod. Subsequently Jim McNeill became a cause célèbre of the Surry Hills theatre/publishing cognoscenti, who were largely instrumental in securing his release. It was easy to see why Robyn fell for Jim McNeill. He was charming and charismatic and amusing. He used to refer to Dylan as 'the little guy with the wonky minces' (Cockney rhyming slang: *mince pies* = eyes, thus *wonky minces* = cross-eyed).

Jim McNeill was also cruel and dangerous and violent, and his mistreatment of Robyn became legend. One night, angry and inebriated, McNeill turned up with a loaded gun at the stage door of the Opera House demanding to see his wife. Robyn and I were sharing Dressing Room 84 and about to go on-stage in *Streetcar*, oblivious to the real-life drama unfolding outside.

After some interaction with the security guards, during which people said shots were actually fired, McNeill was disarmed and taken away. Since that time, getting through the stage door at the Opera House has been like encroaching on Fort Knox. Before that incident, anyone could sail in and out of the building, no questions asked. The late Nick Enright's play *Mongrels* is based on Jim McNeill's life.

One night on-stage in *Streetcar*, through my own mistiming, Stanley, played by Hugh Keays-Byrne, knocked me unconscious. I remember seeing stars as his very large hand missed connecting with my very small hand, and connected with my jaw instead. And I was down for the count.

Around this time Richard directed a very earnest production of the German avant-garde playwright Peter Handke's *My Foot, My Tutor* in the tiny space at Nimrod Street. It was very interesting but full of mostly unfathomable symbolism, including a scene where Peter Carroll and Chris Haywood, wearing masks (of course) remove a tray containing three burning pieces of charcoal from a kiln and present it to the reverential audience as some sort of sacrifice. 'Hot chops!' proclaimed an innocent voice from the audience, which brought the house down, including the on-stage cast. It was three-year-old Dylan sitting attentively on Richard's knee in the second back row.

But by the time we did *The Seagull* at the Nimrod's larger Belvoir Street venue, Richard's and my relationship was in real trouble. Richard's reputation as a director was always that he loved actors and his methods entailed gentle coaxing and collaboration rather than any kind of autocratic bullying or coercion. He ran a good rehearsal room, as Nick Enright used to say. A relaxed and happy and creative workplace. So it was shattering one day in rehearsals when he lost his patience with me because he thought I was being lazy and not trying. He bawled me out in front of some of the other actors and I cried bitterly. But I think he was more distressed than I. It was atypical behaviour from him and I think it shocked him as much as it shocked the rest of us. And I think it's possible that I deserved it.

Playing Masha garnered lots of plaudits for me, and I loved working with that super cast that included John Bell, Anna Volska, Tony Llewellyn-Jones, Drew Forsythe, Maggie Blinco and Peter Carroll. However, I was desperately unhappy, and somehow lost track of things. One could say I went feral. Ruth Cracknell was also in *The Seagull* and in that closely confined dressing room at Belvoir Street she was acutely aware of the turmoil I was going through and was very sympathetic. She quoted the old Spanish proverb: 'Take what you want, said God. Take what you want, but pay for it.'

So I did. And I did.

Richard made appointments with a marriage guidance counsellor in Bondi Junction and he insisted we go together for advice. I hated the thought of discussing my private angst with a complete stranger. The counsellor was a white-haired Presbyterian elder of the church, and even though he was kind and well-meaning, I was too sullen and dejected to derive any benefit from his ministrations. The sadness in our rented Newtown terrace hung around us like cobwebs.

Unable to cope any longer, Richie moved out, even though I begged him not to go. Dylan and I cried for days, weeks. 'I want my daddy,' he sobbed. 'Well he doesn't want us!' I cried.

Dylan was a pupil at Newtown Day Nursery and his teacher Doff Schultze took pity on us and moved in to live with us for a while and take care of Dylan when I had to work. Thank God for Doffy. I love her. She's still a dear friend and came to Dylan's wedding last year.

Soon after Richard left us, a rumour went around Sydney that I heard many times. A rumour to the effect that, even though I had been entirely faithful to Richard, that as soon as we lost our baby, Richard had been unable to deny his true nature any longer and had had affairs with several men. Not true. In fact it was the other way round.

Richard was never unfaithful to me. He forgave me for my treachery. We stayed friends always. One of Richie's finest traits was his capacity for forgiveness, a rare gift and something I've never stopped trying to emulate, with scant success.

chapter six

Show Us Some
Suburban Lust

FILM PRODUCER MARGARET FINK HAD BOUGHT THE RIGHTS TO
David Williamson's play *The Removalists*, which I'd already
been in at the Nimrod Theatre. Margaret Fink is an amazing
woman, with great instincts, true artistic vision and unerring
taste. She's also unflinchingly honest. I love her. Her assistant
producer was Richard Brennan, who's been a good friend of
mine since I was in my teens.

Shooting didn't get off to a good start when the production manager, Sue Milliken, was sacked on the first day
because there were no uniforms for the policemen, a rather
fundamental oversight when there were only six people in
the cast and two of them were policemen. This disaster was
further exacerbated by the fact that Sue was married to the
director of *The Removalists*, Tom Jeffrey, a sad sack given to

malapropisms who had no intention of doing anything but staying put, regardless of loyalties. So there was tension on the set right from the first day's lost shooting.

The set dresser was a stylish girl just out of film school, I think Swinburne. She was terrific. Margaret kept repeating: 'That girl has a great eye, she'll do very well.' Her name was Gillian Armstrong. And of course Margaret later produced *My Brilliant Career*, which Gill directed, thus beginning Gill's brilliant career.

Our production secretary was Lynn Gailey, who is now a valuable official at our union, which is nowadays called the Media Entertainment and Arts Alliance (MEAA). The second assistant director was Errol Sullivan, who is now boss at Southern Star, so we can blame him for *Big Brother*.

Half the cast from the theatre version were changed for the film, and I think at first they wanted Helen Morse to be Fiona, the hapless removee that I had played on-stage. But after screen-testing, they settled on me. Carole Skinner was the original Kate, Fiona's older sister, but she was replaced by Kate Fitzpatrick for the film. The late great John Hargreaves was the constable, originally played by the great Max Phipps, and Peter Cummins took over as sergeant from Don Crosby. Repeating their stage roles were the inimitable Chris Haywood as the removalist and Martin Harris as the husband. Martin is a wonderful actor who's always good in everything he does. It's a shame that we haven't seen more of him over the years.

It wasn't a happy shoot, but then I suppose it wasn't a happy story we were telling. Thank God for Hargreaves' dirty jokes. An adorable man, John Hargreaves, in every way.

There was some silly publicity before and during the shoot. In one *Daily Mirror* article about me the headline read: 'Is This the New Marilyn Monroe?' Another journalist described me as 'rather like a younger, well-scrubbed Brigitte Bardot'. Well I guess it was an improvement on 'Australia's Hayley Mills', which I also copped. Groan. Not that I have anything against Hayley Mills, far from it. However, over the years I've been Australia's answer to everything except Frankenstein's Bride, and even that was possible. In the press I've been called Australia's answer to Goldie Hawn, Twiggy, Felicity Kendall and, only last year, even Meg Ryan. Embarrassingly flattering. Recently, on *This Is Your Life*, Mike Munro called me 'the Kylie Minogue of the sixties'. Someone once said I was Australia's Charlie Drake (a diminutive Cockney comedian who had a big hit with the song 'My Boomerang Won't Come Back'). Maybe that comparison was the most accurate. How depressing—he was a nasty little wart. Whatever the aptness, that kind of comparison journalism is very lazy and unimaginative.

The chore of making the movie of *The Removalists* was in sharp contrast to the experience of working on the play of the same name a couple of years earlier. John Bell had directed the play at Nimrod with his usual energy and enthusiasm, and it was a joy to do. We did it in a double bill with the hilarious Tom Stoppard piece *After Magritte*, directed by Larry Eastwood, now head of design at the Australian Film Television and Radio School. In *After Magritte* I was a tuba-playing grandma, which delighted me as I was only twenty-five.

The original Nimrod Theatre is now of course The Stables, an intimate 120-seat venue which is marvellous to work in, though a little crowded in the compact dressing room. In those days there was no toilet for the cast so the chaps would pee out of the dressing room window onto Nimrod Street below. We women had to hang on until after the audience had gone home.

The graphic violence in the final scene, where the cops beat up my husband Kenny, could be quite an ordeal for the audience when they were so close to the action, with fake blood flying around and landing in the first few rows. One night it all became too much for one pregnant woman, who rushed downstairs and vomited in the foyer, right by the exit where one hundred and twenty people would be walking in five minutes' time. I nicked down and cleaned up the pool of vomit before coming back upstairs to join the curtain call. Wonderwoman? Well, someone had to do it.

I love *The Removalists*, although the women's roles are, of necessity, smaller faceted and less rewarding than the men's roles, which are all great. I made the mistake of saying this in a newspaper interview thirty years ago and I don't think David Williamson has quite forgiven me after all this time.

I've been eight of his female characters:

- Anna in the film *Stork*
- Fiona in *The Removalists* on-stage
- Fiona in *The Removalists* on film (I count these as two because they were quite different from each other)

- The wife in the movie *Petersen*
- The wife in the film *The Perfectionist*
- Kate, the publisher wife in *Emerald City* for the Melbourne Theatre Company
- The sister in *After the Ball* for the Sydney Theatre Company
- Heather, the wife in *Soulmates*, Sydney Theatre Company

In the 2001 Wharf Revue Jonathan Biggins had an idea for a sketch where we did all of David's plays—and there've been more than thirty of them—in three minutes, using the first and last lines of each, rather like the *Complete Works of Shakespeare* in one go. David gave his permission, as long as he could write the sketch himself. It was terrific.

I can't claim to know David well, which may have something to do with being unable to hear any of his conversation at cocktail parties, possibly due to the huge distance between his voice and my ears. (And that's a visual joke that's been done to death by press photographers—David is six feet eight (over two metres) and I'm four feet eleven and a half, dear reader, in case you've forgotten.) However, David does strike me as someone who's easily wounded. But then he's copped some heavy-duty flak for decades, especially from the waspish Melbourne literary mafia. I'll never forget the chilly opening-night reception for *Emerald City* in the beautiful foyer of the Playhouse in the Victorian Arts Centre in 1987. They came to jeer and sneer, but they stayed for the free booze afterwards.

Emerald City was a huge success in both Sydney and Melbourne; indeed we played to full houses again in a return season several months later. I loved playing the publisher/editor. I spent some time at McPhee Gribble being shown the ropes of the publishing business and looking behind the scenes. For an opening-night present, Hilary McPhee and Di Gribble gave me my own authentic blue correcting pencil, which I used for more than a hundred performances on-stage.

The Melbourne and Sydney productions couldn't have been more different from each other, somehow reflecting the huge difference between our two major cities. Richard Wherrett directed John Bell, Robyn Nevin and Ruth Cracknell in the STC's pacy, upbeat, glossy production. John Sumner did it at the MTC with me, Peter Carroll and Maggie Kirkpatrick in a more introspective, darker version of the piece. To my way of thinking, they were both valid readings and served the play equally well. David Williamson wasn't convinced, however, and apparently compared us unfavourably on radio after our first preview, which upset some of the actors. I didn't hear it.

Before we filmed *The Removalists*, I had already shot *Stork*, which was adapted from David's play *The Coming of Stork*, and then, after that, his *Petersen*. Both of these were directed by the indefatigable Tim Burstall, at whose funeral I spoke nostalgically in 2004. When I first met Tim, he was already in his forties. But his boyish enthusiasm made him seem more like an eighteen-year-old. He combined a sharp intellect with a great sense of the ridiculous. He was a serious thinker who loved to laugh, a philosopher prone to vulgarity. He was a great bounding physical presence bursting with energy. A bit like a Labrador on speed.

I found him a joy to work for and to work *with*. It was Tim who first told me that film-making is a truly *social* art, in the purest sense of the word *social*. He was a genuinely collaborative director who made everyone feel that his or her contribution to the storytelling process was of equal importance. I was then only twenty-three and it made a lasting impression. On set Tim's kindness and his affable disposition brought out the best in actors, especially shy actors. His gentle encouragement was constantly in evidence. He always treated me with a great deal of consideration and respect, which was much appreciated, especially when we were shooting some of the more intimate scenes.

I will never forget the day we shot the love scene in *Petersen*. There were dozens of love scenes in *Petersen* but this one was between the hero and his wife—the sweet-natured Jack Thompson and me. This was Petersen's cosy domestic love-making as opposed to, and in contrast to, his adulterous passion with several other characters. The first assistant Ross Dimsey decreed a closed set. Jack Thompson and I were briefed and debriefed, literally. I was very nervous; Jack seemed calm. The camera rolled with Tim's son Dan Burstall operating; the camera was mounted on a crane and Tim was sitting behind Dan. It was a mute shot that would eventually have music over it, so Tim was calling out directions from his vantage point on high throughout the take.

By now the adorable Jack Thompson was on top of me. However, I was so small that I was having trouble being seen by the camera from underneath him. 'Show us your face, Weavs,' Tim instructed me from above.

Finally, with considerable effort, I managed to get my chin over Jack's shoulder and Tim called out in encouragement: 'Good, Weavs! We're on your face! Now show us some suburban lust.'

It was very difficult not to laugh. *Suburban lust!?* 'Chatswood or Glen Iris?' I wanted to ask. Tim's zeal was infectious. His enthusiasm seems to be the quality that most people are agreed on was his trademark.

After the raunchiness of *Petersen* and the raw violence of *The Removalists*, *Picnic at Hanging Rock* was a sedate experience. No, 'sedate' is quite wrong. It was a very sensual film shoot, hot and gum-scented, seething with undercurrents of lust and intrigue, rather like a contemporary reflection of the film itself. It was shot on location in Clare, a small wine-growing community in South Australia, a couple of hours' drive from Adelaide.

Picnic is a very beautiful film, and the set was indeed suffused with a kind of beauty—not just from the plethora of nubile young women, but from the entire design and look of the piece. This was due, of course, not only to Peter Weir's inspired direction and extraordinary eye for detail (he loves unusual props) and Russell Boyd's brilliant cinematography, but also to that amazing art department, which included Peter Weir's wife Wendy, stand-by props man Monte Fieguth (whose house was an eccentric treasure trove of found objects) and Living National Treasure and bona fide genius Martin Sharp, whose very presence lent an ethereal quality to the experience. There was also the incomparable spirit, sunshine and grace of Graham 'Grace' Walker, part of the production design team. I adored Grace Walker, totally and utterly. He's now a successful art director.

Mention should be made of the unfailing good humour and optimism of Pat Lovell, whose determination had ensured *Picnic* had come to fruition. We were all aware that she had some serious power-struggle issues with her co-producers, Hal and Jim McElroy, and sometimes the tension on location was palpable.

The part of the headmistress was originally to be played by Harold Pinter's wife, a terrific actor called Vivien Merchant. But while she was in Hong Kong, on her way to Australia, Ms Merchant had a nervous collapse when she discovered her husband had left her for Lady Antonia Fraser. In an interview Vivien Merchant said: 'Harold just up and left me without warning, took nothing with him, no clothes, not even shoes. But he can wear Antonia's shoes, she's got very big feet.' Vivien Merchant had to be replaced at the last moment by Rachel Roberts, the Welsh actress who'd been married to Rex Harrison and whose life would end tragically in suicide.

We filmed at Martindale Hall, 15 kilometres down a dirt track from Clare and two hours from Adelaide, a sandstone Georgian mansion originally built by a lovesick Australian gentleman to woo the heart of a young Englishwoman. The logistics of its construction would be challenging nowadays, never mind in the nineteenth century with only horses and bullocks to transport so much sandstone and timber all that way. We were told it contained the second biggest chandelier in the Southern Hemisphere (but where, we wondered, was the biggest?). Alas, building the chateau turned out to be in vain. When the young lady in London changed her mind, her broken-hearted suitor returned to South Australia, threw himself into the river beside Martindale Hall and drowned, with only the peacocks as witnesses. Lesson: don't fall for fickle Poms.

In *Picnic* I was Minnie the maid, Tony Llewellyn-Jones' love interest. I think we may have been there for comic relief. Some of my scenes hit the cutting-room floor and never saw the light of the projector. Peter Weir kindly explained they were too amusing and spoilt the suspense.

The beautiful and exceptional Helen Morse played the French mistress. Helen and I were staying out of town at the Clare Motel while the rest of the crew were being put up at the two hotels in Clare township. One day the proprietor of the motel said that she had to ask us to move out for a couple of days due to a previous booking; she added that, when we found out how important the guest was, we wouldn't mind in the least.

'Who is it?' we asked.

'Kamahl!' she exclaimed breathlessly.

Helen said later that if either of us ever wrote a memoir it should be titled: *I Moved Out of a Motel Room for Kamahl.*

Recently I saw Peter Weir's *Master and Commander* and was awed and impressed, as well as being a little wistful that

I never got to work with him again. To this day many people think *Picnic at Hanging Rock* is a true story. Indeed, when the film first came out, those of us who were in it were encouraged to promote that myth, which didn't harm the film at all.

The film *Caddie*, on the other hand, *was* based on a true story, that of a Sydney barmaid. The pulchritudinous Helen Morse was cast in the eponymous role. (I once referred to Peta Toppano as pulchritudinous and she mistook it for an insult. It's true that it doesn't sound like a compliment. I learned this splendid word as a child from my dad, who used to employ it to describe Hollywood's Jean Arthur, amongst others.)

Donald Crombie directed *Caddie* and it was shot around the streets of Balmain. My character was Caddie's fellow barmaid, Josie, a good-hearted innocent with a blighted love life. Caddie takes care of her after Josie undergoes a Balmain backyard abortion. In one scene, Caddie and Josie are on a tram (filmed at the tram museum in bushy outer-suburban Lugarno; it was long after the demise of Sydney's trams). They are discussing the vagaries of existence. It was a long night-shoot and during it a bull-ant bit me on the bottom.

One of the shots took ages—about sixteen takes—and on the sixteenth take, I laughed without meaning to. That's the take they printed and the line of dialogue that prompted my hilarity has gone into folklore: 'Life's a bugger!' Strangers still come up to me and quote it, including young people who weren't even born when it was made. Seen it on video, I suppose.

They gave me an AFI award for *Caddie*, probably for that one line: 'Life's a bugger.'

I bought a little terrace house at 31 George Street, Paddington, in 1974 for $37 500. I had $8000 for the deposit, thanks entirely to my agent Gloria Payten, who withheld a certain amount from my pay cheque every week for about two years. She organised a $30 000 loan from the Earlwood Building Society to be repaid over 30 years. (To be very Sydney-centric for a moment: wow, just think—if I had held on to it, I would have finally paid off the mortgage in 2004 and it would be worth $800 000 conservatively!) It was almost impossible to get that loan. None of the banks would touch me, including the Commonwealth, where I've had an account since 1947, the year I was born. Unmarried mother, actress, bad risk, blah blah. At the time I was still earning more than most of my male colleagues, who had no trouble getting loans. Old prejudices die hard.

Recently Wendy Harmer, the brilliant comedienne and radio queen, told me that Paul Holmes, her former on-air partner, had confided to her that he was a buddy of the late great INXS lead singer Michael Hutchence when they were both teenagers, and they used to see me walk up to the corner shop each afternoon to buy milk with my toddler after kindergarten. They would follow us so they could be in the shop with me and Michael would tell Paul: 'I want that woman, and one day I'll have her.' I hope it's true. Ah, Michael, if only I'd known.

Angry Andersen once told me live to air on national TV, in front of a million people at the AFI awards, that he used to follow me besottedly around Paddington shops. I was surprised and said: 'I wish you'd said something—I would have got you to carry the shopping.'

Even though Richie and I had separated, I was still seeing him two or three times a week when I was in Sydney. Every time we got together I was hoping and wondering if he'd want a reconciliation.

I was also seeing Max Hensser. I had met Max in 1974, when I was still living with Richard and we were working on the film version of David Williamson's *The Removalists*. Max was the boom operator. He was long and lean with a haunted look. He always wore interesting shoes. One morning at tea-break he passed me in the corridor of the studio in Ebley Street, Bondi Junction. He spoke to me for the first time, describing bluntly how he felt about me in one sentence. Such chutzpah deserves reward.

It was a fiery match. Before I bought the house in Paddington he had moved in with Dylan and me to Terry Clarke's house at 15 Newman Street, Newtown. Also living with us were Chrissie Hannan and her boyfriend, Sandy Sharp; they later married and had two sons, Christopher and Edward. Chrissie Sharp and I are still friends. She was 2IC to Brett Sheehy at the Sydney Festival and is now in London with her husband, Michael Lynch, who's running Southbank. I love them both.

The Old Tote Theatre brought out director William Gaskill, one of the shining lights of London's Royal Court Theatre, to direct Shakespeare's *Love's Labour's Lost* at the Opera House. John Bell had already been cast as Berowne and William Gaskill was combing Sydney for an actress to play Berowne's spirited and hard-to-win lover, the feisty Rosaline. I remember sitting opposite Gaskill at my interview, listening intently to him explaining his concept of the production, when he suddenly stopped speaking for a few moments and told me: 'Your eyes are the saddest eyes I've ever seen.' And he gave me the part. Not to cheer me up, I hope.

One day during rehearsals for *Love's Labour's Lost*, in some old workshop in Glebe, about twenty roses were suddenly hurled over the gap at the top of the workshop door, hitting several of us on the head. Attached to the thorny intruders was a passionate note addressed to me. It was from Max Hensser. Bill Gaskill was intrigued, doubly so because he was staying with Richard Wherrett at the time. I was very embarrassed.

It's the only Shakespeare I've done with John Bell, though John has offered me other jobs in Shakespeare, which I have been unable to do due to prior commitments. John was a terrific Berowne, but I was a crappy Rosaline actually, and I looked ghastly in a black wig and Edwardian dress. It's not a style many people can carry off, even when you are whalebone corseted within an inch of your life, ribs and diaphragm; you need to be fully six feet tall, with a chest like a pouter pigeon.

As for having sad eyes, I've long been aware that, in repose, it *is* a saddish face. When you are born with a face that has a tendency to break into a Luna Park grin at the slightest provocation, as mine does, it's small wonder that people assume you're a merry soul and are then taken by surprise to see you *sans* smile.

'Cheer up!' complete strangers will chirp at me. Even when I'm feeling perfectly cheerful, thank you very much.

chapter seven

Nothing's Impossible

MAX HENSSER AND I CONTINUED OUR TURBULENT LIAISON FOR several months. None of my friends thought we were well matched—especially Richard, naturally enough—but I cared for Max and I felt there was something between us that was worth nurturing.

One day in early 1976 when Max was working in Perth, and also having a clandestine tryst with one of his ex-girlfriends, I was in such tumult over him that I could hardly breathe. I was sitting in a make-up chair at ABC-TV's Gore Hill studios at the time, and the make-up artist recommended that I take up yoga, which I did for some years. I'm still convinced that the peaceful yoga sessions I spent learning to meditate, with Joti Brunsden in her lounge room in Harbord, definitely saved me from succumbing to a nervous breakdown.

When Max returned from Perth we decided to marry. If that seems abrupt, never mind foolhardy, that's how my life was in the 1970s. Abrupt and unstructured. Lurching haphazardly from crisis to crisis. Life with Max was so tempestuous that I was hoping that formalising the union might calm it down. I was probably also wanting to show everyone who disapproved, including my family, that I was serious about Max.

Max and I took various hallucinogenics—LSD, mushrooms, whatever was going. Most of our friends did too. They took me to some unexpected parts of my psyche—some good, some banal. One afternoon Max and I took some mescaline and went to visit the actor Lynette Curran, who'd just taken a roast chicken out of the oven. It was a sweltering summer's day and within what seemed like minutes a fly had blown the chicken and maggots were swarming on it. In our drugged state the maggots looked like snakes. It was ghastly.

Then we went to a party at Martin Sharp's enormous family mansion in Bellevue Hill and all the guests resembled hedgehogs. Well, not all of them. Some looked like spinning mandalas and others like milk bottles. It was a bit silly, really. Conversation was at a premium, which, of course, is ideal if you want to avoid conversation. And for most of us, that's at least some of the time. For some of us, like me, it's most of the time.

After the party at Martin's, we didn't sleep for more than forty-eight hours and then I had to go to the opening night of the Stuttgart Ballet at the Opera House. I was sitting beside the Honourable Gough and Mrs Margaret Whitlam and, even though the ballet was brilliant, I kept nodding off from sheer exhaustion. I just hope I didn't snore. I think Mrs Whitlam must have realised something was up. She is a very wise and witty woman. After the opening night of the movie *Petersen* in Sydney, with its notorious nude scene, Mrs Whitlam greeted me with: 'Hello, Jacki. I almost didn't recognise you with your clothes *on*.'

At the opening night of a movie I'd made in Melbourne, my escort and fellow actor 'Ernest Wilde' was off his face on some chemical. And he was lovely. Bright, serene and scintillating—his usual sweet-natured self. Others didn't cope so well with all the recreational drugs during this era and some went slightly—some totally—crazy.

Eventually I had such a bad trip that I was frightened and vowed never to touch LSD again. I was standing on a cliff at Terrigal contemplating flying. I felt certain I could soar out over the ocean like some demented drug-fucked osprey (lots of black eyeliner). I was taking a good squiz at the waves and then planning to make a soft landing on the grassy cliff top when four-year-old Dylan snapped me out of it by saying sternly: 'Don't be ridiculous. There's no way you can fly.'

Oh, the horror. What a useless parent.

A few months previously, Dylan had been on location with me in Melbourne. We were overtired and had had a tiff about his taking a shower, or something equally trivial. It was one of the rare occasions when I smacked him, just once, on the back of his legs. He wept, I wept. 'I'm a terrible mother,' I sobbed. The wise four-year-old said: 'Yes, you are a terrible mother. But I like you.'

That's a story that's been repeated a lot over the past thirty years. In fairness to Dylan—by me, not by him. He's very polite. Very well brought up? I doubt it. We're all a result of accident, not design. Character is impenetrable—multiple layers so deep that who knows what causes what?

Max Hensser and Dylan were great playmates. Max loves children. We included Dylan in the wedding plans, which were highly secret. Then one day I was doing an interview with *Woman's Day* magazine in Paddington. Dylan's excitement was irrepressible and he suddenly announced: 'We're getting married!' He'd blown our cover.

The wedding was conducted by Angela Bowne at Bruce and Sue Moir's house in Carlotta Street, Greenwich, in May 1976. Max and I were in white, as was five-year-old Dylan—in white tie and tails. Kate Fitzpatrick, who'd introduced me to Max, was bridesmaid. There was a party afterwards in Brian and Dawn 'Delta' Fitzpatrick's beautiful top-floor duplex in Cremorne and Brett Hilder took a soft-focus wedding photo of the blissful-looking newlyweds that was on page three of the *Daily Mirror*. Another photo of me with a story announcing the nuptials was on the front page of the Melbourne *Herald*.

Then Max and I went to stay at the Carrington Hotel in Katoomba for a few days while my aunt Georgina and her husband Harry Lozan looked after Dylan. It's a measure of Harry and Georgina's kindness that, even with five children of their own, they still found time to take little Dylan fishing down on a wharf at Brighton-le-Sands on Botany Bay. What's more, so that Dylan wouldn't be disappointed, Harry snuck down under the pier and attached to Dylan's fishing line a small bream that he and Georgina had smuggled from their freezer. The five-year-old fisherman was so thrilled by his catch that he didn't want to leave the pier while the fish were biting. Luckily he didn't notice his fish was frozen stiff. Poor Uncle Harry was frozen too—it was a bitterly cold day, especially under the boardwalk.

My mother wasn't happy at all about my marrying Max, but she was very gracious on the day. She wore a lavender dress, about which she would later say: 'I bought it for *one* of Jacki's weddings.' Oh, the irony of the Cumbrians. My father had now begun to call me The Bolter (see Nancy Mitford) because I kept bolting from men as if I were a recalcitrant filly.

Soon after our wedding, I got a job at St George Leagues Club playing the lead in a 1930s Irving Berlin musical called *Roberta,* which had been a movie starring Fred Astaire, Ginger Rogers and Irene Dunne. I was the Irene Dunne character, Roberta, and John Farnham played the Fred Astaire role. Robert Coleby, Abigail, and John's wife Jill were also in the show. Jill Farnham's a dancer and very tall. When we stood in the wings together waiting to go on-stage, Jill's legs came up to my shoulders. Soon we all became close friends. I still love Jill and John, though I hardly see them anymore.

It was hard going, having to do that show against the racket of poker machines and beer jugs on laminex tabletops, but it was a good lesson in endurance. It wasn't a great production. In fact it was dire. I was also filming in the daytime.

Anne Deveson had written a screenplay about child abuse called *Do I Have to Kill My Child?*, which Donald Crombie directed as a film for TV. Dean Semler, a gentle and very attractive bear of a man, who years later would win an Oscar for *Dances With Wolves*, was the cinematographer. It was a tough schedule—filming all day, while I screamed at a tiny defenceless baby, before going back on-stage at night to be Roberta in Kogarah—but the film turned out well. And they gave me a Logie for it.

Then I played Natasha in Chekov's *The Three Sisters* at the Sydney Opera House for the Old Tote Theatre Company in a production directed by Bill Redmond. *The Three Sisters* is, of course, a wonderful play and I loved doing it.

In most theatres there is a tannoy system—that is, a loudspeaker in every dressing room—that relays what is happening on-stage to the actors off-stage in their dressing rooms, to enable them to keep track of the progress of the play and assist them to be ready for their entrance cues. The tannoy also broadcasts reminders from the stage manager down in the prompt corner that your entrance is imminent ('Miss Weaver, this is your call to the stage'). Some tannoy systems are more sensitive than others, in that you can some-times hear not just the audience's reaction but even the occasional loud remark from the stalls.

One night at the Opera House, I was sitting in Dressing Room 86 of the Drama Theatre having my wig fitted before the show. The play hadn't even started. It was twenty minutes before curtain up. The doors to the theatre had just opened and people were beginning to take their seats. The stage manager's voice came over the tannoy: 'Ladies and gentlemen of the Three Sisters Company, this is your fifteen-minute call. Fifteen minutes to Act One beginners. Ladies and gentlemen, the theatre is open and the stage is live.' The announcement about the 'live' stage is made to warn those actors who may be inclined to undertake a last-minute warm-up on-stage before curtain up that it's no longer possible unless they don't mind making dills of themselves in front of a few early-comers. (Let's face it, there's plenty of opportunity for that once the show's started!)

'Ladies and gentlemen, fifteen minutes to curtain.' Just typing that sentence has sent my blood pressure into an upward swoop. But anyway, back to Dressing Room 86, where my wig's being fitted, I'm powdering my nose, my fellow actors are all busily preparing themselves in the various dressing rooms along the Drama Theatre corridor, the audience members are taking their seats, opening their programs, and there's a quiet buzz of expectant conversation from the stalls. Suddenly a voice rings out from inside the theatre, loud and clear over the tannoy, audible in every dressing room, from a woman who's obviously just discovered to her enormous disgruntlement: 'Jacki Weaver! Oh no, not Jacki Weaver!! If there's one actress *I can't stand*, it's Jacki Weaver!!!'

For me it wasn't ideal preparation for focusing on the work at hand. One of my fellow actors suggested I immediately run down to the stage and announce: 'Whoever said that—you'd better go home now, love, because I'm in every scene!' That was in the mid seventies and I still have an aversion to having the tannoy switched on before the play starts, in case I hear something I'd rather not.

In 1977, Mike Willesee had been a well-known TV journalist for at least a decade and had been the popular and successful host of Channel 9's nightly current affairs program *A Current Affair* where he'd been for several years, before moving to Channel 7 to package and run *Willesee at 7*. Mike had interviewed me on his TV program when I was doing publicity for the film *Caddie* and we got along well, so he asked me to join his team as a showbiz reporter and celebrity interviewer. I also got along well with his wife Carol Willesee, who'd been a model and is now an actress and still my good friend. Also in the line-up of on-air personnel for Mike's new show was a consumer affairs reporter, a very beautiful, highly intelligent and fearlessly dedicated investigative journalist called Helen Wellings, who would eventually meet and marry my brother Rod. Helen was a colleague of mine before my brother even met her.

Willesee's producer was his good mate Phil Davis, a former police roundsman on the *Daily Mirror*—a genial, burly bloke from Bathurst with a rugged athletic build who played rugby for North Sydney and who always got good service in restaurants because people mistook him for a cop. I liked Phil Davis from the moment I met him and the feeling was mutual. We spent a lot of time together at Channel 7, working on the show and spending lunchtimes in each other's company.

During the year I spent on-air at *Willesee*, before leaving of my own volition, I met and interviewed some interesting people, including Burt Lancaster, Sammy Davis Junior, Vincent Price, Susannah York, Liv Ullmann, Douglas Fairbanks Junior, John Thaw, Dennis Waterman, Warren Mitchell, Evonne Goolagong and Fleetwood Mac. I did some good interviews for *Willesee*. Even crotchety actor Warren Mitchell (TV's famed curmudgeon Alf Garnett) who'd been peeved when he arrived at the studio to find that the legendary Mike wasn't interviewing him but rather a tyro reporter/actress instead, grudgingly admitted afterwards, 'That was a surprisingly good interview.' (To which I heard Phil Davis mutter, under his breath, 'Condescending prick.')

I also worked at Radio 2UE for a while as an on-air partner to Mike Carlton. When 2UE offered me a contract, I turned them down. They then offered me a retainer to keep me off any other station, which I also stupidly knocked back, saying I only wanted to act. Much as I enjoyed the stints as a news-gatherer of sorts, I wanted to return to being people other than myself.

The recreational culture of journalism and TV current affairs, certainly at that time, was a culture that involved a lot of hard drinking and I plunged into it without hesitation. Of course I hadn't been a teetotaller before that, but I had seldom entered a state of tipsiness until I turned thirty, which is when I began to move in those social circles. I may have been a late starter to heavy drinking but I certainly made up for it. Big imbibing and merriment just seemed to go with the territory and I enjoyed it immensely. My parents and Max began to express mild concern at the amount I was drinking.

In May 1977 Max, who was now a sound recordist, was away overseas filming a documentary, and I took a month's leave from *Willesee* to accept an acting job in Canberra. I was employed as one of the actors for the National Playwrights Conference when Richard Wherrett was artistic director. The Conference is a terrific, intense experience—workshopping several new plays at once to various stages of readiness and being billeted at the university. It was also a good chance to see more of Richard, whom I was still missing dreadfully. We were even now talking wistfully, hypothetically, about getting back together some day in the distant future.

Dylan's father, John Walters, lived in Canberra at that time so Dylan went to stay with him while I was at the college. One afternoon after work Richard and I turned up to collect Dylan, as arranged, but there was nobody home. After several phone calls, driving all around Canberra looking for them and waiting outside the darkened house for hours, Richard and I finally went to the police. Both of us were tearful, expecting the worst.

It was around midnight. The police were very kind and came with us to John's, where they banged on the door. There was no response and they were talking about forcing the lock when suddenly John angrily opened the door; he said that he'd been ignoring the phone because he'd decided to keep Dylan with him for the night and that he refused to discuss it. I was so relieved they were both alive and not lying dead in a culvert somewhere that without argument I went meekly back to the college dorm with Richard. Meanwhile six-year-old Dylan slept on, blissfully unaware of the drama.

That was the Playwrights Conference where the brilliant but curmudgeonly John Osborne was guest of honour. He was a very disagreeable chap. But I made a good friend of another visiting English avant-garde playwright, Snoo Wilson; we corresponded for years, sometimes in limericks— strictly scanned, of course. Snoo Wilson is still writing radical, droll and highly original novels and plays thirty years later. I miss his limericks.

My husband Max was still in England seeing his family and working on another documentary when Phil Davis and I decided to move into a flat together in East Balmain. I put my Paddington house up for rent and Max arrived home from overseas to find that I'd bolted yet again. An empty house, no wife, no Dylan. I'm not proud of it. Max is a good man and I often think of him. He married another actor, the terrific Wendy Strehlow, and they have a daughter named Sophie.

In the past I have never talked about Max Hensser to the press because he didn't want me to. The same with Phil Davis. I respected their wishes. They obviously weren't followers of the sensible Richard Walsh dictum: 'Privacy is highly over-rated.' But a publisher *would* say that, wouldn't he?

Phil was a keen gambler and attended the races at Randwick every Saturday. The first year we were together we lived off his punting to a large degree. The horseracing world was one I never really became immersed in, although I did grow very fond of some of Phil's racing journalist friends, especially Max Presnall. I finally stopped going to the races after we saw the beautiful champion Hyperno put down with a shotgun on the Randwick track after his leg broke during a race.

Those were also the days when the AJC had a men-only section in the grandstand from which women were banned. There was even a line painted on the floor that females were not allowed to cross. It used to make me furious and brought out the worst in me. I wonder when they abolished it. Surely it can't still be there?

Phil Davis introduced me to the high life—fine restaurants, limousines, Dom Perignon, five-star hotel suites, first-class travel to Europe. When we were staying in Monte Carlo we dined, in evening dress, at a grand restaurant where Phil ordered Dom and the French maître d, wearing tails, replied: 'Would Monsieur prefer something superior to Dom?'

Phil was surprised: 'I didn't know there *was* anything superior to Dom.'

And that's the first time we drank Louis Roederer Crystalle champagne, in the distinctive clear bottle, which is now glass but was originally crystal so the Tsar of Russia could inspect the colour of the vintage before deigning to allow the removal of the cork. It's been my favourite ever since, though of course I can seldom afford it nowadays.

By now Dylan was in Year 2 at Gordon West Public School, the same school I'd attended in the 1950s, so for a month he went to stay with Ede and Art in West Pymble while Phil and I were in Monaco. Phil also took me to Paris, where we stayed at the legendary George V Hotel and visited the Moulin Rouge, Maxim's, Montmartre and the Louvre. He drove me to Rome, glorious Florence, and then to Venice, the most beautiful city I've ever seen. We sipped Campari sodas in Piazza San Marco and martinis in Harry's Bar before he grabbed me a gondola. In Rome we met some expatriate Australians who'd just seen a screening of the Aussie film *Newsfront* with Italian subtitles. They were highly amused when in one scene Chris Haywood's character lets fly with a string of expletives including, 'Fuck off, you mongrel!' The Italian subtitle translated this simply as 'Go to another country.'

We swam and lay in the sun beside the hotel swimming pool in Monaco, where Phil drew my attention to the handsome 'towel boys' who would bring towels, serve drinks and rub sun cream on the backs of single mature ladies, then disappear somewhere into the hotel with them for half an hour or so, after which they would return and repeat the process with other lonely women throughout the day.

I was fascinated. Gigolos! Phil said I could probably get one for free, or at least at a discount, as I was only a young woman at the time. This was 1978. I am yet to experience the services of a gigolo, but it's still early days and at this stage I've learned that nothing's impossible.

By now I'd left *Willesee at 7* to go back to acting full-time. Both Mike and Phil tried to dissuade me and offered me a higher salary to stay but my mind was made up. The Australian writer Sumner Locke Elliott had written a novel called *Water Under the Bridge*, which I had read on the way to Paris. I immediately fired off a note to Robyn Nevin on Qantas notepaper, telling her she must play the lead role of

Shasta in the TV mini-series that was being planned. I didn't know that the producers already had her in mind.

I wanted the role of Maggie and was thrilled when they gave it to me. Maggie's character ages from seventeen to fifty and goes from slender to obese. At the time I was thirty and quite slim, so they made me a huge 'fat-suit' and began planning some ageing and double-chin prosthetics for my face. This involved making a plaster cast of my face, a specialised procedure that is simple if you know what you're doing. But, unfortunately for me, the make-up artist was not prepared to admit that he had no idea what he was doing.

The process should take about twenty minutes. Quick-setting dental latex is applied to the face, and then plaster of Paris on top of that to get an exact impression of your features so a sculpture can be made with fake bits added, which are specially manufactured to fit your face. The methods are no doubt much more streamlined these days, but this was more than twenty-five years ago.

The ignorant make-up people in question—many later accused them of being criminally negligent—applied the plaster, two inches thick, directly onto my face, from the top of my chest to my hairline, with only two straws in my nostrils for air. Then they dried it with a hairdryer. Half an hour later it became horrifyingly apparent that the plaster had stuck fast. I couldn't see or speak, and had only the straws to breathe through. They then realised they had a disaster on their hands and proceeded to remove the plaster, bit by painful bit, with wire-cutters and a chisel. I was terrified and in great discomfort, unable to see or to speak. The plaster had been spread on my face at 2 pm and the last piece was finally removed at 11 pm. Nine hours when it should only have taken a few minutes!

A friend was summoned to come and hold my hand during the ordeal and to give me words of encouragement. My friend likened it to attending a birth; he said it was very worrying for him that at any minute the implements could slip and pierce my eyeball or cheek or forehead. I was quite stoic, I must say, though I wept a little back in the hotel bathtub afterwards and couldn't see properly for a few days. It could have been worse, with a more highly strung victim. I heard that the same mishap occurred to John Hurt during preparations for *The Elephant Man* and he needed a week in hospital to recover from the trauma. The production company apologised and gave me a bracelet. They sacked the make-up man responsible and gave the job to the clever Bob McCarron, who was furious about the incident and said that the culprit should have been struck off the register.

It was quite a good series eventually, with Robyn Nevin and Judy Davis in one of her first roles out of NIDA. They used me to screen-test young actors for the lead role because our characters had a love relationship with each other in the story. David Cameron eventually got this part but one of the many actors who tested opposite me was Mel Gibson, who did a great audition but missed out. I'd already worked with Mel in a comedy half-hour for ABC-TV and thought him very funny, as well as a good sort. And Richie had directed Mel and had taught him at NIDA.

Phil Davis and Dylan and I lived together for about four years, first in the East Balmain apartment, then in a doctor's house right on the beach in lively, gaudy Dee Why, and finally in a house I found for us and persuaded Phil to buy in Fiddens Wharf Road, Killara. I enjoyed that house, with its beautiful garden and swimming pool, and my first proper library room. Every day in summer, in the tiniest of bikinis, I would spend hours in the sun on the floating lounge in the pool reading William Faulkner and Saul Bellow and John Irving. And Alfred Lord Tennyson, who wrote: 'Once he drew,/With one long kiss, my whole soul thro'/My lips, as the sunlight drinketh dew.' I became the Gin Queen of Killara.

I grew to love Phil's family—his mum and dad (Dot and Les from Bathurst) and his brother and family (Rex, Amy, Greg and Jacquie from Narrandera). They would come to stay with us and we'd have great times around the antique snooker table. We had a comfortable suburban life, with two cars (a Ford Fairlane and a Ford Cortina) and two dogs (a blue heeler called Princess and a Cavalier King Charles Spaniel called Luke) and one very neurotic silver Burmese cat called Chloe.

Phil was very generous to Dylan and to me; he was the consummate provider. I felt very secure with Phil, in every way. But Phil could never come to terms with the fact that I was still so attached to Richard Wherrett and that Richard was still a big part of my life and always would be. Phil also resented my working so hard. And I don't believe Phil ever thought I loved him enough. Eventually, after four years, Phil threw me out. Well, told me to leave, anyway.

I wanted to make a fresh start a long way from Killara and Sydney's North Shore, so Dylan and I went to live in Melbourne for a while, where I bought a tiny flat in Lonsdale Street, a stone's throw from one of my favourite theatres, the Comedy, in Exhibition Street. It seemed like a sensible investment as I'd always loved Melbourne, ever since the first day I saw it on that whirlwind visit on my sixteenth birthday, and I'd worked there often over the years and had made some good friends, including dancer/choreographer, now successful impresario, David Atkins.

Now that Phil had given us our marching orders, Dylan's pets had to find new homes as well. My aunt Georgina took Chloe, the Burmese aristo-cat, who soon went AWOL somewhere in Earlwood. Sandy Sharp took Princess the blue heeler, and Luke the Cavalier King Charles went to live with David Atkins' mother Mary and sister Shelley in semi-rural Greensborough, where all the neighbours insisted on referring to Luke as 'Jacki Weaver'. A few years later, when Luke was hit by a car, David told me people were yelling in the street, 'Jacki Weaver's dead!' (Luke and I did bear a passing resemblance.)

After my failure with Phil Davis I swore off men. For a long time. It was not a vow as drastic as radical celibacy (let's be realistic here), but I was certainly determined to give the phallus-bearers of the species a fairly wide berth for as long as I could manage. And I meant it. My mother was shocked and counselled me that loneliness could be in store.

Then I met Derryn Hinch again.

chapter eight

Human Headline Rammed by Battlestar Galactica

'WHAT'S THIS ABOUT YOU AND THAT SHIT HINCH?!'

It's an angry and dismayed John Waters speaking. These are his first words to me after a three-month vacation in London with his wife Sal. (Please note that the actor John *Waters* is not to be confused with Dylan's father John *Walters*.) John Waters has just this minute arrived in Melbourne for yet another return season of our hit show *They're Playing Our Song*, this time at Her Majesty's Theatre. An urgent knock on my door at 131 Lonsdale Street. No hello, no kiss, no hug, just: 'What's this about you and that shit Hinch? Please tell me it isn't true!'

The week before, John Farnham had rung to say: 'Jill and I have heard a rumour that you've got a secret new boyfriend. Why haven't you told us?' I told him that it was because I was sure he and Jill would disapprove of him.

'Darlin', just bring whoever he is with you when you come over to see the baby on the weekend. Jilly and I love ya and if you love him that's enough for us!'

'Okay. It's Derryn Hinch.'

'*Oh no! The man's a cunt.*'

This was the reaction, more or less, of most of my friends. I'd anticipated this and had cravenly referred to Hinch in code as 'Joe'. Whenever anyone inquired about my love life I'd say, mysteriously, I was seeing someone called Joe. It's a moniker that stuck fast. To this day I call him Joe or Joby. In all the years we've known each other, I've called him Derryn to his face only about two or three times, and each time he anticipated trouble. And was not mistaken.

I had first met Derryn Hinch at an awards night he set up when he became editor of the Sydney *Sun* in 1976. For eleven years Hinch had been living in New York as bureau chief for Fairfax; he then had a gorgeous American wife called Eve Grzbowski and had returned to Australia to be the youngest newspaper editor they'd ever had.

In 1976, I was married to Max Hensser and already working for Phil Davis on *Willesee at 7*. My first impression of Hinch was that he was bumptious and very pleased with himself. There are many people who'd say that description still fits him nearly thirty years later, but he's a lot of other things as well. Good things. Someone once said that the only thing bigger than Hinch's ego is Hinch's heart.

By 1980, Hinch was a big star in Melbourne. In the intervening years he had left the Sydney *Sun* to start his own magazine with Terry Hayes and had gone broke. He had also broken up with Eve. As a last resort he had taken a job in Melbourne radio, with Terry Hayes as his producer. Terry was the person who invented Derryn's nickname, 'The Human Headline'; today Terry Hayes is a successful screen-writer in Hollywood, having got started in that line of business when he wrote the screenplay for *Mad Max 2* with George Miller. Hinch was an instant success in Melbourne radio and eventually knocked Bert Newton off his long-standing top rung in the ratings. He was huge.

In 1980 in Sydney Donald McDonald (not the actor, but the future General Manager of the Sydney Theatre Company and Chairman of the ABC) had asked me to audition for a new musical called *They're Playing Our Song*, which was a big hit in New York where it had already been running for two years. Basically a romantic comedy, *They're Playing Our Song* (henceforth *TPOS*) has a wittier-than-usual book for a musical because it was written by the great legend Neil Simon (*The Odd Couple*, *The Goodbye Girl*, *The Apart-ment*, *Last of the Red Hot Lovers*, *Laughter on the 23rd Floor* etc etc).

Then there's a terrific score—about a dozen songs, with snappy music by Marvin Hamlisch and charming lyrics by Carole Bayer Sager. Neil Simon is said to have based the story of *TPOS* on the amusing real-life relationship between Hamlisch and Bayer Sager—a quirky partnership, to say the least, but very winsome.

A big show technically—with about twenty backstage mechanists, a twenty-six piece orchestra, a chorus of six 'alter-egos' who join in only four of the numbers—it is nonetheless basically a two-hander and everything relies on the chemistry between the two protagonists, Sonia and Vernon. In other words, it's a big show for two people.

So I turned up to the Seymour Centre in Sydney for my audition wearing a Tearose grey herringbone tweed jacket with suede elbow patches. I sang 'Nothing' from *A Chorus Line*, another great Marvin Hamlisch musical, with conductor Dale Ringland on piano. And I sang it very well. Then I and another actor read aloud several scenes from the show and they gave me the job. I was ecstatic.

They took longer to find the male lead, and finally whittled the contenders down to two. Then the producers allowed me to make the final choice, because it was crucial that we got along well, being a two-hander. I chose John Waters without hesitation. And what a great choice. John Waters has been one of my closest friends for more than thirty years. To this day some people, including the press, confuse his name with that of Dylan's father but in fact John Waters and I never had a romance. It's always been a fraternal relationship, purely platonic. (*Platonic* means 'play for one and tonic for the other', Betty Hinch once said.)

Donald McDonald met a lot of opposition—indeed, one of the main investors pulled out—for casting two Australians in the roles, instead of American stars. So it was a very sweet victory when we were a smash hit, got great reviews, broke box-office records and ran for several seasons over three years.

In 1980 it was still accepted wisdom that you should only cast actors from overseas (many of them weren't even stars) in big American shows. Thank God the rules were occasionally broken or we'd have missed out on the great Jill Perryman, Nancye Hayes and Julie Anthony. Now there's a new generation of Australian performers who can fill a theatre for long runs in their own right—Hugh Jackman, Lisa McCune, Anthony Warlow, Todd McKenney, Debra Byrne, Marina Prior. The list is endless.

Before we started rehearsing in Australia, I saw *TPOS* in New York with Lucy Arnaz and Robert Klein. I also met their production manager, who was to be our director, Philip Cusack. And so began my friendship with one of the most wonderful people in the world.

The trip to New York in fact had a dual purpose, the main one being to take Dylan, now nine years old, to see Dr Knapp at the Presbyterian and General Hospital in NYC. Dylan's most recent eye surgery (his sixth eye operation) had proven unsuccessful and he was still suffering double vision. The kindly Mosman ophthalmologist, Dr Jim Findlater, who'd been looking after Dylan since he was five months old, told me about Dr Knapp, who was the best in the world.

So we went to see Dr Knapp. But he couldn't fix it either. Dr Knapp felt further surgery was indicated, but not for a few years as there was still fresh scar tissue. Dylan's next and final eye surgery happened when he was sixteen, and was so unpleasant that he resolved never to go through it again. He still has double vision. But he and I had a fun fortnight in New York despite the disappointment of the eye problem.

Rehearsals for *TPOS* began in Sydney, with Robyn Moase recreating the New York choreography and Philip Cusack directing. Sue Nattrass, who was then with the great musical producers JC Williamson's, was running the whole extravaganza. There were a lot of bitchy rumours being spread around town about the show, the main one being that I wasn't up to the singing. My singing teacher Bob Tasman Smith, the musical director Dale Ringland and the producers were firmly convinced that my voice and my intonation were perfectly fine. But my confidence was taking a pounding.

The opening night was a triumph, including my singing. Audiences and critics loved us. 'They're Brilliant, They're Here and They're Ours' crowed the *Sydney Morning Herald*. Eventually we made an album of *TPOS*, which was so popular it went gold.

But the nastiness persisted: that I was lip-synching to one of the chorus girls singing offstage. *WRONG*. That I was miming to someone else's prerecording. *WRONG*. And then the worst one of all: that I only sounded good because there was a special microchip inserted in my body mike that made all my off-notes magically pitch-perfect. Such a technological device didn't even exist in 1980. As far as I know, it still hasn't been invented to this day. Of course, for years, technology has been capable of doing wonders with singing that is pre-recorded but never for LIVE music. Something that can actually anticipate which bum note you'll hit and transform it into the right note as it issues forth? Wonderful. Everyone in the world would be able to sing. Karaoke bars would be temples of bliss instead of such hit or miss chambers of discord.

Then some silly reporter made the mistake of printing this rumour in one of those wanky Sydney glossy magazines for tossers. It was Julie Clarke, Richard Neville's wife. When my agent Philomena Moore made an angry phone call to Clarke, Clarke's response was to gasp: 'Oh dear. You mean it's not true!' Twit!

We sued and we won. An undisclosed amount of money, a retraction and a grovelling apology read in court admitting no such device even existed. But the damage was done. More than twenty years later the rumours still follow me around, with some idiots even inquiring where they can obtain one of those microchip devices. If I seem bitter, it's because it still hurts all these years later.

After the sell-out season of *TPOS* at Sydney's Theatre Royal we moved the show to Melbourne for an equally successful run at the Comedy Theatre. Our opening night party was at a new restaurant called Sardi's, owned by Melbourne radio star and roué Derryn Hinch. It was now four years since I'd first met him at that *Sun* newspaper function.

John Waters and I went to the party with his wife Sally, my paramour Phil Davis and Dylan. Hinch's opening line to John and me as we entered the restaurant was: 'Thank God it was a good show—it would have been bad for my restaurant if you were a dud!' Oh yes, Derryn, it's all about you as usual.

'Who is this jerk?' John Waters muttered, as Hinch got a photographer to take our picture. I'm looking at this photo now—Phil Davis can be seen in the background.

Alan Finney, then working for Roadshow and now at Disney Pictures, always thought Hinch and I would hit it off. Al and his wife Philippa arranged a lunch for several people at Hinch's restaurant, but I begged off at the last minute and didn't turn up. Afterwards Hinch sent me round a Bombe Alaska his chef had specially made for the occasion, with my name on it. It was a kind gesture, but the confection was so revolting I threw it straight down the garbage chute.

We finished that run at the Comedy with a promise to do a return season at Her Majesty's over the road a few months later. John and Sally Waters went off to holiday in England and I did a movie, *Squizzy Taylor*, and a TV series, *Trial by Marriage*. David Atkins played Melbourne gangster Squizzy Taylor in the Simpson–Le Mesurier movie of the same name, I was Squizzy's moll Polly, the brothel madam, and the exquisite Kim Lewis, then only seventeen, played his innocent girlfriend. One night after dinner with the director Kevin Dobson, David and I admitted we had never been in a brothel so, in the interests of research, Kevin took us to Paradise Haven in St Kilda Road, which was a bit worn-out and threadbare as havens go. The girls there were very welcoming and thought it a lark that we actually only wanted to talk to them. One of them, Sandy, took great delight in telling us that her clients often told her that, to look at, she reminded them of Jacki Weaver. Sandy soon had to leave the waiting room to deal with a client but twenty minutes later she was back full of mirth. 'You'll never believe this but that bloke was just about to get on the job when he says to me, he says, hey, love, has anyone ever told you that you're the spitting image of Jacki Weaver? And I was dying to say to him: well, go downstairs and take a gander at who's sitting in our parlour!'

During the Squizzy shoot, I was sitting in the make-up chair at five o'clock one morning when I became very ill with agonising pains in my chest and my skin went the colour of grey parchment. The GP on-set rushed me to a heart specialist, who, after several tests, said the pains in my chest were stress-related muscle spasms. I protested that I was in a placid state and not stressed. 'What's on the filming schedule today?' she inquired. 'I'm due to be gang-raped,' I was forced to admit. Enough said.

I went back to shoot the scene, which was a huge ordeal for all of us, rapists and victim alike. One of the rapists, an extra, had to be released when he couldn't stop weeping. Another begged to be excused, saying his mother would never forgive him because I was one of her favourites. The head rapist Steve Bisley and I had to drink a lot of whiskey to recover from a long and harrowing gang-bang.

After *Squizzy Taylor* I did a second series of seven episodes of the comedy *Trial by Marriage* for ABC-TV with Peter Sumner, Maggie Dence and Terry Bader, written by Michael Aitkens and produced by John O'Grady. It was good fun and hard work, recorded live in front of an audience, always intense and adrenaline-pumping, with not only timing and audience reaction to consider but also having to focus on four cameras and making sure you hit your marks— marks on the floor, usually gaffer tape, to indicate the precise positions you need to be on to ensure the shot is correct.

By now it was time to return to *They're Playing Our Song* in Melbourne, which had already had a sell-out season in both Sydney and Melbourne and was now due for return seasons in both cities, this time in different theatres.

And by now I had split up with Phil Davis. I was sad. And then Megan Tudor reintroduced Hinch and me at Liza Minnelli's opening night.

Hundreds of thousands—quite possibly millions—of words have been written about Derryn Nigel Hinch. Many thousands of them by the man himself. A complex combination of contradictions, he remains one of my favourite people and one of my closest friends. We were married for fifteen years and even now, seven years after our divorce, we still talk to each other every day.

Hinch is the product of a naïve father and a mother who was sharp as a tack, and he takes after both parents. Mercurial, with a quick intelligence combined with a dogged stubbornness; enormous hubris mixed with unexpected modesty; idealistic and highly principled, yet ruthless and reckless—he seldom fails to provoke a reaction in almost everyone.

Polemic may be his profession, but I know that he has never taken a stance on anything he didn't believe in and never expressed an opinion merely for effect. This is where almost all his critics and all the satirists have been wrong about him. Phillip Adams once said to me: 'I think I've worked Derryn out: he's a true innocent.' And I agree. And I know him better than anyone else does. His mother Betty Hinch once remarked: 'Derryn's like April showers.' Depths of sadness quickly followed by glorious sunshine, the tears disappearing as rapidly as they come.

Countless magazine and newspaper articles over twenty-four years have bleated: 'How *can* she love him? Why?' Many women have loved Hinch, and many women still love him and they understand. The corny but unavoidable truth is that I fell for him totally on our first date—a Melbourne Football Club function, of all things, surrounded by boring Aussie Rules officials at a fund-raising dinner.

Having given up on ever living with another man again, stung by my failure with Phil Davis, Dylan, now aged ten, and I had gone to live in that flat I'd bought in Lonsdale Street in the Melbourne CBD, while I did the third season of *TPOS*. Dylan was keen for me to Go On A Date. His favourite garment of mine was a hand-painted silk Pru Acton number, covered in a swirling Milky Way of stars and diamantes that Dylan referred to as my Battlestar Galactica dress.

A week before our first date at the Melbourne Football Club, Hinch had escorted me home, at publicist Megan Tudor's behest, from that Liza Minnelli concert, where Liza told me her sister Lorna Luft thought I was great in *TPOS*. At the front door Hinch asked if I would go to the cinema with him, but it was to be five years before he took me to the pictures. And even then it was a free screening.

Two days after the Minnelli concert, he watched me being a presenter at the AFI awards at Sydney's Regent Theatre, where I wore a tiny strapless gold-lamé full-skirted floor-length gown made for me by Moonyeen McNeilage.

On-stage I did my famous 'Edith Head gives good wardrobe' joke, which brought the house down. And indeed the Regent was demolished soon after.

At the Sebel Town House party after the show, Hinch was with the adorable Georgia Reilly, one of Sydney's most beautiful fashion models. He invited me to the Melbourne Football Club Dinner the following week. Might as well get out of the house, I thought—he's lively, personable, with a positive spirit and, boy, do I need cheering up.

I informed Dylan that I was going on a date. A date, a date, a palpable date! Dylan was extremely excited. He'd been hoping for a date for me for some time. 'I think this calls for Battlestar Galactica!' he trumpeted triumphantly.

So I wore Battlestar Galactica and promptly fell in love, if not in a few minutes, certainly within a few hours. Hinch regaled me with tales of New York, my favourite city, where he'd been living for eleven years as bureau chief for Fairfax. In NYC he'd been thoroughly brainwashed, proselytised, or at least influenced, by the young active feminist women he had wooed, which put him highways ahead of most Australian men. As a journalist he'd interviewed Betty Friedan. He'd even dated Gloria Steinem.

When I met him, he had about nine or ten regular girlfriends and slept with all of them. At that MFC dinner he told me about the feminist movement in the US and how he believed that women are far superior to men. He gave vent to some progressive rad fem views. How enchanting—as a young Germaine Greer devotee who was striving only for equality not superiority, this was music to my ears.

He was sincere, but he certainly knew it was seduction by stealth. And seduction by propaganda. I gazed into his eyes and, somewhere between the appetiser and dessert, I fell absolutely in love with him.

Driving Dylan to Christ Church Grammar in South Yarra the following morning, I eagerly switched on the car radio to listen to my new friend Derryn Hinch. Before long it became clear just what a high profile this man enjoyed in Melbourne. Derryn Hinch had an almost cult-like status. My heart sank at the realisation of what was in store for me if the relationship was to continue and grow. I was used to being in the public eye, albeit sometimes reluctantly, but everything Hinch did made front-page news on a daily basis, and he had no qualms about it. The Human Headline indeed. He had a million listeners every morning, the equivalent of ten full MCGs on Grand Final Day, as Dylan pointed out. Research confirmed Hinch was the most recognisable Australian alongside Prime Minister Bob Hawke. (Even though he was born in New Zealand, Hinch became a naturalised Australian many years ago and refuses to be called a Kiwi.) On top of that he'd recently had a humiliating and very public bust-up and broken engagement with Lynda Stoner. He was still in love with her. An impediment, to say the least.

Hinch had always been a womaniser, perhaps incapable of monogamy, which doesn't make him unusual. What was unusual was that his myriad amours were diligently chronicled in most of the Melbourne media, to a greater or lesser degree. The excruciating *Truth* newspaper always seemed to be putting him on their front page or on their banners. A columnist in the *Toorak Times* wrote that Hinch had 'parted more female fernery than anyone in Australia'. There was never a shortage of nubile glamour girls clamouring to be seen on his arm. The fame, the flashlights, the fun, the French champagne, the flowers, the fast times. Being dumped by Lynda Stoner hurt him in every way, especially his pride. But soon afterwards, his courtship of me couldn't have been more enthusiastic. Wooing me so heartily was no doubt good therapy for him to get over Lynda. Our romance bloomed in the hothouse glare of the media spotlight and the public gaze. I loathed the constant public attention, but I loved Hinch. So I put up with all the fuss.

Hinch was genuinely entranced by *TPOS* and saw it about twenty-five times. Dylan eventually refused to sit beside Hinch during the show because he said Hinch 'always cried in all the mushy bits'. My character, Sonia—gorgeous Carole Bayer Sager, with a mop of curly raven hair—had Hinch totally enchanted long before he became enchanted with me. Watching Sonia on-stage brought back glowing memories for him of all the fabulous Jewish girls he'd dated during his eleven years in New York.

Hinch came by the theatre every night to take me to supper, even though he had to be up each morning at 5.17 to be on radio at 8.30 for three and a half hours. When he didn't watch the show from the stalls, he'd lie down in my dressing room until the curtain call. My dresser had huge admiration for Hinch and, so as not to disturb him, she would dress me in the corridor outside, much to John Waters' disgust.

Cleverly, Hinch was very good to Dylan, even though he's never cared much for kids. After receiving his first drum kit, from me, Dylan spent his eleventh birthday party, organised by Hinch, at Sardi's, surrounded by beautiful chorus girls who made a big fuss of the boy. Betty Hinch darkly predicted that Dylan would turn out badly. For once she was wrong, thank God.

Dylan and I lived in our one-bedroom flat in Melbourne, where we slept in twin beds. There was a sofa in the sitting room that converted to a double bed, but it had never been used because there was a huge marble coffee table in front of it, so heavy that three men were needed to lift it.

Dylan was staying over at a friend's house the first night Hinch came to stay at my place. In a superhuman feat of strength, triggered by lust, Hinch single-handedly moved the marble table. When Dylan returned the next day and saw that Hinch had shifted the table, he was mightily impressed at such physical prowess and exclaimed: 'Just like King Arthur and Excalibur!' From then on, we referred to the table as Excalibur. It took three men to put the table back again. Like Sampson before him, Hinch's strength had dwindled with his lust.

Finally *TPOS* finished its Melbourne run and we went to Sydney for our fourth return season, this time at Her Majesty's Theatre, near Central Station. Hinch continued to shower me with roses, expensive gifts, several daily phone calls and the occasional flying visit. But I was besotted with him and wanted a commitment, something he wasn't ready to give.

Despite his apparent devotion to me, back in Melbourne he'd already resumed his old habits of bedding two or three different women a week. The list was astonishing. An eye-opener. I was devastated.

'Is your heart broken, Mum?' inquired my anxious eleven-year-old.

'No, just aching a little,' I lied.

I cried on Richard Wherrett's shoulder. 'Derryn's not wicked, he's just a man,' said Richie, pouring me a gin and tonic.

I told myself that, once you stop wanting something, that's the moment you get it. I worked hard at trying to convince myself that I didn't want Derryn Hinch in my life.

I hate recalling those times because I think I was such an idiot. A fool for love. One night I spent an obscene amount of money to hire a Lear jet to fly to Melbourne late at night after I finished my show, to surprise Hinch for his thirty-ninth birthday. Front-page news. There were several disappointed women surrounding Hinch when I turned up unexpectedly at the party. The look on his face was like a kid's when he's been caught with his hand in the cookie jar.

Finally I decided to cut my losses and run. I told Hinch we were finished, and I meant it. I sought comfort, briefly, in the arms of a much younger man—a *very* much younger man. (But legal. Just.) John Waters was disapproving of this latest development and chastised me, pointing out that the boy was more suited to be Dylan's playmate than mine, but that boy is still a good friend, more than twenty years later.

Then I gave up men. Yet again.

Months went by. And then one night, while Dylan was staying over with my brother Rod and his wife Helen in Drummoyne, I was out with some girlfriends at Arthur's nightclub in Kings Cross. A waiter who resembled Adonis handed me the menu and asked what I wanted.

'You,' I replied.

'I'm free at midnight,' he said without hesitation.

By the time he returned at the end of his shift half an hour later to take me out, I'd been introduced for the first time to 'Tom', who was now sitting beside me. Tom looked up at the expectant waiter and said: 'Disappear, mate, she's with me.' Adonis departed, disconsolate.

Tom and I talked all night. And by dawn's early light he had asked me to marry him.

Tom was moody, obsessive, dark and troubled, with a tendency to pessimism that was disturbingly infectious. He was also blessed with a brilliant sense of the ridiculous. In fact, Tom can still make me laugh more than anyone I've ever met. And he was extremely beautiful to behold. Very easy on the eye.

Tom loves children, and he and Dylan hit it off straightaway. Big time. Both of them deep thinkers and big laughers, their bond was immediate. Of course I still had unresolved feelings for Hinch, but I was intent on putting him out of my life. Simple self-preservation on my part. And before long I loved Tom very much. Okay, so I'm shallow. 'The heart has its reasons reason doth not know.' Who said that? I just did.

Tom moved in with Dylan and me to our flat in Darling Point. We were very happy in between the occasional bouts

159

of gloom to which both Tom and I were prone. We laughed a lot and had lots of fun, all three of us. Well *four* really, counting Frank, who was Dylan's monkey puppet. Frank was a bold piece of work and Dylan's close mate. Also, Frank often confided in Tom, who would pretend to be shocked as he passed on Frank's revelations.

Tom and I began to plan our marriage, the marriage he'd proposed on the night we met for the first time. I went interstate to meet Tom's parents. And then I was asked to do yet another return season of *TPOS*, a fifth run. John Waters and I had already clocked up more than five hundred performances and worn out three sets of chorus boys and girls. The next season was to be in Adelaide, but John Waters didn't want to do it this time so Barry Quin took over. Barry was married to the very beauteous Peta Toppano.

Meanwhile, in Melbourne one afternoon Hinch happened to be enjoying a post-coital chat with a mutual friend when she dropped the news that I was going to marry Tom. From that moment on, Hinch hunted me down with the dogged inexorability of a heat-seeking missile.

Rehearsals for the Adelaide season began in Melbourne, and Dylan and Tom took me to Sydney airport to see me off. By the time I arrived at Melbourne's Tullamarine airport, Hinch was already waiting for me. Reader, believe me— I protested, I resisted, I begged him to leave me be. I began to have panic attacks whenever I saw his Rolls Royce approaching. I came out in a nervous rash of hives that covered my entire body. Our producer Sue Nattrass became worried that I wouldn't be able to do the show.

Director Philip Cusack, just back from New York, took the unusual and desperate step of publicly upbraiding Hinch and ordering him to stay away from me when Hinch turned up at rehearsals for the umpteenth time. Tom left Hinch a message telling him to grow up. But nobody could withstand the Hinch juggernaut, Hinch the obsessive competitor.

Hinch's personal assistant, Annette Philpott, was one of his most valuable allies. She had remained a good friend to me, and she wanted Hinch and me to reunite. Annette's connivance worked very much to Hinch's advantage.

The *TPOS* company moved to Adelaide to open the show and Hinch followed. Then Hinch took out a full-page in the Adelaide *News* and ran an advertisement that he'd designed himself—a large photo of me and a declaration of love from him: 'I LOVE JACKI WEAVER'. It cost him $5000.

I was in a cafe when I saw it. I was so embarrassed I covered my head and face with the table napkin. I was mortified; Tom was furious; and Hinch was delighted. It made the news everywhere in Australia, not just Adelaide. The Human Headline had done it again. I was reminded of my stage-door johnny (old-fashioned expression meaning 'fan') who'd sent me the tape of himself singing 'I'm Going Out of My Mind'. It seemed an apt way to describe my circumstances.

I didn't enjoy doing the show in Adelaide, and it opened to patronising reviews. I had done almost six hundred performances already and now I was performing it with a new leading man. Barry Quin was a darling and terrific to work with, but all the personal upheaval I was going through only made doing the show more of a chore. Nevertheless, I threw my heart into it and I worked as hard as I could to make the show work. After the sell-out seasons in Sydney and Melbourne and the unstinting enthusiasm of the audiences there, Adelaide's indifference, especially from the press, was disappointing. I've met some lovely people in Adelaide, but generally I have always found it to be a very tough town. A tough town with delusions of superiority, especially on the part of the self-styled intelligentsia.

Tom brought Dylan to Adelaide and they stayed with me for a week but then Tom had to return to Sydney to work. Dylan, Frank the monkey and I sadly waved Tom goodbye as the taxi took him to Adelaide airport. We wanted to go with him.

When Tom arrived in Sydney he threw my television set into the swimming pool. Then he phoned to tell me he'd just taken a huge dose of heroin. The first heroin he'd had in several years. Friends were taking care of him. I was horrified, but I was stuck in Adelaide and couldn't go to him. Dylan and I were frightened by the possible spectre of a drug problem. A few days later, Tom moved out of my flat in Darling Point and our relationship was over. I'd failed again. It wasn't until years later that I discovered Tom had invented the heroin story to get my sympathy. Instead it had driven the final nail into the coffin.

Meanwhile Hinch wanted me to marry him as soon as possible. He kept flying back and forth between Adelaide and Melbourne to see me. Dylan began to feel sorry for him. 'Maybe you should say yes, to put him out of his misery,' said Dylan.

I told Hinch that, if I accepted his proposal, then his days of being a roving serial satyr were over. He swore to me his lifelong fidelity. Which, as far as I know, he kept. Except, perhaps, for some unimportant and minor lapses. Extremely unimportant and minor.

I didn't really want to live in Hinch's Albert Park house, which he had originally acquired under extraordinary circumstances. One night at a drunken dinner party Hinch had offered to buy Mark Day's house for a stupidly inflated sum and Mark had accepted. Poor Wendy Day had gone to sleep to discover, when she woke up next morning, that her house had been sold. To Derryn Hinch. The house wasn't even on the market.

It was an excellent house, but not for me. In the short time he'd been living there, Hinch had already taken part in horizontal folk dancing with many, many women. Their number was equivalent to the entire Ballet Folklórico de México. One day I found a pair of knickers stuffed behind the books in the bedhead shelf. They were not my knickers. Much too big for me. Hinch promised to sell the house and move to a different one.

Also, I was unsure about leaving Sydney, especially now that Dylan was about to start secondary school. But within a few hours Hinch had organised Dylan a place at Wesley College, by all accounts an excellent co-educational (and expensive) school.

At the closing night party of *TPOS* in Adelaide, Hinch announced our engagement. Some were very pleased, some shocked and some even weepy. I was all of the above. A few weeks later, on 25 February 1983, we were married in Hinch's manager's glorious garden in Brighton during a late February heatwave. Ray and Judith Evans gave us a beautiful wedding; twelve-year-old Dylan gave me away and Annette Philpott in pink chiffon was my bridesmaid. The street banner headlines made us laugh:

'HINCH TO WED!' said the Melbourne *Truth* (ignoring me).

'HINCH TO WED JACKI!' said the Melbourne *Sun* (ignoring neither of us).

'JACKI TO WED! PEACOCK BEST MAN!' said the Sydney *Daily Mirror* (ignoring Hinch).

In spite of Hinch being labelled 'The Human Headline', neither of his first two marriages had made the front pages. Both of mine had, in both Sydney and Melbourne. As well as a lot of other things I did. It seemed amusing and worth reminding him that it wasn't until Derryn married *me* that his nuptials made news. This is not a boast, by the way, just a statement of fact. The only conclusion worth drawing is that fame is (a) meaningless (b) an accident and (c) fleeting, although it can fluctuate hugely over the years, usually depending on how much TV you've been doing. And sometimes the most unlikely people know everything about you. The best thing is to try to stay unimpressed with both the praise and the insults. Easier said than done sometimes. I can honestly say I've never chased publicity, but at times I have seemed to attract it like blowflies.

Our wedding reception, for only about forty people, was at the Regent (now the Sofitel) in Collins Street. Just about everyone gave a speech. Most of them were brilliant. As usual, my father Arthur's speech was the best one of all—erudite, witty and entertaining, yet with his own characteristic modesty. He was unbeatable, though Jill Farnham's speech came close.

Richard Wherrett was there, looking strikingly handsome and urbane. Years earlier, when Richie had met Derryn Hinch for the first time, he had expected the worst, but after a few minutes he said to Hinch: 'You're not a shit *at all*.' Derryn had been visibly relieved to have Richie's approval.

Richie brought us a gram of cocaine as a wedding present. However, the groom would not accept the coke (because it's illegal, I guess) so Richie ended up taking all of it himself, later on in his hotel room.

Richie also told me he loved me. He said how pleased he was to see me so happy and he ordered me to remain happy. My agent Gloria Payten was also there looking beautiful, and she too ordered me to be happy. And so did my mother Edith, pretty in pink.

Now I was Jacqueline Ruth Hinch. This time I was determined to make it last until I died. Or until Hinch drank himself to death, whichever came first.

chapter nine

Rollering Through
the Good Times

LIFE AT ALBERT PARK BEGAN AND WE STARTED LOOKING FOR
somewhere else to live.

I've always loved driving. Since I was a teenager, I had
secretly longed to own a truck. Nothing fancy, just a Ford
pick-up or a Holden ute. As a kid, one of my favourite toys
was a Matchbox front-end loader. So it was a slight case of
overkill when Derryn's first gift to me was his navy blue
Rolls Royce Silver Shadow circa 1969 model. Especially
when a truck would have sufficed.

I drove that blue Rolls Royce everywhere, with a great
deal of pleasure. It was a great big hulking gorgeous beast of
a machine and I loved it. David Price once told me that his
wealthy uncle, CO Stanley, only drove Bentleys because he
considered Rolls Royces to be 'too vulgar'. But my Rolls

looked, smelled and felt beautiful, and rode like a dream. If this was vulgar, it was very appealing.

Once I got used to the immense size of the Rolls—and at first it seemed longer than a cricket pitch—I found it was easy to park. Easier even than some small modern cars, which sometimes tend to slope away so much that I find I can't see where they begin and end. My Rolls also had the added novelty of a permanently installed mobile phone, between the front seats, quite unusual in 1983. What's more, calls to London and New York from the car were clearer and easier than most mobile phones seem to manage even nowadays.

Derryn bought himself a newer 1979 burgundy-coloured Rolls Royce to replace the blue one he'd handed down to me. We were now a two-Roller family. From *vieux pauvres* to the most *nouveaux riches* kids on the block.

The Albert Park house didn't have a garage, because it was a pre-automobile Victorian terrace, typical of those in many inner-city suburbs. This meant both Rollers had to be parked in the street, making them an easy target for vandals. Several times we nearly lost the silver ladies off the front of both cars. People would hit our ladies with bricks and hammers, and try to prise them off with all manner of tools. One night someone even used industrial-strength paint stripper to daub anti-Hinch graffiti on every panel of the blue Rolls. They didn't touch his car, but damaged mine right through to the metal. A very sad sight next morning. Burglars and stalkers used to drop by regularly as well. We realised that we had to move somewhere with a little more security.

I inspected more than a hundred houses for sale over the next year, with the help of some very patient real estate agents. Invariably I was more interested in the vendors' paintings and books than in their bricks and mortar. Sometimes Derryn would accompany me to a house I'd recommended to him, only to find it was the paintings and the library that had impressed me, rather than the house itself. However, he was always kind and good-natured about these excursions.

Ironically, the eventual purchase we made was another Derryn folly, a house that I didn't even like or want. Built in 1958 on three levels down a steep slope at the cul-de-sac end of Orrong Road, Toorak, it had a river frontage with a boat mooring, which appealed to Derryn immensely. The fact that recording mogul Mike Gudinski and other luminaries were also at the auction stirred Derryn's competitive spirit, and he was thrilled to make the winning bid. Gudinski said later that, when he saw Hinch bidding, he knew he didn't stand a chance. But this was before Mike had discovered Kylie Minogue, and so he was worth a few billion less than he is now.

The house at Orrong Road was a wreck, and ended up costing more to renovate than it had originally cost to buy. Sitting at the bottom of a treacherously precipitous driveway, it had been the home and consulting rooms of a psychiatrist. TV star Graham Kennedy had lived there in the 1970s. It was a rabbit warren of musty dark rooms with peeling, garish, 1960s wallpaper and damp, rotting mustard-coloured carpet. A severe drainage problem led to inevitable flooding downstairs and sewage overflows whenever it rained, while upstairs the roof leaked so badly that I once counted nineteen buckets dotted about the floor. I always seemed to be buying buckets.

One day the leaks, combined with possums chewing the wiring, caused a fire in the kitchen. Consequently we didn't have a stove or an oven for three years, which is how long it took to make the place reasonably habitable. Even my mother-in-law Betty, a woman not used to luxury, was shocked at the conditions we tolerated for almost four years. Bet told me I'd gone up a great deal in her estimation for my cheerful forbearance. Obviously she'd decided that I was not the spoilt princess she'd initially suspected me to be.

We lived in a flat in St Kilda Road for a few months while the roof was being ripped off and replaced, and the new drains and foundations were being excavated. Architect David Francis did a brilliant job, opening up the house, filling it with glass and light, while maintaining respect for the 1950s original design. Right down to the Hollywood-style pink marble bathroom, which apparently the subsequent owners thought was in bad taste. I laughed when I heard that and wondered what they would have thought of the original lime-green and regurgitation-yellow poky little bath chamber.

David Francis' plans took maximum advantage of the sylvan setting, adding a fourth level with a beautiful view of the picturesque but much-maligned (especially by Sydney dwellers) Yarra River. Almost all the rooms looked out onto the stunning garden. Our swimming pool by the river was heated constantly to hot bath temperature throughout winter and we swam in it daily. The gas heating bill was outrageous. On very cold mornings the combination of the steam rising from the pool, the dawn mist, the winter frost and the rays of the rising sun through the stark, leafless giant trees was an awesomely surreal sight. Especially when you're submerged in hot water. Coming back up the garden steps into the warmth of the house was always a long, freezing journey. I soon grew to love that house with all my heart. I loved it more than anywhere I ever lived. I spent many happy, though sometimes lonely, years there. It broke my heart to lose it and to leave it behind.

We owned it for about fourteen years. At dusk on my last day there, just before the removalists uplifted everything to Sydney after weeks of packing, I remember sitting alone on the stairs, amongst hundreds of cardboard boxes, looking out at the garden, the river, the waterfall, knowing I'd never see them again. Everything changes.

Just before we married, against my advice as usual, Derryn had bought a half-share in a farm with his manager, Ray Evans. He bought the farm one day at a barbecue from a lovely man and dear friend, our GP Dr Richard Ward, and his execrable ex-wife Barbara. The plan was to grow grapes on the slopes of Mount Macedon, on Straws Lane—the famous 'upside down hill', with a view to Hanging Rock about three kilometres away. Yes, *the* Hanging Rock.

There was a rambling five-bedroom farmhouse, part of which had been built in 1842, plus a swimming pool, tennis court and a retired Victorian rail carriage, a 'red rattler' that

Derryn always planned to restore but never got around to. And a vigorously rigorous climate that ranged from 40 degrees in summer to a couple of snowfalls in winter. We nearly lost the farm in the Ash Wednesday bushfires of 1983. Barns, fencing, livestock and vehicles were destroyed but, by some miracle, the homestead remained standing. Both our neighbours' houses burned to the ground.

Dylan and I spent long days helping Derryn clear the bottom paddock of thousands of stones, before the soil could even be turned over. Eventually we planted sixteen thousand vines and Derryn would have tended every single one of them many times over the next fifteen years, working in the dust or mud, in freezing or heatwave conditions, and everything in between. Derryn was a very 'hands-on' farmer, even though he had to employ a farm manager to be there during the week (when he had to be in the city for early morning starts on radio).

For years the three of us would drive up to Mount Macedon, about an hour and ten minutes from the city, on Friday nights and return Sunday evenings. If I was working in a show, I'd join them late on Saturday nights. It was a routine of ours that thieves became familiar with, so we were burgled in the city several times when we were in the country.

I never really suited the farm life. I'm a city chick to the core. Like Woody Allen, I would lie wide awake listening to the deafening silence of the country night, 'waiting for Dick and Perry to come' (see Truman Capote's *In Cold Blood*). But I loved being with Dylan and Derryn, so the farm and the gumboots were tolerable on weekends. Endless games of

Trivial Pursuit around the roaring pot-belly stove and mugs of Derryn's famous tomato soup, laced with brandy. Sometimes with good pals staying over, but often just the three of us being happy families and contented wine growers.

At two thirty one dark morning the three of us, ankle deep in snow and cow-shit, helped deliver a calf with dislocated shoulders to a highly distressed cow in the back paddock. Derryn was the first creature the calf set eyes on, so there was an instant bond between them. Because the calf was crippled and unable to feed normally, for the first few days Derryn even hand-fed her cow's milk from a Veuve Clicquot champagne bottle, which was the only empty bottle handy that morning at 3 am. We named the calf Raspberry Ripple and she followed Derryn around for the rest of her life, convinced that he was her mother.

The palomino mink jacket that I wore to assist during the calf's delivery (it was freezing and I'd driven straight from the theatre) was now covered in blood and placenta and was dispatched to Hammerman's in Sydney for expert cleaning. It was returned spotless a fortnight later accompanied by a note saying, 'Suggest no more midwifery wearing this jacket.'

The vet said we did the right thing. Both animals would have died without help.

Soon after Derryn and I were married in 1983, JC Williamson's, inspired by the success of *They're Playing Our Song*, wanted me to do another show for them and I suggested the Garson Kanin classic *Born Yesterday*. Written in 1949, it had been a long-running Broadway stage hit starring Judy

Holliday, who had then made the movie and won the Oscar in a vintage year in which she beat Bette Davis' performance in *All About Eve* and that dame in *Sunset Boulevard*, Gloria Swanson. Judy Holliday also won the Tony and the Golden Globe for the role. She took over from Jean Arthur (who suffered severe stage fright), my dad's favourite movie star, only a week before the out-of-town try-out and went on to perform it more than 1600 times on-stage.

Phil Cusack was disappointed when Williamson's offered Gordon Hunt from California the director's job. Philip had been saying for years I was perfect for Billie Dawn in *Born Yesterday* and he would've loved to direct it. But instead they brought Gordon Hunt over from America. He was a dream to work with. Sometimes he'd mention his teenage daughter back home, who was an actress. Her name was Helen. Years later Helen Hunt would win an Oscar for *As Good As It Gets*, opposite Jack Nicholson.

Born Yesterday is much more than a comedy. It was way ahead of its time; it dealt with political corruption, the rise of the women's movement, higher education and 'whistleblowing', as well as serving as a metaphor for America's loss of innocence post-World War II. It's also a fabulous vehicle for a female actor: an opportunity to undergo a Pygmalionesque transformation—from shameful exploitation and unhappy ignorance to full-blown self-empowerment through education and good old-fashioned love. Ex-chorus-girl mistress of bullying crooked tycoon becomes campaigner for social justice, and finds true love in the process. Dumb blonde gets wise. And gets the good guy. At one point during Billie Dawn's re-education, as it dawns on her how meaningless her existence has been, she cries out vehemently: '*I hate my life*!' A stark lament that echoes around the theatre, and a turning point for Billie Dawn and for the story.

It's so beautifully written that it's hard to imagine any halfway-decent actress not having a triumph as Billie Dawn. With an excellent cast, which included Brian Marshall, Duncan Wass and Neil Fitzpatrick, we opened at the Comedy Theatre in Exhibition Street, one of my favourite venues. Roger Kirk designed a spectacular set with equally spectacular costumes including a real full-length white-mink coat that was so valuable it had to be locked in the safe after every performance, and a hand-embroidered dress of jet glass bugle beads that was so heavy it was almost insupportable. For my tiny narrow shoulders anyway. The critics were universally enthusiastic. We got rave reviews.

A few weeks into the Melbourne run of *Born Yesterday* my father, sounding shell-shocked, rang from Sydney one Friday afternoon to say my mother had had a massive heart attack and was in intensive care at the Adventist Hospital in Wahroonga. Forty years of cigarette smoking had taken their toll. At the age of fifty-seven my mother needed urgent heart surgery, a triple bypass. I think I became hysterical.

Everyone else sprang into action. My employer, Sue Nattrass, was great. I was dispatched with Derryn on the first flight to Sydney and my understudy, the excellent Taylor Owynns—who, like Eve Harrington in *All About Eve*, was more than ready—did the Friday night and Saturday matinee performances at just a few hours' notice. The Hinch chauffeur, factotum and housekeeper at this time, the late Leonard Cooper (affectionately nicknamed 'Mrs Danvers' after the sinister housekeeper in Daphne du Maurier's wonderful novel *Rebecca*, later brought to life on film by the incomparable Dame Judith Anderson) rang me immediately after the show to tell me Taylor had done a fabulous job as Billie Dawn. I flew straight back to Melbourne the next afternoon and I was back up there on-stage the following night, just like Margo Channing in *All About Eve*. But only after I knew Mummy was going to be all right.

Despite the good reviews in Melbourne, we didn't get good houses. Sadly, *Born Yesterday* was not successful at the box-office. The Firm must have lost a packet because it was a big cast, and it had been mounted so lavishly. Then Richard Wherrett, by now head of the Sydney Theatre Company, sent his literary manager Wayne Harrison to take a look at *Born Yesterday* with an eye to buying the set and costumes and remounting the show at the Opera House. Wayne loved it and recommended it; Richard came down to see it and the STC took it on.

This time Richard wanted to direct it himself, naturally enough. He recast all the roles except for me and Neil Fitzpatrick. My two leading men were now Gary Files and John Allen. It's a fascinating experience to recreate a role with a different director and cast. It's happened to me a few times and it's an invaluable acting exercise—in flexibility, adaptability and maintaining an open mind about the many ways to interpret a role. And trying all the choices available. A fresh canvas.

Richard's production was very different from Gordon's, but both were equally valid and both were equally faithful to Garson Kanin's text. In Sydney we again received rave reviews (with one notable exception), but this time the public voted with their feet. We were a sell-out and we broke box-office records for the Drama Theatre at the Opera House. Brian Hoad was the critic who panned us, viciously, in the *Bulletin*. Brian and Richard were bitter foes for years. Brian Hoad has a fine intellect. He is a first-rate writer. But Brian Hoad is also a first-rate hater and he has a capacity for vitriol that boggles. A waste of a fine intellect.

One night mid performance at the Drama Theatre, we noticed a fair bit of activity going on in the auditorium while we were on-stage trying to thesp. (If Shakespeare's allowed to invent words, I can too.) At the curtain call we realised there were about fifteen security guards and a dozen police officers standing in the aisles.

A well-known criminal had made a death threat against me because of something Hinch had said on-air that day and the authorities were taking it seriously. Very seriously. My Darling Point flat was searched. My dresser Jacquie was asked to spend the night with me so I wouldn't be alone. By the police, not me. Jacquie and I rode home in a police vehicle trying not to giggle, like two naughty schoolgirls. Four armed police saw us onto the premises and again did a search, including the wardrobe. Thank God. And thank God for the police.

This was the first of many threats levelled at me over the years because of Hinch. He was always being threatened with injury by some ratbag or thug and he took it all in his stride. However, whenever I became the target, Derryn was always very upset. So the lunatics knew what they were doing where the psychology of intimidation was concerned.

My dentist, Len Hansen, told me about how he came to see *Born Yesterday* at an afternoon matinee and just managed to get the last single seat in the front row. At the curtain call the little old lady sitting beside him turned to him and said, 'Hasn't she got a lovely smile?'

To which he replied, 'Thank you, I'm her dentist.'

She was a bit startled, to say the least.

Little old ladies have often shown an inordinate amount of interest in my teeth over the years. 'Are they your own?' they would ask. As if I would actually *choose* them. Now that I'm older, the question is seldom asked. It's nowadays gum-bleedin' obvious that these are the teeth I've been saddled with since birth. Well, shortly thereafter anyway.

David Williamson invited me to lunch one day at his and Kristin's beautiful old house in Balmain. They'd liked *Born Yesterday* and David asked me if I would be interested in playing the wife in the film version of his play *The Perfectionist*. It was the role Robyn Nevin had played on-stage opposite Peter Carroll and Hugo Weaving. Filming went ahead with John Waters as my husband, Steven Vidler as the young blond Swedish hunk I run away with, Chris Thompson directing and Russell Boyd, our latest Oscar winner, as cinematographer. I'm quite fond of that movie, even though it only made it to television.

John Sumner, the legendary founder of the Melbourne Theatre Company, offered me Tom Stoppard's new play, *The Real Thing*, but I was already contracted to do something else and regretfully declined. However I adored the play and asked Richard Wherrett if there was a chance he'd consider me for the same role in Sydney. I was thrilled when he said yes, even though Robyn Nevin was by then an associate director at the STC and expecting all the leading roles to be hers.

Robyn Nevin was ropeable that she wasn't doing *The Real Thing* and stopped speaking to me altogether. For the best part of a decade. I was deeply hurt for the first few years and then stopped caring, but not before—in a bout of unworthy ill-temper—I referred to her one day as 'The Grey Nurse'. I'm ashamed to say the nickname caught on. I have since apologised to her. She never apologised to me. Doesn't matter. Her problem not mine.

At this point I must reiterate that Richard and I worked together on only eight productions out of the one hundred and twenty-seven he directed in the thirty years we knew each other. It annoys me that people assume I was part of some imaginary clique of Richard's. In fact he employed hundreds of people and often took big risks on untried actors in the interests of giving someone a break. His generosity towards actors sometimes paid off and sometimes it back-fired in his face. I've always suspected the term 'Mauve Mafia' was invented by some disgruntled macho actor with just a tinge of the homophobe about him who wasn't good enough to crack a big role at the STC.

Richard asked if I had any suggestions for the role of Henry in *The Real Thing*. I lobbied for John Bell; I thought he'd be perfect. And he *was* perfect. John had been acting for twenty years and Henry was his first contemporary role. John's monologue, in which Henry draws an analogy between cricket and literature, was a show stopper at every performance. (John would sometimes give me a lift home in his old Volvo and tell me about the struggle he was having to get his fledgling Shakespeare Company off the ground. It's so gratifying now to look back and see how his tenacity paid off in such a big way. Bell Shakespeare has become one of Australian theatre's greatest success stories.)

Staged in 1985, *The Real Thing* was another record breaker at the Opera House. The publishers of the play sold unprecedented numbers of copies of the text every night in the theatre foyer, so taken was the audience with Stoppard's clever writing.

I was having a wonderful time working in *The Real Thing*. I was also having fun after hours, partying until dawn most nights in bars and clubs with a band of my gay boyfriends, affectionately dubbed 'The Moll Patrol' by my husband. They were very protective of me, though. One night a federal minister (a married man), without any encouragement from me but plenty of it from his hovering lackeys, importuned me in the bar at Kinsela's. The Moll Patrol closed ranks and shirt-fronted the offender. 'She's with us!' they told him in no uncertain manner and he scurried away, his minders at his heels.

I was missing my family in Melbourne terribly, though. Dylan and Derryn always coped very well without me, but

I ached with longing to be with them every day. It's a strange way to live, separated by hundreds of miles because of work. Phone calls, no matter how many, can never assuage the loneliness. Occasionally I would fly home for a Sunday, but would have to be back next day for Monday night's show. This is the problem with a six-day, eight-performance work week. And with an eight to twelve week run plus four weeks' rehearsal, this usually means at least three months, often four months away from home with every play.

The Girl from Moonooloo, an ABC-TV movie musical, was written especially for me by David Mitchell, produced by John O'Grady and directed by Richard Wherrett. It was a little piece of naïve art, incorporating popular songs of the time, set in small-town Australia and Sydney's big-time radio studios in the 1930s, with a twist of Ginger Meggs. I was in my late thirties, playing yet another 22-year-old virgin. But I got away with it. My co-stars were eleven-year-old Ivan Waters, John Waters' son, and David Atkins, who broke his foot in the first week of shooting, leaping from a piano during a dance routine. Although it was only modestly successful, it's a film I still have great affection for.

I especially love the song 'Big Bridge Blues'. We filmed that sequence during a ten-hour all-night shoot one winter's night on a tiny ferry on Sydney Harbour. Sleet was falling, and I was wearing a flimsy silk dress, tears streaming down my face. I've never been so cold in my life, including winters in London and New York. I felt sorry for the crew too, but at least they were rugged up against the elements. Between each take the wardrobe department would swoop on me with blankets and Drizabones. Then, just as my bones began to thaw and my chattering teeth quietened a little, it would be time to unwrap me, expose me to the bitter air and go for another take. The next day's news announced that Sydney had just experienced its coldest night on record. It was a good sequence though, so it was worth the discomfort.

After several weeks' shooting without a break, because I was in almost every scene, I finally got to go home to Melbourne for a couple of days. I was extremely excited and so looking forward to seeing Dylan and Derryn, who picked me up from Tullamarine. In the car on the way to the farm, as promised, I rang Richard, whom I'd just left on the film set in Sydney, to say that I'd arrived safely. I probably rabbited on for a while, being overexcited. For years afterwards Richie used to say that, during that phone call, it struck him that it was the happiest he'd ever known me to be.

Googie Withers and John McCallum are a wonderful couple, brilliant in their professions and in their lives. Both are still actively pursuing their distinguished careers, Googie's for more than seventy years. If that looks like a misprint, she was born in 1913 and made her debut on the London stage in 1929. Since I was a child, I have admired and respected them enormously. So in 1986 when my agent told me that John and Googie had offered me the lead in a play they were producing, I was very pleased. The script duly arrived; I read it and hated it. I read it again and still hated it.

I asked fifteen-year-old Dylan to read it. Dylan has a finely honed analytical sense of humour. Great comic instinct. He wasn't impressed either, though he did smile wanly at the gag where the male hero puts his underpants on his head and says: 'Biggles to base.' So did I. But one slight gag does not a play make. I turned it down. My agent said Googie and John wouldn't take no for an answer and were faxing me the English reviews to try to persuade me to change my mind.

The reviews were good. Googie had seen the play in Bath and fallen off her seat laughing. I read it again. Tried very hard not to hate it. It was called *Having a Ball* and is set in a vasectomy clinic—get the joke? The male hero has to strip naked and a vasectomy is simulated while he's lying on a green operating table that looks like a snooker table, and at one point the character intones: 'There are two balls on the table.' There is also an anti-nuclear theme, probably in an attempt to legitimise the crappy gags.

John McCallum flew me to Sydney, wined and dined me and offered me lots of money. I couldn't choose my leading man, because the playwright insisted the original English actor, David Ross, recreate the role as well as direct, which seemed fair enough. However, John McCallum said I could have a say in the casting of the other parts.

The money offered had become too generous to refuse, so I finally accepted. Then I suggested Maggie Dence for the role of the surgeon, thinking at least Maggie would make me laugh even if *Having a Ball* didn't. I don't think Mag's forgiven me to this day. Maggie's one of those wits who is an asset in any company. Great timing, very funny woman. She didn't think the play was much good either. But I was determined to make it work for John and Googie.

The lead actor/director duly arrived from England. We didn't get off to a swimmingly good start. That night we had dinner, during which he blew cigar smoke all over me. Throughout the meal he was obnoxiously patronising towards me, as only an ignorant Pom can be towards a humble colonial. I was mesmerised by the pronounced sibilance of his speech, combined with his thick Lancashire accent. He explained to me that his nudity was an important and integral part of the text. I vowed to myself then and there that, when I was acting with him on-stage and he was naked, I wouldn't take my eyes off his face. I kept that vow.

Rehearsals were not a good experience. He certainly didn't seem to have any idea what he was doing. While he was acting scenes opposite me, he mouthed my lines at me at the same time as I was saying them, usually something that only a small child or the odd amateur actor tends to do. This too was mesmerising, but I told myself that it would probably only happen during rehearsals and cease during actual perform-ances. It didn't. He did it right through the run of the play in Sydney and Melbourne. He also maintained his air of superi-ority and kept up his condescending attitude towards all of us Australians. It makes me smile sadly even now to recall it.

One night he had the temerity to explain that *The Lower Depths* was by 'a chap called Gorky', as though we were deprived of Russian literature in the colonies. On another occasion he supposed we'd never heard of Brecht. We weren't offended at all. Indeed we laughed. I laughed just a little longer and slightly louder than Maggie Dence. After all, as the vasectomy surgeon, she had to swab his private parts with a sponge on-stage every night. Up until then, Maggie confided, she had only seen the private parts of her husband Graham, the cast of *Hair* and the actor Bob Hornery. (Maggie had been in the Athenaeum Theatre dressing room one night when Sheila Bradley casually remarked that she'd never set eyes on a circumcised penis. Whereupon the ever-obliging Bob Hornery obliged. However, to this day, Maggie has never seen an uncut version.)

But I did try. I really tried hard to make the show work, and I was very sad for Googie and John that it didn't. It must have cost them heaps—I still feel guilty about that. *Having a Ball* is the worst experience I've had on-stage in forty-three years of acting professionally. It was a relief when it finished. I've only seen David Ross once since then—he was playing a villain on *The Bill*.

I received a fair amount of mail from the public who saw *Having a Ball*, all of it negative about the play, some asking me to explain how I could have associated myself with something so bad. The playwright's name is Alan Bleasdale, who wrote the award-winning TV series *Boys from the Black Stuff*. Alan Bleasdale is highly respected. Not by me.

In the meantime my dear husband Derryn Hinch was up to his neck in controversy as usual. He was found guilty on a contempt of court charge. This time he got a custodial sentence. And they sent him to Melbourne's Pentridge Prison.

Did not pass Go. Went to jail.

chapter ten

Hurricane Hinch

WHEN DERRYN HINCH, MY HUSBAND JOBY, WENT TO JAIL IN 1987 it was shattering. A horrendous time for Joby, for me and for Dylan.

Millions of words have been written about it—it was front-page headlines many times over, and it went on for years. Everyone had an opinion on it—the offence, the sentence, the appeals, right up to the High Court. It seemed to drag on forever. For those who were hiding in Patagonia at the time, here it is in a macadamia shell: a priest named Michael Glennon had been molesting children at a camp he ran. Instead of removing him from his position, the church and the magistrate let him continue to run the camp, where he continued to re-offend. While Glennon was awaiting further charges to be heard,

Joby named Glennon in a radio editorial and outlined his previous convictions.

Technically, this is contempt of court because it is illegal to reveal someone's prior convictions when they are awaiting trial on another offence, for fear of prejudicing the trial. Fair enough. But Joby's actions could also be seen as warning parents against sending children to the camp, minimising the possibility of there being further victims and so doing a public service. A service that the church and the magistrate had failed miserably to provide.

Many hailed Joby as a hero; others claimed it was just the usual Hinch grandstanding, publicity-seeking, attention-getting egocentricity. Whatever the rights and wrongs—and I can see both sides—the rule of law is precious in a democracy and must be protected. I believe Joby was rightly convicted of contempt of court, but wrongly sentenced to jail. In his Melbourne *Herald* editorial, Peter Smark got it right when he said that when they jailed Hinch they really jailed him for hubris, not contempt of court. Ostensibly for contempt of court, but in fact for arrogance. It was an inappropriate punishment. The purpose supposedly was to make an example of him, but instead it backfired and had the opposite effect. Going to jail garnered enormous public sympathy for Joby, turning him overnight into a martyr in many people's eyes.

When the sheriff turned up at the Flower Drum, he interrupted us at lunch while hundreds of people from all branches of the media were waiting outside. We were eating sang choy bau, as I recall (or was it Deng Xiao Ping?).

Whatever, they hauled Joby off to Pentridge and I've never seen so many cameras, except for movie scenes in which people get arrested and taken to jail. It led every news service and made all the front pages all over Australia. Joby's popularity soared. Of course many still loathed him, especially amongst the legal fraternity and the press.

All the publicity also brought the lunatic criminal fringe crawling out of the woodwork and out of the gutters. The death threats to both of us increased, including from within Pentridge. Derryn had a lot of enemies in jail, criminals he'd been scathingly critical about, but the authorities kept him in Pentridge for only one night, then for the rest of his six-week sentence moved him to Morwell River Prison Farm, where he shared a cell with a murderer. Because of automatic remissions his sentence was commuted to two weeks but it was still a dreadful time. Radio 3AW employed two full-time security guards to stay at Toorak while Joby was in jail, and they put Dylan and me up at the Grand Hyatt for the duration for our own protection. It sounds flash now, but in fact I spent most of the time in that luxury suite weeping for Joby.

And every night I was working over the road from the Hyatt at the Russell Street Theatre with Bruce Miles and Nadine Garner in Peter Nichols' excellent play *A Day in the Death of Joe Egg*. I think it was one of the first shows that Simon Philips directed for the Melbourne Theatre Company. We even had police attending the play for a few nights because some anonymous ratbag had rung the theatre and threatened me with grievous bodily harm. Maybe it was a critic.

It's no exaggeration to say we received thousands of letters, cards and messages of goodwill. Crates and crates, tea chests and cardboard boxes, all full of presents and mail and tributes. They were stacked up high in our Toorak dining room, overflowing between the buckets that were there to catch the rain from the leaks in the ceiling. It was overwhelming. The dining room was now the mail delivery room and we had to eat in the kitchen.

Teams of Joby's supporters tied yellow ribbons around trees all over Melbourne. Peter Sullivan and Annette Philpott organised for a group of friends—Bert and Patti Newton amongst them—to gather in a South Melbourne recording studio to be filmed singing 'That's What Friends Are For', especially for Joby. I intended to go but, when the time came, I was too upset to get up and leave the seclusion of the hotel suite.

People were very kind to me wherever I went. There were times when I felt that I certainly didn't deserve all the kindness. I just wanted Joby home safely from jail. I think I also wanted him to shut up for a while. Lower his profile. Vain hope.

For Christmas 1987, after his eventual release, Joby took Dylan and me to stay at the Helmsley Palace Hotel in New York. It was about my tenth visit to New York. From the hotel window one night I saw snowflakes falling for the first time in my life. The snow began to fall at two o'clock in the morning so Joby and Dylan took me outside to play in it. Right beside Bergdorf Goodman's.

It was the year I had turned forty and I was perfectly sanguine about it. We were lunching at the Stage Deli one day when I ordered an Irish coffee. The waiter asked for my ID because he thought I was under twenty-one, the legal drinking age in New York State. At first I thought he was joking, and I laughed and thanked him for the compliment.

'This is my seventeen-year-old son,' I boasted to the waiter, indicating Dylan.

Then Dylan said: 'He's serious, Mum.'

Joby added, 'Show him your passport, darling.'

I was forty years old and a complete stranger, who'd never heard of me, thought I was under twenty-one. It made my day. It made my year.

We had a wonderful Christmas in the small town of Cold Spring in upstate New York with Joby's long-time friends Tony and Leonora Burton. Lots of food, presents and trendy bars. I adore New York and always had dreams of settling down there one day. But it was time to go home for my main birthday present. Joby had earlier given me a surprise party at the farm, and one of those new-fangled cellular phones that was as heavy as a brick and cost $5000 dollars. However, my main birthday present was to be breast reduction surgery.

I've decided to discuss my breasts in detail. Something I never thought I'd do in public. This will no doubt be news that is surplus to the requirements of some readers. They couldn't give two hooters. I'm partly motivated to tell all after hearing recently about a little girl of twelve who has suddenly and unexpectedly found herself equipped with a rather large bust that's giving her angst. But for those of you who'd prefer to give birth to a chair than read about my breasts, please skip the rest of this section and move on to page 193.

My breasts began to bud from about the age of ten. My alarmed mother, enviably small-busted herself, took me to a corsetiere in David Jones, Market Street, who, after much measuring and embarrassing fuss, fitted me with my first brassiere. I was eleven years old and the height of an average child aged eight and a half years. The smallest girl in Year 6 and the only one with bosoms.

While not exactly the bane of my life yet, I already disliked my breasts and I was still two years away from being a teenager. In time, as they continued to grow, I grew to hate them. And they certainly grew. From grapefruits into melons. Small rockmelons. My back is narrow. So are my shoulders. Under my bust still measures 31 inches (79 centimetres). Around my nipples is 41 inches or 105 centimetres. That all adds up to a 10E size bra, a most unusual size. By the time I turned forty, those melons were rapidly approaching a shape resembling a couple of rugby footballs. Add to that the regular backaches from the sheer weight of them, and the shoulder discomfort from bra straps holding up parcels loaded with leaden bosomly flesh. I've always had bad posture, directly attributable to being heavy-chested. My mother, on the other hand, had a beautiful carriage, and I don't mean Cobb and Co.

I had had thirty years of practice at minimising my bosom, so many people were unaware just how large it was.

Occasionally I was persuaded to wear outfits that featured my breasts by various friends and employers, but it was always with reluctance that I agreed. I was never comfortable with the unwanted attention my generous mammary glands attracted. I always hoped I had far more interesting assets than my breasts.

I'd never been able to go bra-less. *Cosmopolitan* magazine once warned that a woman must never consider bra-less-ness if she couldn't pass the 'Pencil Test'. In other words, if you can hold a pencil under your breast, you need support. I used to joke that, never mind the pencil, I could hold an entire packet of Textas under my breast. All colours. Or a box of seventy-two Derwents. These mammaries weren't even functional for feeding, their size making it impossible for my baby to nurse properly without being suffocated. Disappointing and frustrating, for both mother and infant alike. So for me my breasts were neither useful nor ornamental, just an ever-increasing nuisance. A source of discomfort and anxiety.

For a long time I'd been hankering for a breast reduction and now I was finally going to consult a surgeon. My family was very supportive. My mother had been urging me to have a breast reduction since I was in my twenties. My dad was too polite to mention the subject, thank God. Joby kindly said that he thought my chest was perfectly fine as it was but, if it made me happier to remove some of it, then he was happy for me to go ahead with the surgery.

I went to see well-respected plastic surgeon Graham Isaacs, one of the kindest and most compassionate medical practitioners I've ever met. He patiently explained the entire procedure in full detail with diagrams, drawings and photographs, and answered my questions. I made an earnest request for small breasts like my mother's. I had always coveted the freedom that went with her A cups. Graham counselled me that with my body type, a C cup would be more suitable for me. I was easily persuaded; I hadn't been a C cup since I was fifteen years old. Then, of course, he asked me to show him my breasts. Stupidly, I was mortified with embarrassment, blushing to the gills. Proof of the extent of my hang-ups, so to speak.

A date was set for the operation and I went home with the brochures. Sitting at home that night Joby was reading the post-operative instructions aloud from the pamphlet:

- Must wear bra 24 hours a day for twelve weeks.
- Must not drive car, exercise or do heavy chores like vacuuming for a fortnight.
- No sex for a fortnight. After a fortnight moderate sexual activity may be resumed, but only if one is wearing a bra.

Joby paused and then said, 'But I hate wearing a bra during sex.'

The surgery went off without a hitch; there was minimal pain. I loved this whole new adventure with average-sized boobs. I even went bra-less sometimes, a great feeling when you've never known it before. I wished I'd had the surgery years earlier.

Now, eighteen years later, I'm back to a size 10E. They grew back within five years and they are very big. However,

Above: Grandfather Jackson Simpson's 80th birthday in Killara. Back row: cousin Gaye, Mum, aunt Georgina, brother Rod. Middle row: my son Dylan, cousins Katie, Carolynne and Diana, with me, Jackson and cousin Joanne in front. *(Author's private collection)*

Right: Darling John Waters and me as Vernon and Sonia in Neil Simon's *They're Playing Our Song,* which ran for more than 550 performances. *(Author's private collection)*

Above: Opening night party of *They're Playing Our Song* at Sardi's in Melbourne with Derryn Hinch, John Waters and his wife Sally Conabere. My chap Phil Davis is in the background just behind my head. I hardly knew Hinch at this stage. *(Author's private collection)*

Right: February, 1983. Wedding to Hinch in Brighton, Melbourne. Hinch's Best Man, Andrew Peacock, is just behind us. *(Author's private collection)*

Above: At my wedding to Derryn Hinch with my two dear loves, Richard Wherrett and my agent Gloria Payten, Carmen Duncan at right. When Gloria died her sister Nina cried, 'Oh Jacki you were her baby!' *(Author's private collection)*

Right: With John Bell in Tom Stoppard's *The Real Thing*, Sydney Opera House. *(Author's private collection)*

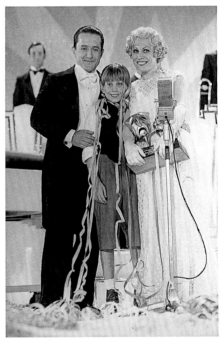

Above: As Billie Dawn in *Born Yesterday,* Sydney Theatre Company (with John Allen as journalist Paul Verrall, who gives her an education and a lot else as well). *(Courtesy STC)*

Right: In Balmain with David Atkins and Ivan Waters, and me in the title role in *The Girl From From Moonooloo. (Author's private collection)*

Above: With Jill and John Farnham at Brook Farm, the vineyard Hinch and I owned at Mount Macedon, near Hanging Rock, Victoria. *(Author's private collection)*

Below: Our TV room in Toorak. There were two other walls full of similar posters. The *Telegraph's* 'How I Felt Jacki' always provoked mirth. *(Author's private collection)*

AUSTRALIA DAY UPDATE

VOL 7 NO 2   NEWSLETTER OF THE NATIONAL AUSTRALIA DAY COUNCIL

TO RUSSIA WITH HOPE
2000 MESSAGES OF PEACE

Two thousand Peace Letters from Australian children aged 8 to 15 have been delivered to Russian children of the same age. The Letters are the central part of the Message of Peace project arranged by the National Australia Day Council.

Message of Peace was created by NADC National President, John Newcombe, OBE, as an Australia Day contribution to the International Year of Peace.

Catriona Thornton, 15, of Clifton Gardens, and Carl Redfern, 14, of Ryde, were chosen to personally deliver the letters.

Actress, Jacki Weaver, a member of the NADC, escorted them on the eight day USSR trip hosted by the USSR Committee of Youth Organisations.

Speaking at the "send-off" function at Sydney International Airport, Mr Valery Zemskov, Charge D'Affaires at the Embassy of the USSR, Canberra, said "These children might give us a lesson on how to be concerned about peace, and how to fight for it."

He said the letters would forge links between the two countries and help promote peace and mutual understanding.

The NADC hopes that many penfriendships will develop from the Peace Letter exchange.

Damien Murphy, 10, of Canberra, wrote, "Is there any way we can achieve world peace? War is a bad thing. If you are interested please help me stop it and we will do it together."

"Let's release the peace from inside our hearts", was the message from Benjamin Goodwill, 11 of Toongarook, Victoria.

John Newcombe told guests at the send-off that the occasion was for him the realisation of a dream of doing something worthwhile for the International Year of Peace that would involve young people.

"This shows that dreams can be realised and you should work to make yours come true," he said.

Cont. page 3

Youthful ambassadors Catriona Thornton and Carl Redfern with Jackie Weaver at Sydney International Airport with the bags of Peace Letters. They were farewelled by young Message of Peace participants holding their certificates of participation aloft.

Above: The media melee outside the Flower Drum Restaurant in Melbourne when the Sheriff arrived to take Hinch straight to Pentridge Prison. *(Author's private collection)*

Right: Going to the USSR, taking 2000 letters from schoolchildren to penpals in Moscow and Minsk. *(Author's private collection)*

Left: At our farm with Dylan, aged sixteen, recovering from his seventh eye operation. *(Author's private collection)*

Below: Cast photo of ABC-TV series *House Rules* where I played an MP. Clockwise from top left, William Zappa, Alex Menglet, Jon Concannon, Mary Siterenos, Marijke Mann, Bud Tingwell, Matt Day, Jacob Kino, Gil Tucker, Nadine Garner and me in the middle in pink. *(Author's private collection)*

THE AUSTRALIAN *magazine*

THE GREATEST CAST OF ALL

Left: The Australian newspaper's weekend magazine. Clockwise from top, John Bell as Cyrano de Bergerac, Garry McDonald, Ruth Cracknell as Lady Bracknell, Judy Davis as Hedda Gabler, Robyn Nevin as Lady Macbeth and me in my *Born Yesterday* beaded dress. *(Courtesy News Limited, 31 December 1988)*

Below: Second wedding to Hinch in Hawaii, on the island of Kauai at Lois and Harold Hunt's cliff-top house. That's them with Nancy Boyer as bridesmaid in white. Bali Hai in the background. *(Author's private collection)*

Above: 8 March 1991, Dad's 70th birthday at the Regal Restaurant in Sydney.
(Author's private collection)

Below: Australian Gothic. Tony Sheldon and I and eyelash curlers, backstage at the Playhouse at Festival Centre Adelaide in Nicholas Enright's *Daylight Saving.*
(Author's private collection)

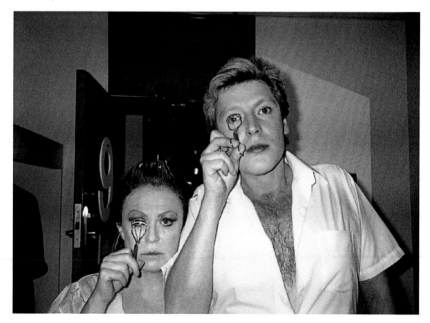

Left: With dear Nick Enright in Michael Gow's *Away* for Sydney Theatre Company. I always have this in my theatre dressing room wherever I go. *(Author's private collection)*

Below: On location for the film *Cosi* by Louis Nowra, with Pamela Rabe, Toni Collette and Barry Otto. *(Author's private collection)*

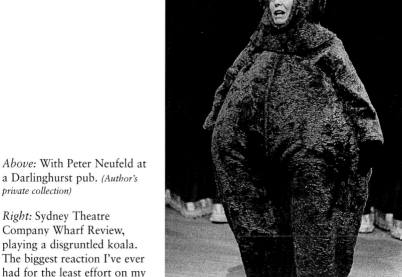

Above: With Peter Neufeld at a Darlinghurst pub. *(Author's private collection)*

Right: Sydney Theatre Company Wharf Review, playing a disgruntled koala. The biggest reaction I've ever had for the least effort on my part. *(Author's private collection)*

Above: December 2000. Dylan and Richie at Aria Restaurant in Circular Quay, for Dylan's 30th birthday. *(Author's private collection)*

Below: Sitting on Richie's blue couch with dear friends: Jennifer Hagen in foreground, Ruth Cracknell, Kirrily Nolan and her husband David Downer. *(Author's private collection)*

Left: Naked publicity shot of me for the Sydney Theatre Company production of Bea Christian's *Old Masters,* a scary ordeal for a 54-year-old. A six-foot tall copy of it hung in the Wharf Theatre walkway for months. *(Courtesy of Jez Allen and STC)*

Below: Old Masters. Outside the Wharf Theatre dressing room, Sydney Harbour in the background. Clockwise from top left: Leanna Walsman, Frank Whitten, Julie Forsyth, Max Cullen, me, Aaron Blabey. *(Author's private collection)*

Above: Backstage during *Old Masters* in the Wharf Theatre dressing room with wonderful Julie Forsyth. *(Author's private collection)*

Below: The family on Channel 9's *This is Your Life*. Left to right: my aunt Georgina, nephew Nick Weaver, son Dylan, me, brother Rod, sister-in-law Helen Wellings. *(Author's private collection)*

Above: My very dear friends and agents Philomena Moore and Pauline Lee of International Casting Service, founded by the late Gloria Payten. *(Author's private collection)*

Right: My gorgeous daughter-in-law Makiko Matsumoto and my darling Dylan. *(Author's private collection)*

Above: October 2003. My husband Sean Taylor and I on the balcony of our honeymoon suite, at the Hydro Majestic Hotel in the Blue Mountains, after our wedding at my brother's house in Birchgrove. My dad used to say that I was conceived at the Hydro Majestic Hotel. *(Author's private collection)*

they haven't dropped down to my waist, which would have been more than likely if I hadn't had the surgery. The nipples are still a reasonable 18 centimetres from the collarbone, much the same as they were the day of the surgery. Melons, not rugby footballs. Most importantly, I don't hate my front appendages anymore, even though they are again unusually large. It took a while—many years in fact—but I now actually like them. Like them very much.

If all this seems petty, trivial and vain in a world full of serious suffering and sorrow, forgive me. Sure, I admit I'm vain. But it was never a petty or trivial matter for me. It caused me years of pain and angst. If I hadn't felt such guilt about what I thought others would judge to be so frivolous a complaint, it might not have taken me so long to do something positive about it. I hope the twelve-year-old girl I heard about recently doesn't suffer the same pain and angst for too many years. It's avoidable.

During the 1980s Barry Cohen, then Minister for the Arts and Environment, appointed me to the board of the National Australia Day Council with John Newcombe, the tennis champion, as chairman. Other board members included Rugby Union international Mark Ella, poet Chris Wallace-Crabbe and Father Brian Gore, the Roman Catholic priest who later became a national hero when he was jailed on a trumped-up murder charge in the Philippines and then finally released. We met several times a year in every state and territory. Our job was to encourage the celebration of Australia Day throughout the nation and, best of all, to choose the

Australian of the Year. During my first year our choice was Aboriginal leader Lowitja (Lois) O'Donoghue, a very gracious and worthy recipient. Other honorees during my tenure included singer John Farnham and cricketer Allan Border.

In 1987, the International Year of Peace, the Australia Day Council sent me to accompany two teenage Australian schoolchildren on a goodwill mission to the then Soviet Union, carrying with us two thousand letters of friendship to children over there. It was around the time of perestroika and glasnost. Before we left Sydney there was a farewell for us at which the Soviet Ambassador, an extremely charming and cultured gentleman, told me that, whatever I wanted to do in Moscow, I should just let him know and he would see to it. I really liked him. When I told my cynical husband, he jokingly remarked: 'He's probably KGB.' Less than a year later this same diplomat was expelled from Australia for spying. I think his name was Ivanov.

Moscow in late autumn was amazing. Magnificent Red Square already glistened with the cold. People waited for hours in the icy wind to file down a staircase beneath the ground to look at Lenin's waxy-looking dead body lying in state, surrounded by strange greenish-tinged lighting on a raised platform. There were no churches then in the Soviet Union—the people's *means* to worship may have been removed, but not their *need* to worship.

In the USSR we were accompanied constantly by a brilliant young interpreter in her twenties, Katya, and a male chaperone, Vlad. We visited several schools and met scores of children and were treated royally. We took an overnight four-bunk sleeper train to Minsk in Byelorussia, where we were woken at dawn by a porter serving sweet black tea from a samovar. In Minsk we met even more children, many of them flaxen-haired. In an impressive and deeply disturbing museum we were shown relics of the horrors of the Great War of 1941–45. Tact prevented me from mentioning that my parents had begun fighting Hitler two years earlier than 1941.

Back in Moscow our Russian minders, Katya and Vlad, were surprised and impressed when we were unexpectedly summoned to the office of a high-ranking member of the Politburo. The five of us sat on the other side of his huge desk while he talked to me about theatre and Australian literature. Occasionally he'd glance at a dossier in front of him that I finally realised must have been about me because he said, 'You have worked in two Chekov plays.'

'No, only one,' I replied.

'You have forgotten one of them,' he corrected me firmly. And he was right. He knew more about me than I did.

That night we were guests of honour at a performance at the Moscow Arts Theatre. A snapshot was taken of me sitting in Stanislavsky's chair and they presented me with an original sepia photograph of the first cast reading of Chekov's *The Seagull*.

Later in 1987, I was offered an interesting new project. I've never been in a soap opera on TV, even as a guest—a soap opera being a daily serial, a melodrama with an ongoing story line. Over the years people would often send me synopses of one-episode-a-week TV series, with me as the central character. However, I seldom, if ever, was asked to be part of a team. It bothered me that maybe I was perceived as not being a team player. For example, I must be one of the few Australian actresses who wasn't in *Prisoner*. Or *Neighbours*. Or *Home and Away*. My cousins in England think I'm not really legit, because they've never seen me in any of the Aussie soap operas which get huge exposure in the UK. And Australians old enough to remember think that I was in the ABC-TV's long-running soap *Bellbird*. But that wasn't me, it was Lynette Curran.

No, I was never offered a soap or a series with a big integrated cast—only loners. But then Ross Dimsey and the ABC offered me a series about a housewife who becomes an MP almost by accident. It was called *House Rules*. It was a novel idea and there were plenty of other interesting characters to relate to, connect with and share the workload with. So I said yes.

There was a great cast, which included Matt Day and Nadine Garner as my children, and Bill Zappa and Bud Tingwell as my political rivals. Nadine had played my daughter with cerebral palsy in *Joe Egg* and she was terrific. High-spirited and intelligent, she was seventeen during *House Rules*. Matt Day was fifteen and we were very close. We spent so much time together at work that Matt confided in me about everything. For my birthday he gave me a record by a group called the Hard Ons singing a song called 'Dick Cheese', with a card that said 'To my other mother. Love from your little bunny.'

Alan Hardy, son of my dear friend Frank Hardy, was engaged as executive producer. There was also a great film crew, who worked like dogs. Cameraman John Pavlovic and his wife Marg are still good friends of mine today. But it was a very hard slog for me—I was in almost every scene. Some of the storylines were terrific while others were downright silly. Some mornings I'd be in that make-up chair at five in the morning and not get out of the Melbourne ABC's Elsternwick studios until seven or eight at night. I was shooting as many as twenty-five scenes a day, from two completely different episodes and all out of sequence. It's something soap actors take in their stride. But not this little tawny duck.

One dark winter's morning around 4.30 am, I'd just washed my hair and was putting on my socks to go to work when a searing pain shot up my spine. I fell on the floor and couldn't get up. My lower back had gone into spasm. Joby called our GP, Richard Ward, who told him to take me straight to hospital.

Joby carried me to the car, then carried me into admissions at The Avenue in Armadale. He then drove to the film set location, where about fifty people including extras were waiting for me, to tell them that I wouldn't be turning up that day. I was still in hospital a week later on an intravenous drip. I was diagnosed with a degenerative disc problem that returns from time to time though never as badly as that first time. A cumbersome steel back brace resembling an instrument of medieval torture was made for me, and I still wear it a few times a year when I feel my back about to go into spasm.

It was great to get back to work a few days after I was released from hospital. The cast and crew gave me a fabulous welcome, even though I'd caused everyone such inconvenience simply because I hadn't put my socks on properly.

One afternoon we were in the middle of shooting a scene in the Elsternwick studios when producer Ross Dimsey arrived to escort me into the inner office of the make-up department for an urgent private phone call. Dylan's father, John Walters, was dead.

John had been an invalid for four years, ever since he'd suffered a haemorrhage during brain surgery for an aneurysm. He'd been in several different nursing homes in Sydney and Canberra, and various friends had taken good care of him. His short-term memory had gone and, when he wasn't under sedation, he was often highly distressed. Dylan and I went to see him whenever we could. Dylan loved his father totally and unconditionally. It was heart-breaking for him to witness his father's slow and painful deterioration, which had begun when Dylan was barely thirteen.

I shot my remaining two scenes for that day, then went home to organise the funeral and our flights to Sydney. When Dylan arrived home from school I said: 'Sit down, Dybie, I want to talk to you.'

Straightaway he said: 'Dad's dead, isn't he?'

Dylan was torn between needing to speak at his father's funeral and not knowing if he was strong enough. Joby gave him excellent advice: 'Imagine yourself in ten years time and whether you'd regret it if you didn't.' So seventeen-year-old

Dylan wrote and delivered the eulogy, chose the order of service, was MC and selected all the music.

Like me, Dylan was blessed with a dad who loved Shakespeare. As soon as he could read, he and his dad would play a game where Dylan had to open the *Complete Works* at any page and quote a line. John would then have to identify the play, the character, the act and scene.

So Dylan chose two Shakespearean pieces to recite at his father's funeral—from *The Tempest*, Prospero's speech ('For we are such stuff as dreams are made on', etc) and, from *Hamlet*, 'Good night sweet prince and flights of angels sing thee to thy rest'. Sitting in the front pew with me watching Dylan being so composed were Joby, my mother, father, brother and Richard Wherrett. We were all proud of him.

When we finished shooting *House Rules* for that year and Ross Dimsey asked if I'd commit to another series, I turned it down. I wanted to spend more time with Joby and Dylan. And I was exhausted.

In 1988, Joby was now rating well on his own prime-time TV current affairs show, *Hinch at Seven*. Christopher Skase had lured him away from Radio 3AW onto his newly acquired Seven Network. I always liked Christopher and Pixie Skase. I thought they were gracious, charming and kind. The scale of the opprobrium Christopher received has always seemed to me to be way out of proportion to whatever he was supposed to have done. And he was never actually convicted. Regardless of the fact that Skase never faced court because he flew the coop, the media and the general public had Skase convicted before he even took flight. So much for innocent until proven guilty. I think I'd have run too, if I were Skase. And I was puzzled at all the sneering by the press and the likes of Amanda Vanstone that Skase was faking his illness. You only had to be around him a short while to realise he always had serious respiratory problems. Amazingly, even after he died people talked as if they still didn't believe he'd really been ill. How dead do you have to be before people believe you're really sick?

I remember Christopher Skase as a visionary who flew too close to the sun and got burnt and was brought down by circumstances, hubris, and taking one risk too many. But it's not a popular view and I never raise it at dinner parties.

By now Joby and I owned an apartment and a house in Hawaii, with the help of a loan from Channel 7. A few months previously, while I was still shooting *House Rules*, we had visited the island of Kauai for a weekend with an eye to buying an investment condo. We saw one, Pua-Poa, on an ocean cliff top and bought it on the spot. A sensible investment. We also looked at a beautiful Japanese-style house and fell in love with it, but we agreed it was out of our price range and left it at that.

I had had to return home a day earlier than Joby because of my filming schedule on *House Rules*. Soon after my plane landed in Melbourne, Joby rang from Hawaii to say he'd bought the Japanese house as well, even though we'd agreed we couldn't afford it. 3912 Namakeha Loop, Princeville, on the island of Kauai was ours for nearly ten years. We always referred to it as Namakeha.

I loved being in Kauai, and never wanted to leave it once I was there. But I never swam in the ocean, not once in ten years. I walked on the sand a few times, but I'm not really a beach person. I gazed out at the ocean for many hours from the cliffs just beside our house. I loved the scented rain that falls nearly every afternoon for twenty minutes around three. The fragrant tropical rainforests, the bushwalks, the pristine atmosphere, the regular rainbows. The mystic spiritual allure of the place.

I loved the spectacular cliffs of the Na Pali Coast. The fresh raw tuna, straight out of the Pacific Ocean. The hibiscus bush and the plumeria tree (the Hawaiian name for frangipani) and the papaya tree in our backyard. Our Japanese garden, with its waterfall and spongy spiky tufts of oriental grass. The rough bars, like The Oarhouse, where they serve margaritas the way they should taste. Joby and I even had a second wedding, or reaffirmation, in Kauai (all his idea). It was a traditional barefoot ceremony on a cliff-top in Harold Hunt's garden, with his wife, Lois, a celebrant, presiding and sixty guests. It was actually bigger than our first wedding. With sacred Hawaiian dancing.

I loved the Hawaiian people, with their laidback attitude and their cool accents and their houses full of dogs and their front yards full of car wrecks. Their good cheap bookstores. Their roadside garage sales, full of unexpected treasures. And the state of Hawaii always votes Democrat.

There's a law in Kauai that no building can be taller than the highest palm tree. So there are no ugly high-rise blocks.

My friend Nancy Boyer visited Kauai from Alaska one weekend, and was still there twenty years later. There are ageing hippies, still living in a 1960s time warp, deep within the rugged Na Pali Valley. Most of them naked.

One year I went to Kauai five times. Once I went for three weeks and stayed for nine weeks. I tried to write a novel there. I tried to write a play there. I didn't finish writing either of them. Maybe I should be there now writing this, and it might come out more quickly. Maybe not. Maybe this would go the way of my play and my novel if I took it to Kauai. Maybe if I went to Kauai just one more time it's possible I might stay forever. I miss Kauai.

The plan was that short-term holiday rentals to tourists of the two properties in Kauai would help pay off the mortgage. A sensible investment plan. There was a big demand for such places all year round and for the first four years the plan worked perfectly. And then came Hurricane Iniki. It was 11 September 1992. Hurricane Iniki was a massive cyclone one and a half times greater than Darwin's Cyclone Tracy. It destroyed much of the island of Kauai and closed down the tourist trade for two or three years.

Houses in our street were flattened into piles of splinters and these were not flimsy beach shacks but sturdy structures worth a million dollars American. Our house remained standing because we had German steel hurricane blinds, but our roof peeled off like Alfoil and was found a hundred metres away. Consequently there was a lot of internal damage to the house. Our condo too was severely damaged, almost totally destroyed.

When Hurricane Iniki hit, Joby was in the Namakeha house with Bob Rogers, Nancy Boyer and a couple of neighbours. He and Bob had gone there intending to spend the weekend with Terry Hayes, but they didn't get off the island for two weeks. Terry never made it; he flew in to Honolulu and was then sent back to LA. All flights to Kauai were cancelled because they knew the hurricane was on its way. Bob and Joby had caught the last flight to Kauai, not realising what lay in store.

At the height of the storm the two-storey house next door collapsed. Joby ran through the debris and dragged out a honeymoon couple trapped underneath the rubble and brought them to our house. During this, Joby managed to break three of his ribs.

Phone communication went. Power, water, everything. After two days Joby managed to call me from a pay phone with a queue of three hundred people waiting to use it. I was rehearsing at the Wharf in Sydney's Walsh Bay and had to run the entire length of the wharf just in time to hear him say: 'Don't worry, I'm OK. I love you. Bye.' Click.

An intrepid Australian TV news crew raced to Honolulu and illegally commandeered a helicopter piloted by a stogie-chomping Vietnam-vet renegade (yes, he did play Wagner in the cockpit). He flew to Kauai at 200 feet to avoid radar detection. The film crew weren't sure where to find Hinch and told the pilot they thought he lived on a golf course. 'Listen, buddy, the entire fuckin' two hundred square miles of fuckin' Kauai is a fuckin' golf course!' yelled the pilot. Not quite true but there are a lot of golf courses. I never played golf either.

When the helicopter buzzed the house, Bob Rogers and Joby were on the roof fixing a tarpaulin. 'That'll be for you,' said Bob sarcastically. The news crew landed in our backyard.

Insurance paid for much of the damage, but recovery was painstakingly slow and so there were no holiday renters to help pay off the mortgage. Back home we were paying huge interest rates on loans taken out to renovate the Toorak house. The cost of the renovations had tripled since their original estimates.

We were overstretched financially. We were starting to go broke. But at least we had shares in Qintex.

chapter eleven

Intimations of Mortality

HINCH AND I WERE WORKING VERY HARD. BUT THE HARDER WE worked, the more steadily our material assets seemed to be sliding away.

It doesn't matter—they're only *things*, I kept telling myself; we still have each other, we enjoy good health. Relatively good health anyway. If you didn't count a dodgy liver each from frequent imbibing and constant carousing. Life was a party. We played hard. But we also worked hard.

After four years Hinch was unexpectedly sacked by Channel 7 from *Hinch at Seven* even though his ratings were good. In no time he was eagerly snatched up by Channel 10, where he fronted his own prime-time current affairs program *Hinch*, five nights a week for two years before being sacked yet again despite consistently high ratings. The general public watched him in their millions but he must have had a knack for getting up the noses of TV executives.

He was splitting his time between Sydney and Melbourne, living in the legendary Sebel Town House in Elizabeth Bay. He was making occasional visits to the other capitals as well, broadcasting his program from all of them. According to research, he was one of the top three most recognisable faces in Australia. He even got a reco once while walking along the Great Wall of China.

During the Melbourne Theatre Company's hugely successful production of David Williamson's *Emerald City* at the Victorian Arts Centre, my parents drove down from Sydney to stay with us for a few days and to see the play. During the interval my mother became so ill that she was unable to go back into the theatre. She had by now had surgery several times following her heart bypass, such was the extent of her heart disease.

After the show she insisted we all drive up to the farm as planned, even though she felt dreadful. When we got there we gave her a hot toddy and put her straight to bed, but by next morning she was delirious and hallucinating and we were all frightened. Derryn called our GP, Richard Ward, who told us to take her to hospital immediately.

That car trip was a nightmare, with my mother lying on the back seat, my father up front and me driving for two hours through blinding torrential rain. Thank God for my trusty old blue vehicle, no matter how vulgar.

At the hospital they were waiting for us and carried her in. My mother had cellulitis, blood poisoning (septicaemia), cause unknown. She spent two weeks in hospital, during which my father eventually had to return to work in Sydney.

My mother was still too seriously ill to travel and she spent another six weeks recuperating in Toorak with us. I had to set the alarm to wake me every three hours to administer her medication. I was so tired, I lurched around the house like a zombie and then tried to buck up on-stage every night. My mother, always the most gracious and appreciative of house guests, apologised constantly for being a burden, despite my assurances to the contrary. To this day I fret that maybe I was less patient with my patient than I might have been.

On top of everything, my poor mother had a pathological aversion to cats. An ailurophobe? And we had two beautiful cats, Tom and Elliott, who were utter hooligans, with no sense of shame. They cannily sensed my mother's antipathy towards them and would take flying leaps at her until they were banned from the house.

I did a Neil Simon farce called *Rumors*. Lynda Stoner was in the cast and I soon understood why Derryn had been so smitten by her. Before long I came to love her too. Lynda is a very dear soul.

When we were performing in the Sydney season of *Rumors*, I got a phone call from Melbourne during the Saturday matinee interval to say Dylan had broken his leg playing football at school. He was in plaster for three months. More grist to the mill for my silo full of maternal guilt.

Beginning in 1990 I did the first of what was to be many performances in many places over the next fifteen years—at venues that included the Sydney Opera House, Melbourne's VAC, Perth Cathedral and Hobart's Theatre Royal—of *Love Letters* by AN Gurney, who had tutored Nick Enright at the Juillard School in New York. It's a clever piece for two actors, male and female, who relate the story of their lifelong relationship from the ages of six to sixty through the simple device of reading by turn their love letters to each other. It's funny, sad and easy to stage at short notice.

Over the years I've performed *Love Letters* with six different actors, including John Waters, John O'May, Campbell McComas, Sean Taylor and, on three separate occasions, for charity in Hawaii with American actors Tom Villard and Wayne Hudgins (later Michael Hart), both sadly no longer with us, dead from AIDS. I remember how moved my mother was after seeing John Waters and me in *Love Letters* at the Opera House. Though not usually given to displays of sentimentality, she seemed to be really deeply affected by that performance. It was to be the last time she saw me on-stage.

During one of my extended sojourns in Kauai, I went to the island's only cinema complex one day with my friend Nancy Boyer (who's from Butternut, Michigan) to see Peter Weir's film *Dead Poets' Society*, starring Robin Williams. It's about a private boys' school where they're all in a production of *A Midsummer Night's Dream*—one of the boys wants to be a professional actor, but his strict father is bitterly opposed to this and things end tragically. It's a beautiful film and I love it. When Nancy and I arrived home from the cinema, Dylan called me from Australia saying that Richard Wherrett had just offered him the role of Francis Flute/Thisbe in *A Midsummer Night's Dream* at the Sydney Opera House, and asking whether I thought he should take it.

Dylan had just left school and was planning to audition for NIDA the following year. I told him it was his decision, but I thought he should do it. This was the highly successful and controversial dance party/ecstasy/Malcolm Maclaren's *Waltz Darling* version, with the wonderful Susan Lyons, brilliant Helen Buday, adorable Rebecca Frith and Luciano Martucci as a terrific Bottom the Weaver. It was the celebration of the hedonistic eighties version, with the magic potion the new drug ecstasy, the fairies a motley crew of cross-dressers, drag queens and eccentrics with much disco-inspired Vogue/strike a pose choreography by Kim Walker. Teenagers not keen on Shakespeare flocked to it and loved it and a new generation of theatre-goers is always a good thing.

It was thoroughly entertaining, and some say it may have inspired Baz Luhrmann's approach to his film of *Romeo and Juliet*. Richard had originally cast Nicole Kidman as Helena but, just before rehearsals began, he reluctantly released Nicole from her contract when she was offered her first Hollywood movie, *Days of Thunder*, starring Tom Cruise. She went with his blessing

It was Dylan's second role in Shakespeare for Richard Wherrett, and he was still only eighteen. When Dylan was eleven Richard had directed him as Young Macduff in *Macbeth* at the Opera House. It was star-studded: John Bell and Robyn Nevin as the Macbeths; Colin Friels and Susan

Lyons as the Macduffs. Also in the cast were Hugo Weaving, Bruce Spence and Heather Mitchell. It was great experience for Dylan and he was very good. Things were looking promising for him.

Nick Enright wrote a play called *Daylight Saving* for his close friend Sandy Gore, who had a success with it at the Ensemble Theatre in Kirribilli. However, Sandy didn't want to tour with it so I played her role in the Melbourne Theatre Company version at the Russell Street Theatre.

I've always felt ambivalent about Russell Street. Even though some terrific work has been done there over the years and it has seen many triumphs, I have always felt that this particular theatre had a haunted vibe about it. I once heard it had formerly been a revivalist meeting house for fundamentalists. It was as though something unfortunate or mysterious had occurred on the premises long before it became a playhouse. For me its very walls reeked of something sinister, even tragic. Exorcisms, perhaps?

But I enjoyed doing *Daylight Saving* there. A light romantic comedy, it had a terrific cast that included Vince Colosimo and John O'May. The following year, 1991, we toured it all over Australia, with Tony Sheldon replacing John O, who left to do three years in *Phantom of the Opera*.

There was a free week or two just before the Perth season, so I went to Sydney to see Dylan, who was now in first-year acting at NIDA. Dylan was boarding with Nick Enright in his Chalder Street cottage called Budgewoi in Newtown. On this occasion Nick was going to be out of town for a few days and suggested I stay at his place too and sleep in his room.

Mummy was about to go into the Adventist Hospital for her fifth bout of surgery. My plan was to stay a few days, see a few friends, visit Mummy, then go home the day before her operation. But suddenly my brother Rod's father-in-law, Helen's father Bert Corkhill, died and Rod had to go to Melbourne to be a pallbearer. The funeral was to be held on the same day as Mummy's operation and Rod suggested I delay my return home to Melbourne a few days, just in case there were complications in what we were convinced was merely a routine procedure.

Dylan and I went to the hospital to visit Mum the night before her operation. We stayed until well after ten o'clock and we were all laughing so much the sister had to tell us to shut up. Mum had asked Dylan to do some bits from the TV series *Blackadder* for her amusement and it seemed to me he ended up doing an entire episode. She was sitting up in bed looking very pretty, rosy, lipsticked and smiling.

The next morning I rose very early from Nick's bed in Newtown and went for a long walk that included a stroll through beautiful old St Stephen's Anglican Church in Church Street, Newtown, sitting on a pew and thinking about my mother. The grounds of that church house the graves of many of Sydney's earliest settlers, including the eccentric woman whose true life story fascinated Charles Dickens so much that he based the character of Miss Havisham in *Great Expectations* on her. Jilted on her wedding day she left the wedding feast on the table and continued to wear her bridal gown for decades. She was obviously in denial, big time. That day in the church, I think I was in denial too.

After breakfast Dylan went to NIDA in Kensington and I went to Marsfield to pick up Dad and take him to the Sanitarium, which is what we called that hospital then. We waited many hours in that waiting room, just Dad and me. Reading, chatting, drinking cups of tea . . . At about 5.30 pm Mum's favourite nursing sister and the Seventh Day Adventist chaplain solemnly entered the room and my heart leapt up past my larynx. Together they told us that she wasn't going to make it. That she'd passed away.

Somehow Dad couldn't get the gist of what they were saying at all. Complete and total denial. 'What do you mean?' he asked several times, like a child.

'Mummy's dead, Dad,' I finally had to tell him as gently as I could. Not easy to be gentle when I was feeling so angry.

They took us into intensive care to see her. The heart–lung machine was still operating and so her chest was still rising and falling as if she were asleep, even though she was officially brain dead.

They agreed to my request that the machine not be turned off until my brother arrived from the airport at seven. He strode into intensive care smiling. I met him at the desk and said: 'She's gone.' His face crumpled like a broken mirror.

Dylan called from NIDA. 'Oh, Dybie . . .' was all I could manage to get out.

'I'm on my way,' he said and hung up. He was there within no time.

Derryn rang at 6.45, fifteen minutes before he was due to go live to air at Channel 10 in Melbourne. 'Hello, darling. How's Ede?'

'She's dead,' I said. His secretary, Suzy Jaeger, managed to get him on an 8.30 flight and he was with us by 10.30.

The nursing sister took Mummy's wedding ring off and put it on my middle finger; all the while I was bawling tears of rage while leaning against the tall chaplain's arm. I remember noticing copious amounts of my snot on the sleeve of his good blue suit and feeling no remorse about it.

My dad was in a sort of daze, like shell-shock. Rod and Dad and Dylan and I clung to each other, weeping softly as the life-support machine was turned off. Gradually her breathing subsided. As she took her final breath, my brother whispered in my ear: 'We didn't get the rice pudding recipe, dammit!' It was a good joke that would have made Mum laugh. It was 2 April 1991.

The funeral happened. Rod spoke. I spoke. Dad was still in shock. We buried her in her favourite silk dress with the roses on it that I had given her for her birthday. She looked beautiful.

Three days later I was opening in *Daylight Saving* in Perth at the Regal Theatre. Everyone treated me very kindly and we did a good show. But my grief was deep and keenly felt. I'd been robbed of a mother and much too soon. We were just starting to get along well, woman to woman, on an equal basis. My mother and I still had plenty of unresolved issues—I was forty-three years old and she'd only just stopped treating me like a child—and now she was gone.

Mum had often said to Rod, jokingly: 'You'll dance on my grave, Rodney.' So a few weeks after she died Rod and I went to Ryde cemetery, where I took a photo of him doing a dainty highland fling on her burial plot. If only she'd seen him, she'd have laughed like a drain.

When we were in Perth one of our cast members, Maggie Millar, asked me to go to lunch at Ann and Peter Carnley's beautiful house in Mount Street. Peter was then the Anglican Archbishop of Perth. He was also the Primate, the elected head archbishop for all of Australia. The lunch in their garden was superb and we became fast friends immediately. Until they retired to their tulip farm in 2005, I usually stayed with the Carnleys in the Archbishop's house whenever I was in Perth, sometimes for several weeks at a time (sleeping in the same bed as Archbishop Desmond Tutu, though not simultaneously). My friendship with Peter and Ann is one I value enormously. We've known each other for almost fifteen years now.

Peter told me about a priest he'd been to theological college with called Ian 'Freddy' Brown, who was rector at St Stephen's Anglican Church in Church Street, Richmond, just a short drive from Toorak. Peter said he thought Freddy and I would get along well and he was right. We hit it off straightaway.

Freddy's no ordinary vicar. Freddy loves the theatre—the more avant-garde the better for Fred. He's also a great cook and a voracious reader, with the biggest private library I've ever seen, as well as a breathtaking art collection. We love going to the cinema together. I've often stayed at Freddy's for weeks at a time while doing shows in Melbourne. He's great company. He's also a good buddy and spiritual mentor.

I was in Rockhampton touring with *Daylight Saving* when Joby rang me from New Zealand to say Betty Hinch had died, from lung cancer. Both our mothers dead within months of each other. Both mothers killed by that filthy disgusting weed: tobacco. A lethal habit. And such a stupid-looking pastime. I loved Betty Hinch and give her the credit for Derryn's good points. I went into Rockhampton's beautiful sandstone Anglican cathedral to meditate and shed a few quiet tears for Betty Hinch. The Dean, Chris Whittall, found me in there and made me a cup of tea in the Deanery. He was wearing a T-shirt that said: *If God had wanted me to be rich, he'd have made me a TV evangelist.* He and his wife Gillian came to see our show the following night. When darling Vince Colosimo was told Chris was a priest but also married, he said, *'That's disgusting!'* The Whittalls and I still keep in touch.

Richard Wherrett left the Sydney Theatre Company after ten years to be a freelance director and Wayne Harrison won the coveted top job and was now running the company. In 1991 Wayne offered me William Nicholson's beautiful play *Shadowlands.* Wayne couriered the script to Melbourne and I devoured it immediately. The minute I finished reading it, still weeping, I rang him to say yes. One of the quickest work decisions ever.

Shadowlands is based on the true-life love story of CS Lewis, Oxford don, Christian philosopher and creator of *The Lion, the Witch and the Wardrobe* and the rest of the Narnia series. I had already read one of his other books, *A Grief Observed*, where Lewis describes grief so eloquently: 'No one ever told me that grief felt so like fear. I am not afraid but the sensation is like being afraid. The same fluttering in the stomach, the same restlessness. There is a sort of invisible blanket between the world and me.' I then read all his other books as well.

In his late middle age, CS Lewis fell in love with a straight-talking, highly intelligent and gifted Jewish poet from New York City named Joy Gresham, who had been a committed Communist. Joy converted to Christianity after experiencing a kind of epiphany when her first husband left her with two small sons to bring up on her own. Inspired by his books, Joy began corresponding with Lewis.

She travelled to England to meet him and they fell in love. Eventually Joy and Lewis married, but their time together was cut tragically short by Joy's death from cancer. Joy's son Douglas, aged nine, figures prominently in the story. He believes his mother will be cured by the magic apple, just like in the Narnia story, which Lewis had written partly as a result of losing his own beloved mother when he was also only nine. I love the complexity of this play. The thematic scheme that intertwines love in all its forms with death, the continuity of life and the nature of God.

I saw Nigel Hawthorne and Jane Alexander in *Shadowlands* on Broadway. They were both terrific, and very charming when I met them afterwards.

For the Sydney Theatre Company, John Bell played CS Lewis and I was Joy Gresham, née Davidman. John was marvellous as CS Lewis. I always find John a dream to work with—so open and easy and generous, yet sharp, sinewy and precise. And such energy.

The role of the child in *Shadowlands* is an integral one and two little boys alternated the part. One of them was ten-year-old Abe Forsythe, son of Drew and Trish, in his stage debut. He was perfect. Totally lovable and deeply moving.

Joy Gresham's son, Douglas, was living in Tasmania with his wife and kids, so Wayne and I saw an ideal opportunity to do some research and gain some valuable insights into Joy's character. We flew to Launceston, then Douglas drove us two hours through rugged terrain to their farmhouse at Ringarooma. Douglas let me read letters Joy had written to him at school. I read her poems and novels, saw several fascinating photos of her, and slept under the crocheted rug that had been her blanket when she was dying and confined to a wheelchair.

Joy was of Polish origin, striking to look at—dark eyes, heavy brows and black hair—and had an educated New York accent. The opposite of me, I guess. The wig, make-up and wardrobe departments transformed me—even some of my own friends didn't recognise me on-stage. The greatest compliment was from Douglas saying it was like watching his real mother.

The critics and the audiences loved it. Many people came to see it several times. Actor Lynn Redgrave, of the great acting dynasty, sent me a note that said:

Dear Jacki Weaver,
Thank you so much for your beautiful, bold, clear, 'Joy'
full and deeply moving performance Saturday night.
I loved the play and you made us understand so
clearly why Jack loved Joy.

With admiration,
Lynn Redgrave

Dying a lingering death eight times a week on the Opera House stage and weeping all those tears so soon after my mother's death was difficult. In retrospect, however, it was probably therapeutic for me at that time to be giving vent to all that grief. And all in the course of my normal working hours.

I was also drinking copious amounts of alcohol, more than I'd ever drunk before in my life. One night I even performed the play drunk. To my deep shame. As I stood, terrified, in the wings, waiting to make my entrance, barely able to see, feeling like a rag doll, I made a promise. I swore that, if I could get through this performance unscathed and without the audience realising that I was inebriated, I would give up drinking. With the support of some good fellow actors, I got through it.

I am certain the audience didn't twig that I was smashed. John Bell didn't, not even when he had to kiss me. When I apologised to John after the show, he didn't know what I was talking about. After that night, I stopped drinking for two years.

In 1992, a year after the Sydney production, I played Joy again in a completely new and reinterpreted mounting of *Shadowlands* directed by Janis Balodis for the Melbourne Theatre Company. This time the wonderful Max Phipps played CS Lewis. Max Phipps' version of Lewis was very different from John Bell's. They were equally brilliant—I was very fortunate to be in two beautiful, and yet so diverse, productions of the same play.

Then Wayne offered me *Six Degrees of Separation* by John Guare, a play I love. It's a tragi-comedy about contemporary relationships in Manhattan circa 1990 and contains the character Ouisa's famous monologue, a summation of the play's theme: that we are all each other's brothers and keepers to varying degrees and it's up to us whether to take that responsibility and to what degree.

OUISA: *I read somewhere that everybody on this planet is separated by only six other people. Six degrees of separation. Between us and everybody else on this planet. The president of the United States. A gondolier in Venice. Fill in the names. I find that A) tremendously comforting that we're so close and B) like Chinese water torture that we're so close. Because you have to find the right six people to make the connection. It's not just big names. It's anyone. A native in a rain forest. A Tierra del Fuegan. An Eskimo. I am bound to everyone on this planet by a trail of six people. It's a profound thought . . . How every person is a new door, opening up into other worlds. Six degrees of separation between me and everyone else on this planet. But to find the right six people.*

I accepted the role of Ouisa, but I decided that before it I would take a sabbatical to London for the first time in twenty years. Then I would spend some time in New York City, in what had become an annual custom, and follow that with a break in Hawaii.

I was away for nearly three months. All by myself. Not drinking. Not an easy task. In London I stayed at Claridge's. (Yeah, yeah, I know what you're thinking: no wonder they went broke.) Hinch had called the hotel ahead of my arrival to organise an upgrade to a suite, to surprise me.

After I checked in (the staff were obviously expecting me to be someone slightly important, or at least far less unprepossessing than I turned out to be), the assistant manager—impeccably polite and resplendent in a tailcoat—ushered me up to the beautifully appointed Lady Hamilton Suite. It was breathtaking—full of antiques, green silk wallpaper, original paintings and a four-poster bed. Never one to be blasé, I was unable to curb my enthusiasm and I very *un*coolly and loudly exclaimed: 'WOW!'

'We are so glad that Madam is pleased,' replied the assistant manager.

The Lady Hamilton Suite included my own butler, who murmured: 'I've taken the liberty of running Madam a bath after your long journey. And then perhaps a gin and tonic? Or some tea and scones?' The scones were hot from his kitchen at the end of the hallway. And the tea was in a silver pot—Regency, I think.

If this is how the other half lives, it's not half bad. I actually became chums with all the staff I met at Claridge's, even though I hadn't turned out to be the countess or heiress they'd been anticipating. Maybe because of that. Clearly, it was evident I was from Downstairs.

It was June and London was in the throes of a heatwave. It was stifling. And while the English may be adept at heating premises, they didn't seem to be terribly efficient at cooling them down. Certainly not in 1992.

Wayne Harrison was in London directing a Michael Gow play in Croydon. While he was in the UK, Wayne was hoping to cast one of the key roles in *Six Degrees,* that of the swindler who pretends to be Sidney Poitier's son, and he asked me to sit in on the auditions. I think about twenty beautiful young men applied for the role and all of them were very good. Wayne eventually chose Dhobi Oparei, who'd already been to Australia for one of the festivals with Théâtre de Complicité.

Wayne Harrison made me buy some suede shoes that looked like dinosaurs—fetching but uncomfortable. Wayne also rescued me from the amorous advances of a surprise visitor. A gallant thwarts a galoot. Galahad Harrison.

I took a train to Carlisle in Cumbria's beautiful Lake District, to meet my cousin Linda for the first time. Linda is a Nordic-looking blonde giant of a woman, with a wit like a razor, the daughter of my mother's brother George. After five hours on the train, I alighted on the platform to see Linda waiting for me right down at the other end.

By the time we reached each other somewhere in the middle, Linda was tearful. 'What's wrong?' I asked.

'I just didn't expect you to be so tiny. You're *minute,*' she explained.

I loved being with my cousin, her husband and children in their lovely house in Workington. Six-year-old Angie, already addicted to Australian TV soap operas, wanted me to sound more Aussie. 'Please talk like an Australian, our Jac,' she'd plead wistfully. So I would willingly bung on my broadest

Oz accent whenever requested, sounding roughly like someone from somewhere between Bourke and Brewarrina.

My aunt Nora could never get over the fact that, for the past twenty-five years, whenever she met Australian tourists abroad—complete strangers—she would ask them if they had any news about me and the answer was always yes, they did, as a matter of fact. Usually just details about some gossip they'd read in *New Idea* on the Qantas flight over to England. But for a while Aunt Nora thought that everybody in Australia knew everybody else.

In Harrington they took me to my grandmother Ruth's grave that I'd last visited in 1949. I saw the tiny terrace house my mother grew up in during the Depression, when my grandfather was working down in the coal mines, where a runaway coal truck had broken his leg in three places, so badly it almost had to be amputated.

I saw the little church where my mother was christened, confirmed and married. I walked along the High Street where Mum's bigoted Granny paraded her, wearing orange clothes on St Patrick's Day as an anti-Catholic statement. When my mother's aunt Mary married an Italian Catholic bank manager, her entire family didn't speak to her for twenty years. Because he was a Catholic, not because he was a bank manager. Nowadays it would be the other way round. Oh yes, the village of my mother's birth, Salterbeck, made West Pymble seem like Paradise.

In the three weeks I spent in New York after leaving London, I managed to see thirty shows. While I was in London I had already seen the excellent Stockard Channing in *Six Degrees of Separation* at the Royal Court Theatre and now I saw it again in NYC, this time with Swoozie Kurtz in the lead.

In New York there's always something playing in a theatre somewhere every night of the week, and you can also manage to find a matinee on a Wednesday, Saturday and Sunday. So, if you juggle your theatre-going schedule cleverly, you can see ten shows a week. This had been my pattern when visiting there for a few years. It takes a certain degree of stamina—up at dawn and on the go until the following dawn. Scurrying like a ferret all over mighty Manhattan Island, beginning at daybreak, looking at people, looking at paintings and buying books. And shoes. Seeing a different piece of theatre every night and on three afternoons. What a dream existence. And just taking in that vibrant city—New York is one of the great loves of my life.

After New York I spent six weeks at our house in Hawaii, slaving over a hot Canon Typestar, trying to write something close to my heart: a one-woman performance piece for myself on Christina Stead, one of my long-time idols. Eventually I chucked it in. I was bitterly frustrated. It was great subject matter and I had some reasonably good ideas, but I think I just lost heart. How dare I even attempt such a thing? And I was a little lonely.

Dybie and Joby were both pleased to see me home again. While generally tolerant and indulgent of my sprees abroad, they did seem to miss me after I'd been absent for more than a few weeks. And of course I missed them—we exchanged several phone calls daily and from Kauai lengthy faxes every day as well.

Roger Hodgman asked me to play Doctor Gorgeous in *The Sisters Rosensweig* by Wendy Wasserstein. It was a big hit on Broadway and I saw it with the incomparable Madeleine Kahn as Doctor Gorgeous. *Incomparable*!

I realised, a while back, how gushy and actressy I sound putting superlatives before so many names. *Incomparable*, *excellent*, *fabulous*—whatever. Gushy? Maybe so. But hey, I'm an actress. For forty years. Sometimes I even address complete strangers as *Darling*. Unashamedly. It's actress's licence—there have to be some perks that go with the job. And it's handy when you forget people's names: *DARLING! May I introduce you to Darling!* And Madeleine Kahn *was* incomparable. In a TV interview recently the *legendary* Mel Brooks told *clever* Andrew Denton that Madeleine Kahn was *great*. And she was. One of the greatest.

In the MTC production Genevieve Picot and Judi Farr were the other Sisters Rosensweig. It was a big cast that included Max Gillies, Tony Sheldon and Rachel Griffiths in one of her early roles, just before she hit the big time overseas. I became good friends with Gerald Lepkowski, who played Rachel's boyfriend in the show. Gerry has another unusual talent apart from acting: he can make an anagram of people's names that describes their natures. (Jacqueline Ruth Weaver is Caviar Jewel Queen—well almost.) We did an extensive tour with the show all over the country, including a season at the Wharf in Sydney. Doctor

Gorgeous was a gorgeous character based on the play-wright's real sister, actual name Georgette, who'd only ever answer to the name Gorgeous.

The three sisters are very different: one is a cynical atheist banker, another a hopelessly romantic writer and Dr Gorgeous is a would-be glamorous talkback radio psychologist who is deeply religious. Again, as when I played Sonia Walsk in *They're Playing Our Song* and Joy Davidman in *Shadowlands*, many members of the Jewish community embraced me as one of their own—I was asked to be guest speaker at various Jewish fund-raisers and was always flattered to do so. And then sensed their undisguised dis-appointment when the inevitable moment arrived that I had to admit I was merely a *shiksa* from Pymble. *West* Pymble, what's more.

By this time Hinch had been sacked by Channel 10, in spite of good ratings. Personal animosity overcoming sound judgement. Channel 9 picked him up and gave him the job as compere on the *Midday Show* recently vacated by Ray Martin. Rumour had it that Mike Munro had been promised this job and was very angry about being gazumped by the parvenu Hinch. Several staff members on *Midday* weren't happy with the decision either, as became clear from the way they treated Hinch. Very unwelcoming. Hinch worked hard but he wasn't happy. Miserable in fact.

During the year that Hinch compered the *Midday Show*, 1994, we lived in the 36th-floor penthouse at Sydney's Regent Hotel in The Rocks near Circular Quay. Through our kitchen we had private access to the roof. Spectacular.

It is probably now apparent where all our money went, to those who wonder about this and who constantly inquire about it (as a journalist did only yesterday). Or at least where some of it went, anyway. Money that we both had earned and both had worked hard for. And spent. Love of luxury is a persuasive vice, especially when you've known penury. Luxury is certainly one of the benefits of wealth. However— at the risk of sounding like some obnoxious Pollyanna—the best part about having money is being able to afford to give it away. Especially to those who least expect it.

It hadn't been a great year in many ways. Dylan suffered a recurrence of a medical condition that needed surgery—a few years previously, he'd undergone four operations to remove a mysterious cyst that grew in his jaw, but now it was back again and he had to endure another three operations, and much pain. Joby proved to be a good nurse, though he occasionally overdid the brandy in the eggflips.

The three of us spent that Christmas in Hawaii. After New Year, Joby returned home and Dylan and I went to New York during one of their worst winters on record. There was a blizzard so severe that for three days people were warned to remain indoors. Many people died from the cold.

Dylan and I were staying in one of the cheapest hotels, to save money, and it wasn't the best place to be trapped in. But we still managed a lot of laughs, some fine meals, excellent theatre, long invigorating walks and we listened to some great music, especially jazz down in the Village.

Hinch was sacked from *Midday*, but Channel 9 kept him under contract for a year in a kind of limbo, not giving him anything to do. Not that he was ever idle. Joby is incapable of idleness—not an idle bone in his body. I, however, am an expert at idleness. Could write a thesis on the subject. With practical demonstrations.

One of Australia's best-loved plays, and deservedly so, is Michael Gow's classic *Away*, which must have been produced more times than almost any other Australian play. Many Australian actors have been in *Away*. I was offered a couple of different versions of it before I was finally available to play Coral for the Sydney Theatre Company in about their fourth mounting of it, this time with Wayne Harrison directing.

I had a call from playwright Nick Enright to say he'd heard about it and he'd love to play Coral's husband, which surprised me as Nick had been so busy with his successful writing and teaching career that his acting aspirations seemed to have been put on the backburner. Minutes after hanging up from Nick, Wayne rang to ask, 'Who would you like to play your husband?' 'Nick Enright,' I said. 'What a good idea,' said Wayne.

I loved working in *Away*—it's a truly wonderful piece of writing and it was a lovely cast. Written in 1986, *Away* is about three separate families who go away for their Christmas holiday by the seaside in the summer of 1967. It's deeply moving, very funny, and the dialogue uses language that is both poetic yet also sharply observed Australian vernacular with classical references, especially to Shakespeare's *A Midsummer Night's Dream*. The main protagonists are the teenagers Tom and Meg, played by David Campbell and Beth Champion. Meg is struggling to cope with her unhappy termagent of a mother and her hen-pecked father, played by Maggie Dence and real-life husband Graham Rouse. Tom and his parents, played by John Hamblin and Julie Hamilton, are facing the tragedy that Tom is dying of leukaemia. Coral and Roy are mourning the recent death of their conscript son in the Vietnam War. A violent thunderstorm brings the families together and thus begins their process of healing.

Maggie Dence took a photo of me and Nick in costume, which I framed and always have in my theatre dressing room. Nick Enright was a prolific playwright whose work included the Broadway hit *The Boy from Oz* and an Oscar nomination for the Susan Sarandon film *Lorenzo's Oil* which he co-wrote with director Dr George Miller, and Neil Armfield's Belvoir Street production of Tim Winton's *Cloudstreet* which Nick co-wrote with Justin Monjo. Nick was also an actor, director and a teacher with an exceptional gift for friendship. I knew him for many years and we worked together on *Daylight Saving* and *The Real Thing*. We also worked together on some excellent lunches and dinners. After a valiant battle with cancer Nick died in March 2003, aged only fifty-two. Such a waste and so unfair that Nick died so young. He was a good man with so much left to do. I miss him.

In 1995, Mark Joffe was about to direct a movie of Louis Nowra's play *Cosi*. I love Louis Nowra's writing and always have. I think Louis quite possibly fits the description of that overused word *genius*. I don't really know Louis that well, but I like the way he laughs.

The American company Miramax was producing *Cosi*. The rumour was that, for the part of the homicidal nympho-maniac Cherry, Miramax had suggested Whoopi Goldberg. When they were persuaded that an Australian might be a better idea, they lobbied for Elle Macpherson. I'd seen both Christen O'Leary and Celia Ireland play Cherry on-stage in Melbourne and Sydney respectively, and they were both fantastic. It still baffles me why neither of them got the job. Dozens of women screen-tested for Cherry. I was definitely a last resort.

I hadn't done a film for a long time and I was glad to get it. It was a terrific movie and a lovely cast which included Colin Friels, Barry Otto, Ben Mendelsohn, Pamela Rabe, Toni Collette, Rachel Griffiths, Colin Hay, and David Wenham as the pyromaniac Doug. We had some good fun shooting it.

And I enjoyed looking ghastly. Only a few minutes in the make-up chair each morning and then climbing into clever Tess Schofield's bizarre costumes (literally *climbing*, because donning my opera costume was like getting into a block and tackle). But I wasn't really as out of shape as they made me appear—that Bananas in Pyjamas T-shirt was a six-year-old's size and the overalls a ten-year-old's.

One night we were sitting in the kitchen in Toorak when John Waters rang. He'd had an idea for a musical based on British rock classics of the 1960s and he wanted to know if I was interested. I certainly was.

Life was about to change radically.

chapter twelve

Twilight of the Gods

JOHN WATERS ENJOYED WIDESPREAD SUCCESS WITH HIS SHOW
about John Lennon, *Looking Through a Glass Onion,*
when he first performed it with Stewart D'Arrietta in 1991.
Since then the show has had many successful re-runs and
reincarnations, right up until the present day.

In 1995 John and Stewart had an idea for another
musical show, *Reunion.* As told to me over the kitchen phone
in Toorak that night, the concept sounded appealing—
former rock singer in his forties reminisces about the past,
sings some great British rock classics of the 1960s and
reunites with the girl he left behind. There was some terrific
new original music by Stewart, plus a rock'n'roll band made
up of some first-rate musicians. Stewart and John produced
the show, John's sister Fiona (Fizzy Waters) was stage manager

and Peter Neufeld, who had also worked on *Glass Onion*, was the lighting designer.

I didn't expect to lose my heart to Peter Neufeld but, after three months on tour with the show, that's what happened. I was forty-eight and Peter was thirty-three. After the tour finished, I went to live with Peter in his house in Paddington. We were together for seven years.

For the first six months we kept our romance secret. My husband Derryn Hinch asked me to deny all the rumours and the gossip. Derryn was hoping that I might change my mind about Peter and return home after a few months. Derryn and I had been happily married for twelve years and he thought this might be just a small blip we could get through unscathed. It was Richard Wherrett who insisted that I confess to Derryn about Peter and me. Richard hated deceit, especially coming from me. But Derryn had already guessed something was amiss.

And my father was now dying of cancer. My brother had wisely counselled me to keep the breakdown of my marriage quiet for Dad's sake. Had Dad known, he would have been deeply upset and he had quite enough to cope with already.

I felt enormous guilt over the hurt I caused my husband, leaving him for another man. I fled from a husband I still loved; I did yet another runner. I wasn't proud of it—I was a cruel strumpet and I knew it. But I wanted to be with Peter. I was in love with him and that was that.

Over the years the press often referred to the age difference between Peter and me, but it was never an issue for us. At first being fifteen years older than Peter was just a bit of a novelty, but very soon it became irrelevant for both of us and we honestly never thought about it. The epithet 'toy boy' was bandied about a bit, which niggled me. A man of thirty-three is not a 'boy', and to refer to him as a mere 'toy' is downright offensive.

I did blush when I imagined Peter's family's reaction back in England. A married actress fifteen years older! Worse than that—an Australian!! I felt sure they must have been appalled. But I needn't have worried. Eventually I met Peter's parents when they visited Australia, and they were perfectly charming and gracious. Peter's mother is one of the most beautiful women I've ever met—a sort of cross between Ava Gardner and Cyd Charisse—and his father looks like a more handsome Douglas Fairbanks Junior, whom I had once inter-viewed when I was a reporter on *Willesee* (he was seventy-eight and gorgeous).

Peter always referred to me as his 'girlfriend' during our seven years together, which at first seemed a little strange, given my age. But I soon got used to it and always called him 'my boyfriend' without a qualm. I've never liked the word 'partner'. 'Partner' is too businesslike to describe one's heart's companion, one's live-in sweetheart. Spouse, husband, wife, de facto, beloved, paramour—anything is preferable to that dry old word 'partner'.

In deference to Peter, I want to protect his privacy from any further details about our seven years together. Suffice to say he treated me very well, like you'd treat a marchioness, if indeed you knew a marchioness. Peter took very good care of me. He is naturally affectionate and truly generous in heart and spirit, the consummate gentleman. He's a great host as well, a talent he probably inherited from his generous Austrian father. Peter also happens to be the most inventive gift-giver I've ever met. He obviously puts hours of thought into every present he gives and it is always a treat to receive. It's a rare gift to be good at gifts. I always seem to give the wrong thing.

I'd been living with Peter for several months when Derryn signed a contract with John Singleton's Radio 2GB in Sydney to do the mid morning shift up against John Laws. I found Derryn an apartment in Highgate in Kent Street in The Rocks. At his behest we were still behaving as though we were together, but some people were starting to suspect it was a sham.

Finally it seemed pointless to keep it a secret any longer and one morning, without warning anyone except me, Derryn announced our separation on the radio. None of his staff was expecting it. One of his researchers on the program was so shocked she burst into tears: 'You always seem so happy together,' she explained. Many people were surprised by the news, including people who were close to us.

It was a good thing that we'd managed to keep my father from finding out about our separation during his last days. Dad, however, had had a bombshell of his own to drop on me, a dark secret he'd never revealed even to my mother. When he was a child, between the ages of seven and twelve, he had been systematically and constantly sexually abused by his foster father in their family home. This was a foster father who was a pillar of the community, married with three children of his own.

I spared my Dad the knowledge of my own childhood experiences with a sexual abuser. It would have caused him untold distress. My tormentor was long dead anyway, so there was nothing to be gained from dobbing him in. I never told my mother either. And I'm glad neither of my parents had to go through the anguish of finding out.

Not long before he died, my father married Judy, who had been his heart's companion for two years. She made him very happy and it wasn't fair that they had so little time together. We organised both his wedding and his funeral in the space of ten days. When he first became very ill Judy and I nursed him at home but he spent his final couple of days in a Greenwich palliative care unit where we kept a round-the-clock vigil by his bed and where I could see at first hand what exceptional human beings those nurses are. I was holding his hand and whispering in his ear that I loved him and not to be frightened when he finally took his last exhausted breath and slipped away. It was 5.30 am and my husband Derryn Hinch, who had come up from Melbourne to lend me support, took me and Dylan to breakfast at the Sebel Town House. Then Derryn delivered me back to Paddington where my boyfriend Peter Neufeld was waiting anxiously for me. Derryn was still hoping I would change my mind about Peter and come home to Melbourne.

My fiftieth birthday was celebrated with 150 guests, whittled down from 600, at John and Sal Waters' house in Mosman. Sal and John gave me a fabulous birthday party. John, my brother Rod, Derryn and I all made speeches.

Ruth Cracknell was there. Nick Enright was there. Richard Wherrett was there. All gone now.

I went on tour with the wonderful Christen O'Leary in a play called *Girl Talk* by Patrick Edgeworth, produced by Hit Productions. Over a period of nine months we played more than two hundred performances in sixty-nine different venues all over Australia. Sixty-nine different venues! Whenever I tell people that, they seem surprised that there *are* that many theatres in Australia. There are actually many more than that. *Girl Talk* didn't play in Geelong or Newcastle or Canberra or Adelaide or Brisbane or the Sydney Opera House. But we still played sixty-nine venues, the smallest for one hundred and twenty people, the largest for nearly two thousand. We opened in Mount Isa, and finally closed the show nine months and many thousands of miles later in Werribee. Sold out The Playhouse in Perth and packed out Glen Street Theatre in Sydney. Sold out in Darwin, sold out in Hobart's Theatre Royal (as I've mentioned before, it's my favourite theatre, closely followed by Her Majesty's in Ballarat, His Majesty's in Perth and the Comedy Theatre in Melbourne—love them all).

It's a huge country, and nothing could make that clearer than visiting so many places in less than a year. Albany, Mandurah, Geraldton, Port Hedland, Broome. Then over to Queensland: Cairns, Townsville, Rockhampton, Mackay, Nambour. Places I'd never heard of, like Chinchilla and Capella. And beautifully restored theatres, like those in Toowoomba and Charters Towers. In fact some of the most unlikely places have state-of-the-art performance spaces. Like Karratha in the middle of that searing red sand, in the north of Western Australia. And Esperance right down at the other end, the tail end of WA, with the spectacular turquoise Southern Ocean rolling in all the way from Antarctica and the breathtaking natural pink lake, rose-coloured by some mineral mystery of nature. And Kalgoorlie, with its multi-million dollar new modern theatre, which the locals assured us was erected as a cynical piece of vote-buying (let's have more such cynicism, I say).

Sixty-nine venues means sixty-nine times you pack your suitcase, sixty-nine times you unpack your suitcase, in sixty-nine motels, ranging from grotty and damp to cosy and pleasant. Occasionally even salubrious. Very occasionally. Sixty-nine venues also means travelling thousands of miles. Usually by station wagon, driven by the stage manager; sometimes by airline, while the two-man crew does the long haul in the six-tonne truck carrying the set and the costumes. Once we spent two hours in a rancid-smelling light plane, mostly used for transporting abalone and baiting feral dogs, to take the show to Carnarvon.

In some of the regions the audience dresses up as if it's a special occasion. Sunday frocks and patent leather shoes. In some towns they bring lamingtons and pikelets, and share them with the cast afterwards. In Proserpine it was a huge elaborate supper and the punters got so involved in the nar-rative of the play that they started to call out advice to the protagonists on-stage. I loved it.

In one tiny Victorian town where we were performing at the School of Arts, there was a homemade sign in the window of the hall advertising the show and offering as an extra inducement: 'Enjoy A Glass Of Sherry With The Cast After The Show!' I wonder if that sold more tickets.

In Alice Springs and Dubbo, some of the audience had driven five or six hundred miles just to see us. It was very touching. It was good to feel so appreciated in so many places. It also brought home to me the fact that live theatre is not dead yet. No matter how technically advanced and brilliant the storytelling becomes in cinema and on television, there will always be an audience for actors doing it on-stage, in person, at that very moment.

I made a point of exploring every town as much I could. I'm a big ambulator. Well, more accurately, a small ambulator who's big on ambulating. Christen was heartsick and homesick for her horn-blower sweetheart, so she worked out her frustration in every country town gym.

In Bathurst I received a letter from a woman called Lalage Gabb, who told me that in 1949, when she was seventeen, she had sailed to England and grudgingly shared a cabin with two last-minute passengers, a Mrs Weaver and her infant. Whenever Lalage saw me in the press or on television over the next fifty years, she wondered if I had been that infant. I certainly was. The infant terrible. Though she did say that I was fairly well-behaved for a two-year-old.

In Wonthaggi another dear woman wrote to say she knew me in England when I was a child, and could we meet after the show. When she showed me her precious photos and outlined the details, I realised it was a case of mistaken identity. But she was so excited, and her friend said she'd always talked about knowing me, that I didn't have the heart to tell her she had the wrong Jacki. Later, when I returned to Sydney, I wrote to her and told her the truth. In return she thanked me, but said she would still always think of me as the little girl in the photos.

I wrote earlier that my unhappiest professional experience in more than forty years was doing Bleasdale's *Having a Ball*. The second most miserable time I've ever had was doing *Navigating* by Katharine Thompson. She had written an excellent play called *Diving for Pearls*, so her credentials were good. She'd also been married to the much-maligned *Sydney Morning Herald* critic Bob Evans, but you can't judge people by their husbands.

Navigating was about a worthy subject: whistleblowing. Dobbing in villains. About devious evil-doers working within the accepted systems, and conspiracies that destroy people's lives. Katharine's research was awesomely thorough—I found journalist Quentin Masters' book *Whistleblowing* particularly enlightening and helpful. *Navigating* had some good structural ideas, some interesting ideas for characterisation, some engaging complexities of plot. But to my mind the dialogue ultimately turned out to be dull, banal and witless.

Richard Wherrett was engaged to direct a joint Queensland/ Melbourne Theatre Company production and so he cast three Melbourne actors and three Queensland actors. Richard was very keen for me (a *Sydney* actor, heaven forbid) to play the part of Bea. Katharine Thompson had originally written the role of Bea for the brilliant Anne Phelan but Robyn Nevin, who then ran the Queensland Theatre Company, vetoed Anne for some reason. Robyn was equally opposed to my doing it, though I didn't know this at the time, and she wrote an impassioned letter to this effect to Richard. He didn't tell me about it until well after the run of the play was finished, many months later. And even then he refused ever to allow me to see Robyn's letter, because he said it would hurt me. He said that, if I'd known about it during the actual run of the play, it would have crushed me so much I would have been unable to do it.

I've always been curious about its contents and over the years I've gleaned a little of what it contained. People who've seen it have told me it was a libellous document designed to prevent me from getting a job the director wanted to give me. Bewildering even now, for me anyway. Apparently Robyn tried to involve Roger Hodgman, then head of the Melbourne Theatre Company, but he wouldn't be drawn, saying that Richard, as the director, had the right to make the final casting decisions. And Richard threatened to walk out of the deal if I wasn't in it. Thank God I didn't know all this was going on behind my back. I worked hard on *Navigating*. Very hard. Total one hundred per cent commitment.

How clearly I remember standing at the back of one of those 'subscriber briefings' where Katharine did her very convincing spiel about the play, explained her impressive research technique with charts and time frames etc, and her general modus operandi. She then answered questions from the audience.

'How do you go about writing dialogue?' she was asked.

'Oh, it just writes itself,' she responded blithely.

My heart sank. Oh no it doesn't, Katharine. If only it did write itself—especially for those who have to utter it.

I actually received some rave reviews, as it turned out. The review in the *Sunday Mail* was headlined: 'Wonderful Weaver Wows 'em!' But I hated doing it. In the dressing room after the opening night performance in Brisbane, Katharine thanked me profusely. 'You're a genius, Jacki,' were her actual words.

In spite of a very warm response from the audience, I was feeling a little bereft as neither Richard, the director, nor Robyn, the artistic director, was there at the opening. The absence of both of them was understandable—Richard was at the funeral in Sydney of a very dear friend of ours, Dean Essing, and Robyn was performing in *Master Class*, the Maria Callas play. Robyn was furious that Richard wasn't there, and said she'd 'never forgive him', which baffled me. Especially considering the domestic dramas she herself had been through when married to the criminally inclined Jim McNeill. Like the time when McNeill, using violence, had prevented her from going on-stage because he wanted her to stay home and watch TV with him instead of going to work at the theatre. Thank God Peter Neufeld and my son Dylan flew up from Sydney during *Navigating* to give me some support.

I loved the rest of the cast, especially Janet Andrewartha, who played my sister. How grateful I was for those fragrantly balmy Brisbane nights, which Janet and I would spend after work on her hotel balcony sipping Scotch. Her soothing voice and me full of angst. I was perplexed that some members of the Queensland Theatre Company seemed to be making a point of ignoring me and it was a relief to get the production down to Melbourne, where at least everyone in the company spoke to me.

I enjoyed the way I looked and sounded as Bea. Dowdy, pale, rheumy-eyed and pudgy, with my hair dyed dark brown. My hair had to be dyed because Robyn said she didn't like actors to wear wigs. I was a lumpy sad sack in a big old cable-knit cardigan, speaking with a solid rustic twang. And it was gratifying that many people didn't recognise me on-stage, especially as the gist of Robyn's objection to me, apparently, was that I wasn't capable of transformation. Amongst other shortcomings. (I sometimes wonder where that letter is now. Maybe Peter Wherrett has it amongst Richard's papers. I don't want to see it. Not really. What's the point?)

The irony was that Robyn never came to see *Navigating*. Not once, in either its Brisbane or Melbourne seasons. Even though she was artistic director of the company that commissioned it. As I've said before, I honestly don't care. Many months after *Navigating* had finished, Robyn rang me to express her appreciation. She said she was reviewing the year and had just re-read the excellent press notices I received. I was surprised and touched.

The Sydney Theatre Company, with Wayne Harrison at the helm, did their own production of *Navigating* with Noni

Hazlehurst as Bea and Marion Potts directing. Reluctantly I attended the opening night at the Opera House. In the foyer afterwards, Katharine Thompson came up to me and said, ever so sweetly: 'I'm sorry you were in the dud version, Jacki.'

I was speechless. Not just at the lack of tact, but also at the fact that she could even think such a thing, never mind say it. Many people, myself included, thought the Sydney version was an even bigger dud than our QTC/MTC production.

Later, when Robyn finally got the gig as artistic director at the Sydney Theatre Company, I was engaged for Mary Anne Gifford's production of Beatrix Christian's *Fred* at Wharf One. Just before rehearsals began, Robyn invited me into her office and said we had some issues to address, or words to that effect.

Obligingly, I thought, I apologised for my unkindness several years previously, for my acerbic tongue and for inventing That Nickname. I apologised sincerely.

'Yes I was very hurt, Jac,' Robyn intoned reproachfully. 'Very hurt indeed.'

I waited for her to apologise to me and slowly realised this would not be forthcoming. So I gently reminded her that she had also hurt me, deeply, and on more than one occasion.

'I have no recollection of any such thing,' she replied. And that was the end of that. Maybe she really does forget such things.

I had a wonderful time in a very unusual and witty play called *The Falls* written by gifted playwright Hilary Bell, who is a truly original woman. Her father John Bell directed it and it starred his other gifted daughter Lucy Bell. I played Lucy's sister, but in the end I turn out to be her mother. There were numerous bizarre twists of plot and character and some very aberrant behaviour. There was quite a large cast, including Barry Otto, Peter Cousens and Jennifer Hagan, so it was a tight squeeze in the tiny Stables dressing room. Barry had to get made up in the toilet. We had a lot of fun and the audiences and critics loved it.

At the same time I was rehearsing the STC Wharf Revue for Wharf Two with Jonathan Biggins, Drew Forsythe and Andrew Ross. At one point, sporting a white wig and a deeper voice, I did an impersonation of Robyn Nevin. I was a little nervous when she watched the first run-through, but she laughed heartily and saw the show several times. Robyn's heart's companion, Nicholas Hammond, told me he loved my take-off of Robyn. 'You even got the way she holds her arms exactly right,' he said. It was for the same show that Drew Forsythe and Andrew Ross wrote me the Koala Song. Graham Wills, head of STC wardrobe, designed me a terrific koala suit, as wide as my height and very awkward to get into. With a big separate head and ears, but with my own face. I've never received so great a response for so little effort. A crowd-pleasing pushover.

Beatrix Christian is a wonderful playwright, with a unique impression of the world, which she conveys beautifully in her highly original storytelling. Her language and her characters are fascinating. Her play *Fred* is a murder mystery with laughs. My character was a financial adviser trying to become pregnant. Matt Day was my husband. Only ten years earlier, Matt Day had been my son in the TV series *House Rules*. The gorgeous Claudia Karvan was also in *Fred*. So were Kirstie Hutton and Aaron Blabey. I could tell they were going to fall in love with each other as soon as we started rehearsals. And they did. Shrouded in secrecy. Except from me. I was awake to them from the start. After all, I've practically got a PhD in Clandestinity. Kirstie and Aaron were married not a few months later.

It was during the run of her play *Fred* that Bea had the idea for *Old Masters*, a play for three divas, Lillian, Dotty and Fleur. At the closing night party for *Fred*, Bea told me she wanted to write a character for me who was totally amoral but universally likeable. Fleur. I almost didn't do *Old Masters*. Robyn was having difficulty scheduling it around competing work commitments she and I had. We were both contracted to do other things during that year but it finally worked out that I could do it, with Benedict Andrews directing, Robyn as Lillian and Julie Forsythe as Dotty.

One day during a rehearsal for *Old Masters* at the Wharf, I suddenly felt faint and had to lie down on the floor. Everyone was very kind to me, especially Robyn. I was embarrassed at the fuss and for holding up rehearsals.

They drove me to the doctor, who said I was obviously stressed. About Richard's health, among other things. The doctor was also Richard's GP and so he knew that Richie was not well. And that he was not going to get better.

I knew it too, but refused to accept it.

chapter thirteen

Fear No More

It's October 2001. My eyes are closed, and my sunlit upturned face wears an expression of utter bliss. I'm dressed in delicate floral silk chiffon and standing barefoot in thick black dusty soil. Gordo is kneeling in the dirt with his head under my skirt pleasuring me with cunnilingus.

An hour later I'm in a sleazy motel room, making love to Gordo's 25-year-old son Ford, who's also been my secret lover for ten years and who demands to be suckled at my breast like an infant. My close colleague of thirty years, Lillian, who also happens to be Ford's mother, is about to dump me cruelly and in my hysteria I try to rip my clothes off in front of three hundred people before Dotty can cover some of me up again.

All this is, of course, a piece of fiction, the play called *Old Masters*, by the amazing Beatrix Christian which we were performing for the Sydney Theatre Company at Wharf One in 2001. Some friends say it was one of the best things I ever did; others hated it and left at interval. I love the stimulation of working on something that polarises opinion.

When playwright Bea Christian had described Fleur to me as 'a totally amoral person whom we all can't help liking, no matter what she does', my friend Freddy the Vicar assured me it was a compliment. Fleur was a rich gift of a role which, astonishingly, won me a best actress Mo Award for 2002, when all five nominees were women over a certain age: Wendy Hughes for *The Graduate*, Kris McQuade for *Cloudstreet*, Amanda Muggleton for *Master Class*, Tina Bursill for *Up For Grabs* and me. A significant line-up in this era of youth worship and a perceived dearth of good roles for middle-aged women. Anyway, I was sure I was a rank outsider amongst that field and was thrilled and surprised to win, and said in my acceptance speech: 'I'd like to thank everyone I ever married.'

Playing Fleur in *Old Masters* was tiring—she sprinted everywhere, even backstage. She seldom stopped talking, singing, dancing, fighting, and having sex all over the stage for three hours, eight performances a week. (During each performance while Max Cullen was simulating this aforesaid intimacy under my skirt on his knees, he soon developed the habit, probably out of boredom, of chatting quite audibly while I faked pleasure. Indeed one night a man in the front row roared with laughter when Max was heard to mumble from beneath all the silk chiffon: 'Ah, I see you drive a Volvo!')

All this was happening while Richard Wherrett was dying and I was living with him, going home to him every night after the theatre to take care of him and, at his insistence, to sleep alongside him in his bed until he could finally settle, sometimes not until dawn. It was an exhausting and heartbreakingly difficult time. From the moment I woke, I knew I'd be more or less running, or at least scurrying, for the next twenty or so hours. I lost 10 kilos in six weeks. And all the while I was trying (and mostly succeeding) to stay cheerful.

Except for one night, when I arrived at work. Suddenly, in the dressing room before the show, I quietly but absolutely lost my optimism. In my little cubicle behind the Wharf Theatre's skimpy drapes, Julie Forsythe held me in her arms until I stopped crying and my chest stopped heaving. And the show, of course, went on. Thank God for that great cast and that backstage crew who kept me going.

The previous year Rich had directed the torch-lighting sequence at the Sydney Olympic Games Opening Ceremony; he'd done a smash hit new musical, *Shout*, about the great Australian rock star Johnny O'Keefe, written by David Mitchell and John-Michael Howson and starring David Campbell, Tamsin Carroll and Trisha Noble (formerly Patsy Ann Noble, who began her career on *Bandstand* in the sixties). He had also directed a terrific production of *As You Like It* at NIDA and insisted I see it. The character of the melancholic Jacques resonated especially for him and played on his mind. Richard identified with the melancholia Jacques was enduring after a life of licentious excess, and also with

Jacques' hints of an illness that had befallen him, probably an Elizabethan version of the pox.

He was also writing a multimedia performance piece with Justin Fleming, plus putting the finishing touches to a sound and light show (a project he'd been working on for Harry Miller for two years) and writing a show for me, in which I would play four characters and be joined on-stage by a chorus of beautiful young men(!). He was also working on a novel, a comedy/thriller. So he was far from idle.

He'd also completed and launched his second memoir, *The Floor of Heaven*, a beautiful book about his life in the theatre, which he'd been writing when I stayed with him in Port Douglas for a short time in 1998. He had rented a house up there with some friends for a few months and asked me to join him for a while and share the drive home to Sydney.

In his earlier book, *Desirelines* (1997)—an 'unusual family memoir' he had written jointly with his brother Peter about their childhood and the dark secrets it contained—he had written: 'I can't imagine anyone not being attracted to Jacki Weaver. Delightfully pretty, tough and realistic, gentle and generous, deliciously wicked and witty, the intelligence shines out of her like a laser.' He had also declared: 'I decided if I couldn't make it with Jacki, I couldn't make it with any woman.' And although there were to be many women he would love (and I will admit to the occasional pang of jealousy) nonetheless, true to his word, when we broke up he didn't become romantically involved or physically intimate with a woman ever again. I helped proofread both books for him and, when I came to his confession of having had (before me) 'affairs with various actresses', I crossed out 'affairs' and wrote 'meaningless dalliances' in the margin.

I was very touched when he dedicated *The Floor of Heaven* to me with the words: 'For JACKI, who makes the skies blue'. One of my prized possessions is a copy of that book, to which he has added in his distinctive handwriting on the dedication page: '. . . and whose blue eyes, bright smile and long time companionship have supported me so much for thirty years. With all my love, Richie 25/X/00'.

Fortunately, Richard and Peter Neufeld liked each other; they even worked together a few times. And Peter was right beside us during Richie's illness and at his death, giving his total support and love.

Richard and I always confided in each other about our respective amours, omitting no detail, however slight. I liked all his sweethearts, with one exception. He felt much the same about mine, with one exception.

When he fell in love with Wayne Hall, a stunningly attractive and sweet-natured young man from West Virginia, I was very happy for him. Wayne was very special and we got along famously when he came to stay in Australia. We shared a birthday, 25 May, and were born twelve years apart, so we also shared a Chinese Zodiac sign. Both Gemini Pigs: highly ethical, but self-indulgent. If you care about such things. We certainly hit it off immediately we met.

In an unbelievably tragic circumstance, Wayne was killed in a motorcycle accident in Los Angeles just hours after happily saying goodnight to Richard. Richie couldn't bear to tell me himself and delegated Brett Sheehy, who was then his assistant, to break the news to me. Similarly, it was Wayne Harrison who had originally been given the job of telling me Richie was HIV positive, because Richie couldn't bring himself to be the one to upset me. This was back in the early eighties, when such a diagnosis was a virtual death sentence, so it was a small miracle that he lived until 2001 and, ironically, didn't die of AIDS but of cirrhosis of the liver. Indeed I've lost many friends to AIDS, both here and in America.

On 10 December 2000, Richard turned sixty with much fanfare, surrounded by scores of friends and family and past lovers. That day John Bell launched Richard's book *The Floor of Heaven* at a smart cocktail party at NIDA in Kensington. A week later there was an even more lavish party at the Wharf Restaurant with star-studded entertainment, produced by Tony Sheldon; it included Drew Forsythe doing his wickedly accurate Wherrett impersonation and great singing from Tamsin Carroll and Simon Burke.

Richard also asked for speeches from his brother Peter, Robert Alexander, me and Brett Sheehy to talk about his life in the fifties, sixties, seventies and eighties respectively. His sixtieth birthday was a milestone he hadn't expected to reach. There had been so many health crises so often, but we seemed to take them and the attendant dramas in our stride. Actually, considering the punishment his body had gone through over the years, Richard had the constitution of an ox.

Ferrying him hither and thither, to this specialist and that specialist, on hospital visits, sitting for hours in waiting rooms or at his various bedsides, we all saw him through so much that it didn't seem possible when we realised that the downhill run was finally approaching. Even though it's almost four years since he died, the memory of Richie's suffering during those last months is so raw that it's unbearable to think about. Like the night he sat on the edge of the bed, hunched over with his face in his hands and sobbed, 'I can't bear this any longer.' I felt useless. Not that I was alone in the flat with him. Far from it. In the weeks leading up to his death, Richard was surrounded by love. Literally hundreds of visitors came to the hospital and then to his home.

Several months before that, I had been lying on the purple cushions at his place when he asked of me four things. Firstly: 'When I'm dying, will you move in and look after me?' I said of course, but that that was years away yet.

Secondly: 'What do you want of mine after I'm dead?' I began to cry and said all I wanted was for him to stay alive. When he pressed me to choose something, I opted for the mask of him in the perspex box, which is beside me as I write this. I've always been fond of this mask, though many of his friends dislike it and find it a little weird. It was fashioned by the Australian sculptor Susan Rogers for an exhibition and is taken from an actual imprint of Richard's face; it was painted in the manner of an Arab prince or sheik, complete with headdress. It is sitting on the bookshelf where my old scripts and photo albums are kept. I'm also surrounded by several framed photos of Richard, two of them hanging on the wall.

Thirdly, he asked me that day: 'If you wanted to pre-empt your death, how would you go about it?' I fended that one off by saying that suicide had long ceased to be a viable option for me, out of consideration for Dylan.

And lastly, the fourth wish: 'Will you marry me?' I said I'd think about it, but probably not. Nonetheless, he wouldn't let go of the idea of our marrying right up to the end.

Over the thirty years we'd known each other, he'd asked me to marry him several times, the most recent being when we were at Port Douglas together. We had taken five days to drive home to Sydney, drifting down the coast and staying in roadside motels, where he would ask for one room with separate beds. 'Because she's my ex-wife,' he'd inform the receptionist.

He had also proposed to me a couple of years before that, when we were staying at Ed and Fiona Manier's place in Cow Bay near Mossman in far North Queensland, on the night when a spider the size of a dinner plate invaded my room. I certainly wished we'd been sharing a room that particular night.

And now here it was, 2001, and he was asking again. He organised a celebrant, set a date, and booked tickets to Bali with Qantas for our honeymoon. To anyone who came to the flat he'd announce triumphantly the impending nuptials. He derived such joy from the prospect that I was quite prepared to agree to anything that would make him happy provided it was all right with Peter Neufeld, who was, after all, my live-in boyfriend. And Peter said whatever made Richard happy was fine with him. I remember being in tears in Lucio's restaurant with Chrissie Sharp and Brett Sheehy counselling me not to go ahead with the wedding. I didn't and, in retrospect, I suppose I made the sensible decision. It probably would have seemed a bit bizarre.

By now I'd been living with Peter Neufeld in his house in Paddington for more than six years, since the break-up of my marriage to Derryn Hinch. Peter had always admired and respected Richard. The four of us had become a small family unit: Richard, Dylan, Peter and I. We shared dinner together once a week, and usually spent Christmas, birthdays and holidays together. Lots of laughs and secrets, plus the occasional disagreement. We were a solid little family unit with an inner circle of dear close friends—Robert and Barry, Lezzy, Brett and Steve, Duncan, Corby, Peter B, Tony, Simon—extending ever outwards, like a ripple in a lake, to touch those hundreds of good friends who comprised Richard's community and who rallied round to help take care of him.

Richie was dying of cirrhosis of the liver from hepatitis C, so he wasn't shrinking and wasting away, but instead growing bigger. Moving around became very awkward and painful for him and, though we had 24-hour nursing care, with Irish nurses who were nothing less than saints in uniforms, he became so heavy that we needed at least two or three able-bodied chaps on hand around the clock to help lift and move him. Someone drew up a roster in four-hourly shifts and people were amazing, all wanting Richie to be as comfortable as possible in his last few weeks.

I have an image of Richie smiling contentedly on the purple cushions, surrounded by six beautiful, adoring women—two of them holding his hands, two rubbing his feet, one stroking his forehead and one feeding him grapes. I couldn't get near him. Karen, the nurse, suggested to me: 'I think you could sneak away for a quick nap.' But I could never be out of his sight for long before he was calling for me, sometimes just to make sure I was there.

One night he woke me at 4 am and, frustrated that his wedding plans seemed to have stalled, told me to get his citrine ring from the dressing table. I couldn't find it. 'Oh, any ring will do,' he muttered impatiently. So I brought him the silver ring with the cross on it.

'Now hold out your hand,' he ordered. 'With this ring I thee wed. I, Richard, take you, Jacqueline, to be my wedded wife. Repeat after me . . .'

Which I did. 'That will have to do until I can get Jan Morice to do us properly,' he explained.

Karen came to help him back into bed. 'Jacqueline and I are married,' he told her.

The next night he was so restless that he rolled against me and I fell out of bed with a thump onto the floor. After that Karen made a rule that, as soon as he was asleep, which sometimes wasn't until dawn, I had to leave Richie's bed and sleep in the other bed, for my own safety.

One afternoon, too weak to stand unaided, he was sitting on a chair in the shower recess with the hot water streaming down on him when Karen said: 'He wants you to get in the shower with him. Do you mind?' So I took off my clothes, stepped into the shower and put my arms around him. He buried his face in my chest and sobbed as if his heart were breaking. Which it was.

It was with great relief that I finished working in *Old Masters* on 1 December. I was exhausted.

The morning of 4 December, Dylan's birthday, Richie woke early as usual and I asked what he wanted for breakfast: 'A large glass of prognosis negative,' he smiled. When I praised his wit, he said, 'Not me. Bette Davis—*Dark Victory*, 1948.'

Later that day he said: 'Don't forget you have to speak at my funeral.' I demurred yet again, and wept slightly. 'Get some beta-blockers from Tony [our GP]. Musicians take them for nerves. You'll be fine, I promise.'

That night we celebrated Dylan's birthday around the glass table. Robert and Barry made bouillabaisse and a lemon cake; Richie was in fine form, sipping Cointreau on ice from a brandy balloon with the blue velvet blanket around his knees.

He asked to be taken to bed at around nine and then decreed that he wanted a bedside chat with each of us 'one by one and in alphabetical order'. There were about ten of us—Robert first and me last, alphabetically. We waited anxiously as each returned in tears from the bedroom.

Rich told Dylan: 'I hope you know that I've loved you since you were a baby. I wanted to be the father to you that I never had.' And: 'Your mother's a good woman, but she needs pushing. Make sure she does the one-woman show I had planned for her.' (The one he'd been writing earlier that year.)

Then it was my turn. I waited for his words of wisdom. But all he said was, 'Get into bed and cuddle me.' Which I did until he fell asleep in my arms.

The next morning he was surprised and disappointed to wake up. He'd been hoping to die that night after saying his farewells to us. He was bitterly miserable.

Later that morning the doctor told us that it was impossible to predict, that Richie could last another three weeks or maybe only five more days. Luckily for him, it was to be only two days.

He died just as he wanted, lying on the blue couch, in sight of his beloved Sydney Harbour view, surrounded by most of us in the inner circle—me (holding his hand, whispering in his ear), Robert Alexander (kneeling beside him), Lezzy McDonald, Peter Neufeld, Tony Scotford, Peter Bridges, Brett Sheehy, Steve Nichols and Duncan McGregor.

It was 3 pm on Friday, 7 December 2001, and at that very moment an Anglican priest arrived unexpectedly at the door and was able to anoint him. Father Peter Kurti had planned to visit me the following day, but by chance he had called in earlier than expected.

In death Richie looked more handsome than ever. Peaceful at last, he seemed to be smiling and merely asleep. About forty friends arrived and paid their respects over the next couple of hours; we drank champagne and loved him. It was a spontaneous celebration, amazingly joyful. We kept him with us for several hours; I didn't want him to be taken away immediately.

In a movingly fitting tribute, Michael Lynch, then General Manager of the Opera House, dimmed the lights on the Opera House sails.

Brett Sheehy and I together consulted Richard's handwritten instructions for the funeral, an event which Brett produced and directed, even though he was now CEO of the Sydney Festival and it was only days off opening. I had the unenviable job of whittling down the potential list of twenty eligible pallbearers to the permissible eight.

Brett Sheehy and I read our eulogies, Simon Burke sang; Luciano Martucci, Robert Alexander, Peter Wherrett and his grandson Jackson all spoke. Father Greg Thompson officiated and Michael Lynch lent us the Opera House ushers in their uniforms to direct the audience at St John's Anglican Church, Darlinghurst.

John Bell read Shakespeare's great sonnet: 'Fear no more the heat o' the sun/Nor the furious winter's rages,' with its insistently repetitive refrain, 'Fear no more the frown o' the great/Thou art past the tyrant's stroke,' and its penultimate stanza:

Fear no more the lightning-flash,
Nor the all-dreaded thunder-stone;
Fear not slander, censure rash;
Thou hast finished joy and moan;
All lovers young, all lovers must
Consign to thee, and come to dust.

Brett mentioned the fact that Richard had once said, 'All I'm afraid of is the possibility of lacking courage.' I cannot ever remember Richie being anything but courageous. Always brave of heart. Richard the Lionheart.

The coffin was covered in a blanket of golden sunflowers with a single blue iris, and the 800-strong congregation burst into spontaneous applause as Richie was carried out to the sound of Thelma Huston singing 'Don't Leave Me This Way'.

And then he was gone.

chapter fourteen

And the Show,
of Course, Goes On

RICHIE DIED LESS THAN A WEEK AFTER WE FINISHED *OLD Masters*. I was adamant I never wanted to act ever again. If he wasn't there to see me, then there was no point doing it. Losing him meant losing my passion to work. A passion that had long been on the wane anyway. I was also very weary. Retirement was a very appealing prospect.

In February 2002, two months after Richie died, Robyn Nevin and the Sydney Theatre Company instigated a Richard Wherrett memorial concert at the Sydney Opera House, written, produced and directed by the brilliant Tony Sheldon, drawing on excerpts from Richard's own writing. There was a huge cast acting scenes and singing songs from plays and shows Richard had directed. One of the highlights was those two great women, Maggie Dence and Linda Nagle, doing a song Linda had written that mentioned all one hundred and twenty-seven shows Richie had directed. It was a highly emotionally charged night, with much hilarity, many tears.

Two weeks beforehand producer Tony Sheldon had asked me if I thought I would feel strong enough on the night to do a song called 'Old Friend' from a show called *I'm Getting My Act Together and Taking It On the Road*. I was unfamiliar with the song but as soon as I read the lyrics I understood why Tony had asked if it would distress me too much to sing it at that heartfelt celebration of Richard's life. But I was determined to get through it for Richard's sake; Richard, who thought courage to be the most important of character traits. I spent most of the day's rehearsals at the Opera House in a state of sheer terror, but, standing in the wings that night, waiting for my cue to go on-stage, I felt a palpable calm descend on me as I walked out and began to sing 'Old Friend'.

Every time I've lost another lover
I call up my old friend
And I say let's get together
I'm under the weather
Another love has come to an end.

The refrain I sang that's repeated after each verse and finishes the song goes:

Love is rare
Life is strange/
Nothing lasts
People change

The last two lines of Richard's memoir *Desirelines* arc:

Nothing lasts
People change.

❧ ❧

When the STC, with Gale Edwards directing, offered me the role of William Zappa's wife in David Williamson's *Soulmates*, my immediate reaction was to turn it down. I was determined not to put myself through the ordeal of getting back up on-stage. I wanted to mourn for Richie. At home alone. Upstairs in my cubby in Peter's house in Paddington.

My good friend Susan Lyons had been offered the role before me and she knocked them back. But I was talked into it. Get back to work. Take my mind off the life-changing trauma of the past few months. Family and friends thought it would do me good. So I accepted.

And I met Sean Taylor, a recently arrived South African actor of impressive repute, who'd been cast in the role of my seducer. And I fell in love with Sean Taylor.

Reader, I married him.

Epilogue:
Living National Trevor

BACK IN THE 1980S WHEN I WAS STILL MRS HINCH, GOUGH Whitlam was presenting me with an acting award and referred to me as 'A Living National Treasure'. Hinch said it made him feel like a curator. A curator of miniatures.

So here I am, still a miniature at four feet eleven and a half inches. And the only way to grow now is downwards or outwards. I've never minded being small, even nowadays when it's more fashionable than ever to be tall. I avoid the word 'short'; I've never been short of anything. Except perhaps restraint.

Years ago, whenever anyone remarked on my height, occasionally with undisguised condescension, my mother Ede would say, 'Who wants to be an Amazon?' What good psychology. And though I've often felt inadequate for various reasons, it's never been because I'm small.

However, my smallness could be accountable, in no small way, for the disagreeable fact that many people still refer to me, in my late fifties, as being *cute*. Even when I was in my teens, whenever anyone said I was *cute*, which was often, it was always a source of great annoyance to my mother Ede, who once went so far as to retort: Jacki's about as cute as a hatful of razor blades!'

One of my enduring obsessions throughout my life has been with the essential scent of everything I encounter. My sense of smell has never been inadequate. It's my most evocative tool when it comes to conjuring up the past. Nowadays I wear Nirmala, the nineties was JOY, the eighties was Tea Rose and Chanel No. 5, the seventies was Arpège and Youth Dew, the sixties was Miss Dior. That was when I could afford them, which very often was not the case.

My mother wore Diorissimo, and even now the slightest hint of it in my nostrils summons up a hundred memories of my mum. As does the scent of gardenias. The distinctive scent of daphne makes me think of Margaret Roseman teaching me to ride a two-wheeler in Livingstone Avenue, Pymble, where her mother's garden was packed with daphne. And just a whiff of Clarin's Eau Dynamisante and I can feel Richard Wherrett's arms around me again. A famous curmudgeon was once quoted in the *Sydney Morning Herald* as saying he hated the smell of JOY, and I was rather chuffed, pleased that the actual *smell* of me might have had the capacity to offend him if I had come within his olfactory range.

Nowadays I live on Parramatta Road (recently named by the *Herald* as the worst street in Sydney) in inner-city

Camperdown and I love it. The inverted snob who is lurking in my heart of hearts derives great satisfaction from boasting that I now reside on the most undesirable thoroughfare in all of Australia.

From a fifth-floor flat in a concrete bunker-like block, Sean and I waken to birdsong and a view of the gleaming spires of Sydney University's St John's College, surrounded by ancient Moreton Bay fig trees and gigantic jacarandas. Accompanying the birdsong are the screaming diesel engines of hundreds of city-bound peak-hour buses and the occasional Care Flight helicopter landing on the college's football oval, the occupants bound for Royal Prince Alfred Hospital just around the corner.

Of the many places where I've lived—which has to be about forty-odd—Camperdown is one of my special favourites. Glebe is our backyard and our local is the Forest Lodge Hotel, where my long-time friends Bruce and Sue Moir first met while uni students. John O'Grady remembers going to the Forest Lodge as a boy with his mother in the late 1940s, when musk-scented women with ample cleavages sipped shandies in the Ladies' Parlour, wisely segregated from the gentlemen.

In his recent memoir, *My Life As Me*, Barry Humphries makes a case for the value of omission and cites Voltaire, who defined a bore as someone who leaves nothing out. Lord knows what Voltaire would have made of Proust and his *Remembrance of Things Past* (or, more accurately, *Every Single Tiny Minutia of Things Past*). Even Proust's staunchest fan would have to admit he left very little out.

Clearly Voltaire's advice would be: don't give any reader good reason to say 'This is news surplus to my requirements', as journalist Christopher Hitchens wrote when the British Prime Minister announced that his youngest child had been conceived in a royal castle. So this humble tale is deliberately incomplete. Much more has happened in this particular life than you'll find in these pages. Nonetheless, there are secrets herein that the reluctant memoirist was certain would be carried to her grave. Secrets that even her son and her brother still didn't know at the time of writing. Secrets that will have to be revealed to them before this goes to press.

The last thing I wanted was for this story to become some sort of carnal confession. This is despite my reply to Geraldine Doogue, when I was being interviewed once on her ABC radio program 'Life Matters'. Geraldine asked me, 'What would you call your memoir, if you ever wrote one?' Absolutely certain at that time that I would *never* write a memoir, I replied: 'Um, I dunno . . . *A Slave to My Libido*?'

I wanted to make Geraldine laugh and, luckily for me, she did. I was horribly hungover that morning. I had heard at midnight, in a phone message from Kirrily Nolan, that Ruth Cracknell had just died and then, having finished work for the night at the Opera House, I sat alone at the nearby bar in The Basement nightclub, weeping into several dozen double Chivas Regals. A private mourning for Ruth.

In a recent interview on *Enough Rope*, Andrew Denton brought up one of my long-ago smart-arse quotes in which I had said, 'I'm not promiscuous. Promiscuous implies that

I'm not choosy. In fact I'm very choosy. I just happen to have had a lot of choices.' Ha ha.

Once, long ago, when trying to explain sexism to a stupid young reporter from the Melbourne *Sun*, I came up with a similarly glib one-liner: 'Men are good for sex and not much else.' I uttered the phrase ironically, but irony never translates well into tabloid print and, oh boy, did that quote come back to haunt me. Many times over three decades. Thus my reputation as 'some kind of bizarre femme fatale' (to quote Neil Simon) was constantly reinforced, a reputation I sometimes quite enjoy but which, to be honest, outstrips the facts. When he was courting me, my husband Sean Taylor was warned by a well-meaning fellow South African that I was 'a man-eater', and I was secretly delighted.

As I pointed out to Andrew Denton in that interview, I've turned down a lot more men than I've said yes to. Many more. A woman I know has had, by her own reckoning, three times as many lovers as I have, and yet she claims to not even enjoy sex. An accusation that could hardly be aimed at me. However, even I, not easily shocked, was surprised when Miranda in *Sex and the City* admitted losing count of all her lovers when she reached number forty-three. Implying she'd had many more than that. And she was only in her mid thirties. The low tally of notches on my revolver can be partially attributed to laziness. As Dylan's dad, John Walters once told me: 'You would have made a fine nympho, but you failed your practical.'

Having said that, it cannot be denied that I've had my fair share of sweethearts. And I do feel a tinge of regret that, for reasons of confidentiality, I haven't mentioned several of my paramours, lest relating the circumstances of the liaisons would give too much away, even if I changed their names. One I should mention, though, is 'Barney' (he knows who he is) who stuck patiently by me for twenty-five years and saw me through many major crises while remaining anonymous, yet supportive, when we were both in several concurrent relationships. Duplicitous, yes, but Barney was an important element in my life until about four years ago. We seldom see each other anymore, and then only by accident. Barney's a good man and at last he's happily married, and deservedly so. Another of my ex-lovers is 'Feste' who, along with his wife 'Michaela' and five grown-up children, I still love dearly. Feste's oldest daughter is fond of telling people that I could have been her mother. Feste and I were an item only *before* he met his wife Michaela, I hasten to add.

Since I was a toddler, I've loved the opposite sex, who, generally speaking, are a fine gender. Sure, I've known a lot of creeps, but only a couple of genuine villains, and one of those was when I was a small child. All my life I've enjoyed many close friendships with men: straight men, gay men and vacillating men. And ninety-five per cent of those relationships have been and still are platonic. A girlfriend asked me recently how to seduce a man and I had to admit to being without any technique in that area. Instant gratification being my middle name, I don't beat around the bush, so to speak. If I fancy someone, my feminine wiles don't run to much more than 'how about it?' So if I've never said that to *you*, dear reader, then chances are that I *don't* fancy you. Sorry. Or, on the other hand, I was scared that you might turn me down. Refusal May Offend, as the sign in Rothman's grocery used to say.

My possible vocation as a courtesan would have been stymied by the fact that I've never made love to a man I wasn't attracted to, except for, admittedly, a few where sympathy was involved. And, anyway, isn't it true that ultimately most courtesans invariably become lonely and disillusioned, or worse? Like that poor wretch Nana created by Zola. Irresistible Nana who, through her sexuality, was once so powerful, so adored and feted, and yet who ended her days sadly: ignored, diseased and destitute.

In the great playwright Arthur Miller's memoir *Time Bends*, he mentions his aunt, whom he cites as his muse and inspiration. He describes her as 'bleached blond, loving, vulgarly candid, worldly and uncultivated' and then he adds, 'I never wanted her to leave the theatre disappointed'. This description fills me with the warmth of recognition. It could sum me up. Except for the uncultivated bit. I'm not uncultivated; I just *pretend* to be uncultivated. But I never leave the theatre disappointed after one of Arthur Miller's plays, even when they're badly acted or miscast.

No one's stories are free from theft. A friend purloined one of my personal anecdotes and made herself the central character. My reaction was not the indignation that might be expected of a plagiaree, but rather fascination. What a peculiar thing to do. Another friend not only pinched one of my stories and passes it off as her own, but also tells it to me as though she's forgotten its origin, as I'm sure she has. You have to laugh, as Mrs Haycox used to say. I never steal other people's stories and then pretend they happened to me. It's much more fun to retell good tales, leaving the central characters where they belong and giving them the credit they deserve. Good gossip.

This reluctant memoir has been a long time coming, for various reasons. In 1999 I was first approached to write it, but it was not until 2002 when I was in Melbourne with the play *Soulmates*, going through yet another series of personal upheavals, that eventually I allowed myself to be persuaded to start writing by a persistent publisher, my long-time dear friend Richard Walsh, whom I've known for more than thirty years. Even with his unflagging patience and encouragement, I was, nevertheless, 'glacially slow', to use Mr Walsh's own phrase. It was like squeezing haemoglobin out of granite. To be fair to myself, I was working incredibly hard at my *real* job in the years 2002–05 and there was often simply not the time to sit down at the laptop and dredge up my past, painful and otherwise. Especially when I had no intention of doing a tell-all. And yet I've told rather more than I originally intended. And like most remembrances, it's not strictly chronological. It darts about, skittering back and forth over time frames like a ferret in a pantry; impressionistic rather than historical, like most people's recollections.

Numerous publishers and entrepreneurs tried to talk me into doing an autobiography for more than thirty years and I always resisted adamantly. Richard Wherrett used to tell me that a memoir has to be fearlessly candid or it is a pointless exercise, which I must have taken to heart, as I had no wish to expose my own nightmares to complete strangers, so my vow never to do a book seemed to be set in concrete. It was enough that I was frequently obliged to talk frankly to the press when I didn't really want to, in order to publicise productions I was in. There was no way, especially when my parents were still alive, that I was prepared to reveal any more. Or so I thought. But Richard Walsh kept urging me to change my mind, and finally I did. Shrugged my shoulders and bought an iBook. And wrote a sentence beginning with the first person singular. And hovering in my mind were the words of Henry Handel Richardson who wrote: 'How I do hate the sleek biography! I'd have every wart and pimple emphasised, every tricky trait or petty meanness brought out.'

I've been lucky to have been a jobbing actor for more than four decades. Sure there are characters I'd love to have played—like Juliet, Viola, Eliza Doolittle, Nora in *A Doll's House*, to name a few—but they passed me by, and I've no regrets. I've been fortunate in my working life and I've worked with some marvellous artists. Dozens of them. Just being around Garry McDonald's perfectionism, for instance, is totally inspiring.

In 2004 I was a Jewish South African social worker in a moving piece of verbatim theatre called *Through the Wire*, dealing with the refugee situation in Australia and written by Ros Horin for the Griffin Theatre Company. In 2003–04 I played three women opposite Max Gillies in Neil Simon's *Last of the Red Hot Lovers*, directed by Jennifer Hagan for Hit Productions, which toured to sixty-two different venues.

I also managed to squeeze in an eighteen-venue tour of Reg Cribb's multiple award-winning *Last Cab to Darwin*, directed by Jeremy Sims for Pork Chop Productions. In 2004–05 I did a one-woman show, Robert Hewett's *The Blonde, the Brunette and the Vengeful Redhead*, in which I play seven different characters including a man and a four-year-old boy, which I produced myself with the help of my brother Rod Weaver and my good friend Stewart D'Arrietta. Jennifer Hagan directed *Vengeful Redhead* and my husband Sean Taylor co-directed. Thus in an eighteen-month period I stayed in more than ninety-two different hotels and motels.

2005 also saw Reg Cribb's *Ruby's Last Dollar* open at the Sydney Opera House and go to Perth. I think Reg wrote Ruby for me partly as consolation for having to delete my role of Deidre the Trollop from the original version of *Last Cab to Darwin*. I wasn't fussed about losing Deidre—after all, I still had five other characters in *Last Cab*—but some people grew quite attached to Deidre and were disappointed at her demise. There were eight actors and three crew on *Last Cab to Darwin* and we all became quite close. The blokes had a nickname for me: Trevor, as in Living National Trevor. Better than Buried Trevor. One thing is certain—I'm sick of packing my suitcase.

My baby brother Rod grew up to get his law degree from Sydney Uni just like our dad, and Rod is now a barrister, after flirtations with acting and scriptwriting for TV. He has a son, Nicholas, with Helen Wellings and another son and daughter, Ashley and Amy, from his first marriage. Rod and

I have always been very close. He takes a concerned interest in my affairs, business and otherwise. I once had a dream where Ede and Art were telling him to look after me when they were gone. Perhaps it really happened. I don't know.

My dear son Dylan is a quiet, thoughtful, private man, very ethical and decent, with a great sense of humour. Although he's a good actor with a lovely tone to his speaking voice, he hasn't pursued a life as an actor. He plays music, he can write well and he has a quarter of a law degree with not much interest in getting the other three-quarters. In 2004 he married Makiko Matsumoto in Helen and Rod's Birchgrove garden, which is where Sean Taylor married me in October 2003.

I adore Sean Taylor.

I still speak to Joby every day and his radio career is again thriving in Melbourne, and he still has a plethora of paramours.

And, as our accountant once complained in the 1980s when we were rapidly going broke, I still buy too many books.

The trouble with being a voracious reader of quality stuff is that your standards are so high that nothing you write yourself is ever good enough. There was that frustrating year in the eighties that I spent trying to write a performance piece for myself about Christina Stead, which ended in tears and abandonment. Actors and writers share the umbrella of storytelling. It's possible that everyone can write and everyone can act to a degree; but few people can do either excellently, never mind both.

My most recent attempt at a novel was just a few years ago. After months of research and copious notes I went to a hideout for a while to try to pull it all together. (As Frank Muir said: 'I've just been to Corsica to finish my novel—I'm a very slow reader.') But, alas, despite a cracker of a plot and intriguing characters, I just couldn't make it work, not to my liking anyway. Only three other people read it—they claimed to enjoy it, but I didn't trust their bias so that manuscript is now gathering dust in a storage room in Alexandria (Sydney, not Egypt) and there it stays.

I'm not a bad actor though, some of the time. And although I'm not particularly gregarious, I like the fact that acting is a communal and less solitary way of telling stories than writing is. I do love my solitude, but maybe my need for company is greater. I love people.

And at last I've discovered that I love my life.

Professional biography

1947	Born 25 May at Hurstville, Sydney.
1962	Began professional career playing lead role in *Cinderella* at Phillip Theatre, Sydney.
1963	*Hansel and Gretel* by Humperdinck, ABC TV opera. Played Gretel.
1964	*Mother Goose and the Three Stooges*, pantomime, Palace Theatre. Played Jill.
	Once Upon a Surfie, Palace Theatre. Played Gadget.
1965	*Split Level*, ABC-TV drama. Played dysfunctional child.
1966	*Wandjina*, seven-part ABC-TV drama series. Played juvenile lead.
	Lady Precious Stream and *Little Red Riding Hood*, Arts Council tour around New South Wales schools.
	Homicide, Crawford Television. Played the first of many victims.
	Ten Bob in Kitty, satirical revue, Copenhagen Theatre Restaurant, Sydney.
	Be Our Guest, ABC-TV variety series. Compere.
	Peter Pan by James Barrie, Independent Theatre, North Sydney. Played Peter Pan.
	The Schoolmistress by Arthur Wing Pinero, Old Tote Theatre, Sydney. Played Dinah.

1967   *A Taste for Blue Ribbons*, ABC Radio serial. Played juvenile lead.

The Runaway Steamboat, children's play, Adelaide Festival. Played 12-year-old-boy.

Hay Fever by Noël Coward, Marian Street Theatre, Sydney. Played Jackie.

1968   *The Imaginary Invalid* by Moliere, Old Tote Theatre. Played Louise.

You Never Can Tell by George Bernard Shaw, Old Tote Theatre. Played Dolly.

1969   *The Knack* by Ann Jellicoe, Hobart Theatre Royal. Played Nancy.

Would you Believe, ABC-TV panel game show, ran for five years, Sundays prime time.

Division 4, Crawfords Television. Played Bud Tingwell's daughter.

1970   *The Bandwagon* by Terence Frisby, Phillip Theatre, starring Peggy Mount. Played Aurora.

1971   *Stork*, feature film, screenplay by David Williamson, directed by Tim Burstall. Played Anna.

The Removalists by David Williamson, Nimrod Theatre, Sydney. Played Fiona.

Customs and Excise by Jack Hibberd, Nimrod Theatre, Sydney. Played a husband swapper.

After Magritte by Tom Stoppard, Nimrod Theatre, Sydney. Played an 80-year-old tuba-playing granny.

The Roy Murphy Show by Alex Buzo, Nimrod Theatre, Sydney. Played Sharon the Rugby League Maid.

Caste by TW Robertson, Marian Street Theatre, Sydney. Played Polly Eccles.

1972   *Legend of King O'Malley* by Bob Ellis and Michael Boddy, Old Tote Theatre. Played several roles.

Forget-Me-Not-Lane by Peter Nichols, Old Tote Theatre. Played Young Ursula.

Alvin Purple, feature film, directed by Tim Burstall. Played Emily.

1973   *Tom* by Alex Buzo, Nimrod Theatre, Sydney. Played Tom's wife.

          Petersen, feature film, directed by Tim Burstall, screenplay by David Williamson. Played Jack Thompson's wife.

          The Engagement, ABC-TV comedy with Mel Gibson. Played a ditzy virgin.

1974   *The Removalists*, feature film, screenplay by David Williamson, producer Margaret Fink. Played Fiona.

          The Seagull by Chekov, Nimrod Theatre. Played Masha.

          Love's Labour's Lost by Shakespeare, Old Tote Theatre, directed by William Gaskill. Played Rosaline opposite John Bell as Berowne.

1975   *Picnic at Hanging Rock*, feature film, directed by Peter Weir. Played Minnie.

          Caddie, feature film, directed by Donald Crombie. Played Josie.

          Polly Me Love, telemovie for Eric Porter Productions. Played Polly.

          Rush, ABC-TV drama series. Played Yvette.

          Seven Ages of Man, ABC-TV series. Played the teenage seducer of Supreme Court judge.

1976   *A Streetcar Named Desire* by Tennessee Williams, Old Tote Theatre. Played Stella.

          Do I Have to Kill my Child? Telemovie, Film Australia, directed by Donald Crombie, producer Anne Deveson. Played lead.

          Roberta by Jerome Kern, musical. Played lead opposite John Farnham.

1977   *The Three Sisters* by Anton Chekov, Old Tote Theatre. Played Natasha.

          The Faces of Dick Emery, ATN7 TV comedy series. Various roles.

          Australian National Playwrights Conference, directed by Richard Wherrett. One of the stable of actors taking part in the conference.

          Death Cell, telemovie. Played a terrifying ghost.

1978   *Rockola* by Tim Gooding, Nimrod Theatre and Adelaide Festival. Played Blue Velvet.

Bedroom Farce by Alan Ayckbourne, Elizabethan Theatre Trust. Played Kate.

Lots of TV work.

1979   *Three Blind Mice*, ABC-TV comedy. Played various roles.

Cop Shop, Crawfords TV. Played a dangerous kidnapper.

Patrol Boat, ABC-TV drama. Played an obnoxious journalist.

Cappriccio, ABC music series.

1980   *Water Under the Bridge* by Sumner Locke Elliott, television mini-series. Played Maggie.

1980–81   *Trial by Marriage*, ABC-TV comedy series. Played lead, Joan, fourteen episodes.

They're Playing Our Song by Neil Simon, Marvin Hamlisch and Carol Bayer Sager, musical, JC Williamsons. Played lead, Sonia, opposite John Waters.

1980   *Squizzy Taylor*, feature film by Simpson Le Mesurier. Played Dolly.

1983   *The Girl From Moonooloo* by David Mitchell, ABC-TV musical telemovie. Played lead.

Born Yesterday by Garson Kanin, JC Williamsons, Comedy Theatre, Melbourne. Played Billie Dawn.

1984   *Born Yesterday*, directed by Richard Wherrett, Sydney Theatre Company, Sydney Opera House.

1985   *The Perfectionist* by David Williamson, telemovie, directed by Chris Thompson, producer Pat Lovell. Played Barbara.

The Real Thing by Tom Stoppard, Sydney Theatre Company, Sydney Opera House with John Bell. Played Annie.

1986   *The Challenge*, TV series, Channel 9. Played Rasa Bertrand.

Having a Ball by Alan Bleasdale, Australian Elizabethan Theatre Trust. Played Doreen.

1987   *Emerald City* by David Williamson, Melbourne
        Theatre Company, plus return season. Played Kate.
        Blithe Spirit by Nöel Coward, Melbourne Theatre
        Company. Played Elvira.
        A Day in the Death of Joe Egg by Peter Nichols, Mel-
        bourne Theatre Company. Played Sheila.

1988   *House Rules*, ABCTV sit-com series devised by Barbara
        Bishop. Played lead, Julie, twenty-six episodes.

1989   Tried to write a novel and a performance piece. Failed.

1990   *Daylight Saving* by Nick Enright, Melbourne Theatre
        Company. Played Felicity.
        Rumours by Neil Simon, Garry Penney Productions.
        Played Chris
        Love Letters by A.R. Gurney, with John Waters,
        Sydney Opera House. Played Melissa.

1991   *Shadowlands* by William Nicholson, Sydney Theatre
        Company. Played Joy Gresham opposite John Bell.
        Daylight Saving by Nick Enright, return season and
        national tour.

1992   *Six Degrees of Separation* by John Guare, Sydney
        Theatre Company. Played Ouisa.

1993   *Away* by Michael Gow, Sydney Theatre Company.
        Played Coral.
        Shadowlands by William Nicholson, Melbourne
        Theatre Company. Played Joy opposite Max Phipps.

1994   *The Sisters Rosensweig* by Wendy Wasserstein, Mel-
        bourne Theatre Company and Sydney Theatre
        Company. Played Dr Gorgeous.

1995   *Reunion*, a rock musical by John Waters and Stewart
        D'Arrietta, national tour. Played the ex-wife of a
        fading rock star.
        Cosi, feature film, screenplay by Louis Nowra,
        directed by Mark Joffe. Played Cherry.

1996   Various compering, small film and TV gigs.

1997   *Navigating* by Katherine Thompson, Queensland
        Theatre Company and Melbourne Theatre Company.
        Played Bea.

1998   *After the Ball* by David Williamson, Sydney Theatre Company. Played Judy, both younger and older versions.

Fred by Beatrix Christian, Sydney Theatre Company. Played Antoinette.

1999   *Silhouette* by Simon Brett, Marian Street Theatre, Sydney. Played Celia.

2000   *The Falls* by Hilary Bell, with Lucy Bell, directed by John Bell at the Stables for Griffin. Played Nellie.

The Wharf Review by Jonathan Biggins, Andrew Ross and Drew Forsythe for Sydney Theatre Company.

2000–2001 *Girl Talk* by Patrick Edgeworth, for Hit Productions, sixty-nine venues with Christen O'Leary. Played Julie.

2000   *Old Masters* by Beatrix Christian for Sydney Theatre Company. Played Fleur.

2001   *Soulmates* by David Williamson, for Melbourne Theatre Company and Sydney Theatre Company, directed by Gale Edwards. Played Heather.

2002   *Through the Wire*, verbatim theatre piece devised by Ros Horin on refugees in Australia for Sydney Festival at Parramatta. Played South African Jewish woman.

2003–2004 *Last Cab to Darwin* by Reg Cribb. Jeremy Sims' Pork Chop Productions, Sydney Opera House and twenty-venue tour nationwide. Played six roles.

Last of the Red Hot Lovers by Neil Simon, a two-hander with Max Gillies, national tour of sixty-two venues for Hit Productions. Played all three women: Elaine, Bobbi and Jeannette.

2004–2006 *The Blonde, the Brunette and the Vengeful Redhead* by Robert Hewett. A one-woman play, playing all seven characters, eight weeks for Melbourne Theatre Company, then regional and national tour into 2006.

2005   *Ruby's Last Dollar* by Reg Cribb for Pork Chop Productions, Sydney Opera House and Black Swan Theatre Company, Perth. Played Ruby.

Acknowledgments

To my dear friend and publisher Richard Walsh for his encouragement, good humour, kindness, patience and faith in me, without which I may have lost heart and given up by the time I arrived at Chapter Two.

And to my husband Sean Taylor for his gentle coaxing whenever I felt like throwing in the towel, and for laughing in all the right places.